200 Hote

Britain's Coolest Hotels and B&Bs

NORTHUMBERLAND
SEE BRITAIN BY TRAIN

Contents

Country Comforts

Food Glorious Food

Dog-Friendly

Eco Warriors

Boutique Chic

200 Hotels - An Introduction

A quiet revolution happened in the United Kingdom between the late 1980s and the noughties. Back in the day, hotels and B&Bs were often places of convenience rather than comfort. Luxury, such as it existed, came at an enormous price, and upmarket hotels often rested on their laurels, focusing instead on keeping the wrong kind of people from enjoying their tired rooms and intimidatingly posh French food. Hospitality was simply something Britain wasn't very good at: if you wanted to experience good food and service, you had to go abroad.

Fast forward to the 2020s and Britain is a different country, packed full of great places to stay often run by passionate people who live and breathe good hospitality. The dread word 'boutique' was the first indicator that things had changed, and of course is now an over-used term. But it does give a flavour of a new kind of British hotel or guesthouse that began to appear 30 or so years ago – small, independently owned, and putting the guest experience front and centre. There was a new sense of contemporary style in guest rooms, where luxury didn't necessarily mean antique furniture and four-posters. The renaissance in Modern British food made an appearance too, with lots of places revamping their restaurants and basing their menus on locally sourced, seasonal ingredients. And service was authentic, never trying too hard to please but always on hand if needed.

Like all good revolutions, change has continued, with new trends and activities emerging – wild swimming, food foraging, art classes, yoga and wellness retreats – and many establishments offering alternative accommodation: shepherds huts, lodges with hot tubs, even treehouses. The best places now have an eye on the environment too, with renewable energy sources, discounts for those arriving on public transport and kitchen gardens saving on food miles.

This book doesn't pretend to include all of Britain's best places to stay but instead aims to provide a curated selection. Our choices are deliberately eclectic, driven not so much by budget as by the uniqueness of the property, its location, facilities, decor – or just its owners and the extra mile they often go for their guests. We avoid the usual global brands that dominate accommodation in many towns and cities, the point being that it's not always about what you spend on a room, it's where you spend it, with plenty of surprisingly affordable options if you know where to find them. We also aim to provide a range of choices in most corners of England, Scotland, Wales and Northern Ireland.

Above all, we are confident that this book doesn't include anywhere that could be considered average. If you've had it with chains and can't be bothered to wade through the piles of choice on booking.com, browse our collection of hotels, B&Bs and contemporary guesthouses: you will not only find what you need, it will also be somewhere special.

*Eagle-eyed readers might notice there are actually 288 properties. The title is homage to the 1971 album by the late musical maverick Frank Zappa. Famed for his eclectic style, like Frank we've tried to showcase a rich variety within these pages.

Families, Resorts, Spas

Home from Home

Pubs & Coaching Inns

Sheer Luxury

Seaside Style

Too Cool for School

Love is All Around

One-Offs

Historic Hideaways

Great Outdooors

London

You shouldn't come to London just to stay in a fancy hotel. Firstly, there's so much to do and see it would be crazy to spend all your time in your room. Plus London hotels are eye-wateringly expensive so you need to choose carefully to find good value. Ultimately it's about finding somewhere comfortable enough to return to after a hard day's sightseeing, yet not so comfy that you never want to leave. Look instead for a touch of character – London hotels tend to be identikit chain properties that all look much the same – a good location and service that's a cut above the norm: a warm welcome goes a long way in the big city!

Aragon House, p.12

Artist Residence London

A brilliantly located, affordable and very cool boutique hotel bang in the centre of London

We're big fans of the Artist Residence hotel group, which also has places in Brighton, Cornwall, Bristol and Oxfordshire. They're good-value, well-run and strive to be different, and their London flagship property is no exception. Indeed it deservedly won the Good Hotel Guide's 'London Hotel of The Year' a few years ago and is a stylish yet friendly place, small in scale and welcoming in tone, with just 10 individually decorated guest rooms and suites, plus a café, all-day restaurant and a basement cocktail bar.

Arranged across three floors and divided between Small, Medium, Loft rooms and a couple of Suites, the decoration of the hotel's guest rooms is delightfully random, with reclaimed floorboards, a mix of furniture that blends vintage and contemporary, and – naturally – a good selection of art on the walls. They also have fast wifi, air-conditioning, flatscreen Freeview TVs and digital radios, well-stocked fridges, Nespresso coffee machines and complimentary tea, coffee and biscuits. The beds are big and bouncy, and all the rooms have en-suite bathrooms with powerful rainfall showers and Bramley toiletry products, while the larger rooms and suites also have free-standing baths and walk-in showers, super-king-size beds and seating areas. Some of the rooms are dog-friendly, and lucky pooches get a bed, bowl and a selection of treats.

Public areas are similarly artsy and shabby chic, and the reception very low-key, accessed via the ground-floor restaurant, making it a nice place to stay without the drama of a big hotel lobby. The restaurant serves food all day and offers a very accessible menu, with burgers and salads, sandwiches and snacks, as well as a full dinner menu in the evening, featuring similarly hearty and affordable main courses.

Pimlico is perhaps not central London's most interesting district, but it is a proper neighbourhood and you are super-central – very well located for public transport options but also within walking distance of any number of major London sights – Tate Britain is close by, as is Buckingham Palace and a couple of the capital's most beautiful parks, and the Battersea Power Station development is just across the river. But the hotel has also been deliberately designed for people to hang out in, so once you're done exploring the city, you can sip cocktails in the bar and eat well in the hotel's busy restaurant. Your choice – and your very cool home from home in the centre of London!

CONTACT 52 Cambridge Street, London SW1V 4QQ • 020 3019 8610

HOW MUCH? Double rooms from £180 a night, not including breakfast.

ROOMS 10 Guest Rooms & Suites.

DELTA OSCAR INDIA
HOTEL ALFA VICTOR
ECHO TANGO
OSCAR SIERRA PAPA
ECHO LIMA LIMA
INDIA TANGO
OSCAR UNIFORM
TANGO FOXTROT
OSCAR ROMEO
YANKEE OSCAR
UNIFORM

Aragon House

A stylish and welcoming pub with food and rooms that makes the perfect west London stopover

Sometimes, nothing else but a pub will do, and if you're looking to stay in central west London then you're in luck, because Aragon House does everything a boutique city inn should do. It's an attractive Grade II Georgian building offering generously proportioned and stylish rooms with comfortable beds, excellent food and drink, a pretty sheltered garden, a snazzy subterranean cocktail bar – and most important of all, a friendly, welcoming vibe.

The hotel's 15 individually designed hotel-quality bedrooms offer all the amenities you might need, including mini Smeg fridges, Nespresso coffee machines, air-conditioning and en-suite bathrooms with Bramley toiletries. There's good wifi, flatscreen Smart TVs and Roberts Radios, complimentary still and sparkling water, and you can even bring your pet – Aragaon House is dog-friendly throughout. Rooms vary in size from 'Cosy' (larger than you'd expect) through 'Comfy' and up to 'Deluxe', but there's not a huge variation in price. The main differences between the types of room are space and the fact that the Deluxe rooms have super-king-size beds, easy chairs and a separate bath and shower. Twin rooms and inter-connecting rooms are available; there is also an accessible room with space for a wheelchair, and some of the Comfy rooms have space for an additional bed.

Aragon House's guest rooms are extremely good value by London standards, and there's also a convivial bar and restaurant to tempt you downstairs, with an array of eclectic artwork adorning the walls. Food-wise, it offers upscale and rather vogueish gastropub fare with seasonally changing menus. They do a mean line in cocktails too, in the Green Room bar. Aragon House is also well-equipped for weddings, parties and corporate events – the Richardson Room holds up to 60 seated and 80 standing, and their picturesque and spacious walled garden holds up to 150. Home to booths and sofas, with blankets, heaters and hot-water bottles provided come winter, it's a lovely spot at any time of year.

Parsons Green is also a proper London neighbourhood (if a rather gentrified one) so you can feel like a proper well-heeled Londoner while you're here. You are surrounded by bars and restaurants, close to Kings Road for shopping, and also well placed to see more or less everywhere in London, with the Tube station just a two-minute walk away.

CONTACT 247 New King's Road, Parsons Green, London SW6 4XG • 020 7731 7313
HOW MUCH? Double rooms from £109 to £139 a night, not including breakfast
ROOMS 15 Guest Rooms.

Hotel Amano

A cool look and low prices in the heart of London's Covent Garden

'Amano' means 'they love' in Italian, and what is there not to love at the London location for this well-established and rather cool German hotel brand, which has set up shop in the heart of Covent Garden? First of all, the location is terrific, just around the corner from Drury Lane's Theatre Royal, but the hotel is stylish and personable too, which is something central London hotels often are not. The rates are also moderate by central London standards.

The hotel has 141 guest rooms, spread over six floors, each designed to the same exacting, contemporary specifications and style, complete with high-quality furnishings, clean lines, flatscreen TVs and Daluma eco-toiletries. The building itself is 19th-century and full of architectural quirks, so no two rooms are exactly the same: categories start at 'Cosy' and move up through 'Comfy', 'Roomy' and 'Roomy Plus', with Cosy being perfect for a solo traveller or a couple on a budget and Roomy Plus large enough to accommodate an extra roll-up bed if needed. Try to snag a corner room if you can (room numbers ending in 17), which are extra spacious and have floor-to-ceiling windows. For a touch of glamour, the hotel's four 'Goldy' rooms have a free-standing golden bathtub – slightly Brothers Grimm, we grant you, but perfect for a treat or romantic occasion. They also accept dogs in some rooms, and provide all sorts of cute amenities for furry friends. As for other facilities, the hotel's restaurant – Penelope's – offers top-notch Spanish-Middle Eastern cuisine, plus there's a fabulous rooftop bar on the 7th floor, which has some of London's most spectacular panoramic views, DJs spinning tunes and cocktails on tap – an ideal spot for both an early evening aperitif or a nightcap.

Finally, there's the hotel's location – crucial in a large city like London, where it's important to be based in the neighbourhood that suits you and your holiday plans. Covent Garden is not only as central as you can get in London, but it's also a vibrant, must-see part of town for anyone who enjoys shopping, theatre, restaurants and bars, as well as a spot of history and culture. Based here, you're within walking distance of major sights like the National Gallery and Trafalgar Square, Theatreland, Soho and Chinatown, plus you have a multitude of places to eat and drink on your doorstep. A perfect place, in short, to base yourself for an unforgettable trip to London.

CONTACT Drury House, 34–43 Russell St, London WC2B 5HA • 020 3739 8900

HOW MUCH? Double rooms from £159 to £229 a night, not including breakfast.

ROOMS 141 Guest Rooms & Suites.

BAR

Karma Sanctum Soho

London's original rock 'n' roll hotel!

Billed as London's original rock 'n' roll hotel – owned by music biz insiders – the Karma Sanctum Soho is the capital's most hip and happening boutique hotel. It's partly down to its famous regulars and casual superstar visits – pretty much everyone has been seen here at some point – but also because there's a vibe here that you just don't get anywhere else. You might not get into the Inner Sanctum private members' bar, or catch a secret after-hours DJ set, but the famed rooftop terrace and bar and Japanese-inspired street food restaurant are in-the-know London destinations – and residents get preference.

Occupying knocked-together Georgian townhouses on the Regent Street edge of Soho, it's a cool location for anyone in town for gigs, exhibitions or sightseeing. It's as boutique as hell, which means 30 elegantly styled guest rooms and suites, ranging from 'Compact' to 'Loft Suite'. Space is tight unless you're in the mid-range rooms and upwards, but we're talking deep, bold colours, big beds and bathrobes, original art, designer lighting, marble bathrooms and sound systems – in fact, pretty much everything you can imagine when you combine the words 'London' and 'boutique'. The Junior Suites have an eye-catching Art Deco style, with their mosaic-mirrored glass columns; bag the Loft Suite and you have your own private entrance to the rooftop terrace. And while you could find these things in other city hotels, what sets the Karma Sanctum apart is that un-stuffy rock 'n' roll attitude, whether it's the hot tub on the roof terrace, the 24-hour bar, the Chrissie Hynde artwork on the restaurant walls or the hugely knowledgeable staff. Plus you're a short walk from some of the capital's best eating, drinking and music venues, and you never know who might be sitting in the bar when you get back late at night. For those who fancy a beatnik weekend in the country, there's a Karma Sanctum in Berkshire too!

CONTACT 20 Warwick Street, London W1B 5NF • 020 7292 6100
HOW MUCH? Double rooms from £159 to £500 a night.
ROOMS 30 Guest Rooms & Suites.

The Pilgrm

Not a misprint but a stylish hotel in W2 with contemporary furnishings and great prices

This snazzy Victorian-era hotel in Paddington with an unusual name has a no-frills outlook: it's a pooch-friendly spot with no front desk, room service, baths or minibars, but don't let that put you off – their refreshing approach is appealing and the place is certainly not without charm and warmth.

Fusing contemporary with vintage, the 73 rooms are divided into four categories: Bunk, the dinkiest; Small, ideal for budget-conscious couples or friends; Medium, a more capacious space complete with a floating double bed; and Large, with kings or super-kings, plenty of space at 14sqm and with views over the neighbourhood. With Jason Catifeoglou – formerly of the Zetter collection – at the helm, style is at the forefront, with cast iron reclaimed radiators, soothing tones, Egyptian cotton sheets and towels, original

artwork, mattresses handmade in Devon and a selection of books and magazines featuring in the bedrooms. All the rooms except Bunks have Freeview TVs, real plants, USB sockets and Marshall bluetooth speakers. Guests have free rein over the pantry on each floor and can grab water from there as and when they please (just ask for your own recyclable bottle), and at ground level Workshop Coffee is a casual setting for a steaming cup of joe. Up on the first floor, lounge guests can enjoy a bite to eat, with the likes of Le Swine bacon sarnie or fluffy pancakes for brekkie, and their signature toasties with fries or baked chickpeas with chorizo served with crusty bread for lunch. Drink-wise, there's a tempting array of cocktails to choose from, including their in-house signature Spritz.

Located just by Paddington station, the hotel lies in an excellent position: sitting next to Norfolk Square, close to Marylebone and Notting Hill and just a 15 minute stroll to Hyde Park and the scenic Serpentine, it's a top-notch choice for a stay in the capital, not to mention easily accessible to Heathrow.

CONTACT 25 London Street, London W2 1HH • 020 7667 6000
HOW MUCH? Double rooms from £150 a night.
ROOMS 73 Guest Rooms.

The Athenaeum

A unique five-star hotel in the heart of Mayfair, classically English with strong eco-credentials

At Cool Places HQ, we are convinced that there is something very special about London's cityscape, and The Athenaeum's sweeping views of London landmarks over Green Park's treetops are something unique. If green living and ecology are important to you, you'll also love The Athenaeum's vertical living wall, now a symbol of the hotel. In keeping with the outside, the inside décor is geared towards calm and relaxation from a natural colour-scheme palette to the compact but luxurious spa. All this is a departure from the 1980s when The Athenaeum was a hot spot for celebrities in search of a party. In homage to its previous life, a portrait of Joanna Lumley as Patsy in 'Absolutely Fabulous' greets the guests from the elegant lobby area.

The other thing we like about this hotel is that – unusually for this part of London – it is not part of a global chain, and we think that makes a difference. It's not cheap by any means, but is also not one of the capital's most expensive properties. Since its extensive refurbishment, it has been listed in the Condé Nast Traveller Readers' Choice Awards. While the hotel retains its Art Deco features, the rooms and suites have been brought into the 21st century with some style and they feature Hypnos beds, large flatscreen TVs, Nespresso coffee machines, wifi and minibars championing small British brands. They also feature unique works of art inspired by the local area and landmarks, British icons and pieces of history – think Winston Churchill and the Queen's corgis at Buckingham Palace alongside Andy Murray hitting a tennis ball off the roof! The more you look, the more you see.

All in all, the design aesthetic of the rooms and suites at The Athenaeum creates a feeling of space and light, and great views too. It's unique, classically English, a little eccentric and captures a sense of place in the city, with plenty of nods to Mayfair and Green Park. One more thing, where else would you find family rooms and residences with their own dedicated children's concierge, a toy store, nannies and babysitters? While The Athenaeum staff are taking care of the little ones, why not settle in at '116 at the Athenaeum' – the hotel's excellent restaurant – or sip a well-earned cocktail in the bar or on the terrace… ? Those views again!

CONTACT 116 Piccadilly, London W1J 7BJ • 020 7499 3464
HOW MUCH? Double rooms from £350 a night.
ROOMS 111 Guest Rooms & 12 Suites.

THE ATHENAEUM
HOTEL & RESIDENCES

Brama

Sleek guest rooms that offer one of London's coolest and most affordable places to stay

London is a city of neighbourhoods, and it's becoming increasingly popular to stay outside the city centre, not only to experience a bit of real London life but also to save quite a lot of money! One of the newest and best places to do just this is Brama, which occupies a landmark building in the southeast London borough of Bromley. It's a very cool boutique hotel, with a great bar and restaurant on-site, and is only 18 minutes by train from London Victoria.

Bromley Town Hall dates from 1907 and has been beautifully renovated, retaining buckets of period style, not least the elegant art deco staircase where local hero David Bowie posed for the media back in the 1970s, and even a nuclear bunker underneath the building. Furnishings are cool and well-chosen mid-century items, and perfectly in keeping with the style of the building. The hotel is deliberately informal, offering what they call 'luxury as you like it', with no reception, online check-in and a mobile key to your room, making it as private or as welcoming as you like. The 23 guest rooms range from Shoebox and Snug to Spacious, Studio and Suite. Even the smallest are a decent size, and they're all quite contemporary and slightly playful, decorated with a sleek minimalism and provided with excellent wifi, Smart TVs, tea- and coffee-making facilities, bottles of filtered water, biscuits, good-quality hairdryers, steamers for clothes, and air- and regular USB chargers. Even the smallest rooms have king-size beds, while others have super-kings; mattresses are Hypnos and very comfortable. Bathrooms come with robes, refillable Bramley toiletries and 'Bumboo' sustainable toilet rolls. There are also two accessible rooms, both spacious and with adapted doorways and bathrooms, one of which has a bath.

All in all, with room rates starting at just over £100, it's hard to find better value anywhere in London for accommodation of this quality. And guess what? Bromley isn't a bad base, with a lively vibe and lots of places to eat and drink, including the on-site Dorothy and Marshall bar and restaurant, which is open for breakfast, lunch and dinner. It occupies the large and airy space of the original court chamber and has an outside terrace in the adjacent courtyard – head there to sample one of their 'Rebel Rebel' cocktails, named in honour of Bowie!

CONTACT 6 Court St, Bromley, London BR1 1AN • 020 3989 9090
HOW MUCH? Double rooms from £100 to £329 a night.
ROOMS 23 Guest Rooms & Suites.

City of London Club

A unique and very special place for a stay in the heart of the City of London

Situated in the Square Mile, the capital's most historic quarter, the City of London Club is quite unlike anywhere else to stay in the capital. It's first and foremost a private members' club, with all the elegance, history and sense of privilege that implies. It boasts a grand entrance hall with a suitably sweeping staircase and any number of cosy bars and lounges and private dining rooms. Unusually, it's also home to some rather swanky – and very contemporary – guest rooms that anyone can stay in on a visit to London: just the ticket if you're looking for comfort and elegance in a central London location at an affordable price.

The rooms occupy two floors at the top of the building. Members obviously get preferential rates, but even the prices for mere mortals are a fraction of what you pay for a similar level of comfort at even the most ordinary central London hotel. And – let's be honest – there's nothing ordinary about the City of London Club. The rooms break down into four categories – Club, Double, Junior Suites and the top-notch Prince Philip Suite. Given the shape and age of the building, each room is different, but they've all been thoughtfully designed and furnished and are very comfortable and well-equipped – each with large Hypnos beds, high-quality bed linen, desks, wifi, air-conditioning, tea- and coffee-making facilities, minibars, Smart TVs and en-suite bathrooms with toiletries and robes. Some have their own dressing rooms, too.

It's a short stroll from your room to the sleek haven of Churchill's Bar, with its own rooftop terrace, where you can enjoy a cocktail before descending to dinner in the Club's members' restaurant, where the food is traditional yet contemporary in style and presentation. In summer, tables spill out into the Club's atmospheric private courtyard and although no catering other than breakfast is available on weekends, there's no shortage of places to eat nearby.

Because the City is relatively quiet at weekends, the Club is available for exclusive use then, and it will come as no surprise that it is available for wedding hire too – the lavish interiors are a photographer's dream. Either way, whether you come as a group, a couple or a family, you couldn't be better placed to enjoy the sights of the City, or, for that matter, trendy Spitalfields and Shoreditch – both just a hop, skip and jump away, as are a choice of Tube stations for travel to the West End.

CONTACT 19 Old Broad St, London EC2N 1DS • 020 7588 7991

HOW MUCH? Double rooms and suites from £215 to £440 a night.

ROOMS 20 Guest Rooms & Suites.

Batty Langley's

A historic haven in the heart of Spitalfields set between Shoreditch and The City

One of a trio of London boutique hotels that self-consciously blends 18th-century elegance with contemporary style, Batty Langley's is as comfortable an East End bolthole as you'll find. Situated a stone's throw from Spitalfields Market, it's handy for both the City of London and for Shoreditch's hip restaurants and clubs, while the West End isn't too far away either. One of the most distinctive hotels the capital has to offer – a pair of renovated weavers' houses on a street that was colonized by Huguenot refugees in the 17th and 18th centuries – it's comfortable, bursting with heritage, rather cool, and utterly unique.

Batty Langley was one of the most influential interior designers of his day and he advised rich folk on matters of taste, in particular how to decorate their houses. The hotel is well named, as it's not only a soothing place to come back to after a day's sightseeing, but an elegant one too. Like its sister hotels, Hazlitt's in Soho and The Rookery in Clerkenwell, it boasts several welcoming lounges decorated with antique furniture, oil paintings from the owners' extensive Georgian art collection and lots of books, along with well-stocked honesty bars and comfy sofas to flop on to. There's also a sweet little courtyard to sit and relax in. With just 29 guest rooms, the hotel's ground-floor areas never feel crowded, which suits the urban home-from-home feel perfectly, and although it has no restaurant or bar, you don't really need either in this neighbourhood, where there's so much choice on your doorstep.

The guest rooms are spread across five floors and are decorated with handsome antique furnishings, big oak beds – some of them four-posters – and en-suite bathrooms, many of which have rolltop baths. Like the group's other two hotels, the feel is private and rather special (as if it was your own secret), yet the rooms are relatively affordable, spacious and well-equipped with all the modern amenities you need – wifi, air-conditioning, minibars and Smart TVs cleverly concealed within the period furnishings. Tea- and coffee-making facilities are also provided on request. While rooms vary in size, all are decorated in an equally lavish manner. Whichever room you opt for, Batty Langley's is ideal for discerning guests who like their hotels with a healthy heritage factor and style in spades.

CONTACT 12 Folgate St, London E1 6BX • 020 7377 4390

HOW MUCH? Double rooms from around £300 a night.

ROOMS 29 Guest Rooms & Suites.

South Place Hotel

Cool foodie hotel in the heart of the City of London that is also dog-friendly

You'd expect the food offering to be pretty good here, at the only hotel of the restaurant focused D&D Group, and the South Place Hotel, in the heart of the City of London, doesn't disappoint. Not only does it have an excellent and very busy restaurant on its ground floor, The Chophouse, it also boasts one of only half a dozen Michelin-starred restaurants in the City in Angler – a sleek affair at the top of the building where the views are only surpassed by the quality of the food. The hotel also boasts several convivial bars, including an outside terrace that is as good a place to drink a cocktail in summer as anywhere in the City that you'll find.

But the South Place is not just about food. It's one of very few hotels to be built in the Square Mile in the last 100 years, and has 80 very comfortable rooms, ranging from entry-level Loft rooms to Studios and Suites; all have ultra-fast wifi, high-end TVs with Freeview, digital radios, minibars and Nespresso machines and apart from the loft rooms all have decent sized bathrooms with baths. The hotel also has as a good-sized gym, sauna and steam room – and a fleet of bikes for guest use.

The hotel's location just off Moorgate naturally means that it's a top choice for corporate folk, but really this would be a good place to stay for anyone. There is no more historic part of the capital than the City, which stretches out from the hotel in all directions; and you are close to the Barbican arts centre in one direction and to the hip and happening Shoreditch and Hoxton in the other. Moorgate Tube is also just a two-minute walk away so you can be anywhere in no time.

But perhaps what we like best about the South Place is the fact that all of its 80 rooms are dog-friendly, and that they don't just tolerate dogs and their owners, but lay on beds, towels and treats as well as providing a mapbook showing the best dog walks nearby – of which there are plenty!

CONTACT 3 South Place, London EC2M 2AF • 020 3503 0777

HOW MUCH? Double rooms from £350 a night.

ROOMS 80 Guest Rooms & Suites.

Hoxton Southwark

Perhaps London's coolest place to stay south of the river – and dog-friendly too!

The burgeoning Hoxton group has two other hotels in London (in Shoreditch and Holborn), but this is maybe our favourite, and perhaps the coolest place to stay south of the river that you'll find. It's in a great neighbourhood, two minutes' from the river and the Thames path which you can take in one direction to nearby Tate Modern, the Globe and Borough Market and in the other to the South Bank and Westminster.

With 192 rooms, Hoxton Southwark is the smallest (just) of the London Hoxtons – despite being in the largest building, half of which is given over to co-working office space. Rooms vary from Shoebox to Biggy and take in Snug, Cosy and Roomy along the way, and come equipped with air-conditioning, tea and coffee, digital radios, fridges with fresh milk and water and Smart TVs. You can buy drinks and other essentials from reception at non-mini-bar prices, and even the smallest rooms have high ceilings (only the Shoeboxes don't have space for a chair or desk). Bathrooms are decent sizes without too much variation between categories. The first and second floors are home to their dog-friendly rooms, and dogs go free, as well as being provided with a dog bowl, bed, treats and toy and a dog-friendly guide to the local area – something all the Hoxton hotels do. Rather sweetly, they also tend to ask the dog's name so they can give him/her a proper sort of welcome.

The ground-floor lobby, bar and restaurant form a deliberately sociable space, with a vibe that is a bit gentler than its Shoreditch cousin. The hotel offers a good range of food and drink options, from the relaxed Albie's restaurant in the lobby, which serves burgers, salads, sharing boards and snacks all day and evening, to the rightly popular Seabird restaurant on the 11th floor, which specializes in Mediterranean seafood and has one of the best views in London from its large terrace. There's also a mezzanine bar that's a great little hideaway and a good place to meet friends.

CONTACT 32–40 Blackfriars Road, London SE1 8PB • 020 7903 3000

HOW MUCH? Double rooms from £279 a night.

ROOMS 192 Guest Rooms & Suites.

One Aldwych

A super stylish London hotel with a pool, spa, cinema and a terrific Theatreland location

For a London hotel, One Aldwych just about has it all. Set in a landmark building, the former home of the Morning Post enjoys a perfect position in London's West End, on the edge of Covent Garden and Theatreland. It's awash with facilities, with its own pool and spa, a cinema screening room, and has a terrific restaurant and destination hotel bar. Yet, despite all this and a set of cream-of-the-crop guest rooms and suites, it manages to retain a boutique feel – not just in its rooms and public spaces, but in its staff, who are assured, knowledgeable and experienced in going the extra mile for their guests.

Divided between Superior, Deluxe, and Suites, the bedrooms come with Smart TVs, Dyson hairdryers, tea- and coffee-making facilities and complimentary water, soft drinks and snacks – all drinks in the minibar (including beer and wine) are also complimentary. In the en-suite bathrooms, you'll find cosy robes and thoroughly British Mitchell & Peach toiletries. All boast a walk-in shower, with many Deluxe rooms also equipped with a bath, and are superbly well sound-proofed from the street outside.

At street level, the Lobby Bar is a destination in itself – perfect for that pre-dinner cocktail. It's overlooked from the mezzanine by the hotel's Indigo restaurant, which serves a delicious and inventive menu built around British ingredients. Seasonally-themed tasting menus are the big draw here, as is Indigo's reputation as one of London's top gluten-free restaurants. Downstairs at One Aldwych is the mouthwatering world of Charlie and the Chocolate Factory with afternoon tea inspired by Roald Dahl's iconic story. The biggest secret is the subterranean health club where you can indulge in a spa treatment, visit the gym or take a dip in the 18-metre swimming pool – a rarity in central London, as is the underwater music that soothes you as you swim in its chlorine-free waters.

As a high-end hotel in the heart of London, a stay at One Aldwych comes at a price. It naturally goes without saying then that you'll be incredibly well looked after here, but your hosts also understand that you're not in London just to spend time in your room, so a rich array of cultural events are laid on for guests – everything from theatre packages at the nearby Donmar Warehouse to bespoke London tours with a historical expert: basically, experiences you won't forget – much like the hotel itself.

CONTACT 1 Aldwych, London WC2B 4BZ • 020 7300 1000
HOW MUCH? Double rooms from £700 a night.
ROOMS 101 Guest Rooms & Suites.

The Laslett

A stylish, hip and dog-friendly hotel, The Laslett, made up of five Regency townhouses located in the heart of Notting Hill, is somewhat hidden away yet just moments from the hustle and bustle of Portobello Road. Named after Rhaune Laslett, the founder of the Notting Hill Carnival, it's a thoroughly comfortable and very cool place to stay – special enough to feel you're staying somewhere nice, but comfy enough to make you feel right at home, with pictures, photographs and sculptures by local British artists and old Penguin paperback books adding to the homely vibe. They have 51 spacious en-suite bedrooms, decorated in shades of grey and white, all with good wifi, a flatscreen TV and tea- and coffee-making facilities. Food is classical with a twist, using local and British ingredients, and you can eat on the outdoor terrace where brunch is served at the weekend. There's also a great bar and live music on Sundays!

CONTACT Pembridge Gardens, Notting Hill, London W2 4DU • 020 7792 6688
HOW MUCH? Double rooms from £380 a night.

Hazlitt's

Named after the late-18th-century writer William Hazlitt, who lived in a boarding house here, and part of a group of three boutique London locations, Hazlitt's is hands-down one of the capital's most gorgeous and unique places to stay, providing a superb and very characterful hideaway in the heart of Soho. A warren of rooms in a row of wonky Georgian houses, it exudes history and literary associations from every nook and cranny, with wood panels and four-posters, faded rugs and fine old paintings. The wildly sloping floors, ancient books and objets d'art at every turn give the place a feel that's delightfully unpretentious, sort of like staying with your richest and most eccentric London aunt or uncle. Overall, it couldn't be further away from the experience of staying in a chain hotel, and that's exactly the point: just soak up the atmosphere and think yourself lucky to be staying in such a unique location, at the heart of Europe's most exciting city.

CONTACT 6 Frith Street, Soho, London W1D 3JA • 020 7434 1771
HOW MUCH? Double rooms from £300 a night.

The Rookery

One of a group of three London hotels that blend Regency charm with a thoroughly contemporary sensibility, The Rookery was formerly the site of one of London's most notorious slums when the building went up in 1764. Thankfully, it's changed quite a bit since then, and Clerkenwell is now at the heart of London's creative industries. With buzzer entry, the hotel has an exclusively private feel, and characterful and cosy ground-floor lounges with antique furniture and wood-panelling. The intimate atmosphere continues in the 33 guest rooms, which are decorated in the same slightly theatrical style. Some rooms have four-posters, others roll-top baths, and all come with good wifi, minibars and other modern amenities, including Smart TVs cunningly concealed to preserve the 18th-century ambience. The show-stopper place to stay is the fabulous two-level Rooks Nest suite, with a four-poster bed and a separate living space in the turret above.

CONTACT Peter's Lane, Cowcross Street, London EC1M 6DS • 020 7336 0931
HOW MUCH? Double rooms from £300 a night.

The Portobello Hotel

Part of the small Curious group, it's no accident that The Portobello is one of the capital's most alluring boutique hotels – indeed it virtually invented the term when it opened in 1971 when it was perfectly in keeping with Notting Hill's at-the-time slightly edgy vibe. It's still a convenient and stylish base for the capital while at the same time retaining some of the feel of a bohemian outpost. The hotel has 21 bedrooms, each individually and quirkily designed: ranging from Box through Jolly Good to Roomy, Splendid and the ultimate Signature' they all come with wifi, mineral water, minibars and en-suite bathrooms with Green & Spring toiletries and robes and slippers. Downstairs there's a comfy sitting room with honesty bar, and although the hotel has no bar or restaurant, you can order snacks and drinks from their well-priced room service menu. Unusually for a London hotel of this quality, a buffet breakfast is also included in the room rate.

CONTACT 22 Stanley Gardens, Notting Hill, London W11 2NG • 020 7727 2777
HOW MUCH? Double rooms from £250 a night.

Lucky Dip

The Ampersand Hotel

10 Harrington Rd, London SW7 3ER

One of very few privately owned five-star hotels in this part of London, this is not only an extremely comfortable place to stay in a good location, it's also dog-friendly, so you can bring the whole family. The rooms are great for humans too – each individually styled and all boasting comfy beds with bespoke headboards, tea- and coffee-making facilities, Freeview TVs, robes and slippers, and either bathtubs or walk-in showers in spacious bathrooms. Naturally, the more expensive rooms are bigger and some have free-standing baths in the room, but all are large enough for a reasonable stay. There's a café that serves food all day, including an award-winning afternoon tea and a relaxed and contemporary restaurant.

Bermonds Locke

157 Tower Bridge Rd, London SE1 3LW

At the funkier end of Bermondsey Street on Tower Bridge Road, this apartment-hotel epitomizes the Locke Living group's mission to provide cool, affordable urban accommodation for those who want to stay a bit longer, and offering all the amenities you need to do so – including kitchen facilities, discounts for stays of a week or more, even a lobby that doubles as a co-working space. The hotel's style is relaxed and self-consciously stylish, but also very practical and budget-conscious, with crisp, contemporary bathrooms with showers (no baths), well-thought-out kitchen facilities, Smart TVs and 'Who Gives a Crap' toilet paper. As for food, the Shaman coffee bar in the lobby serves drinks and snacks and turns into a regular bar in the evening, while Robin Gill's Bermondsey Larder serves as the hotel's in-house restaurant.

Chateau Denmark

Denmark St, London WC2H 0LA

The spiritual home of music in the capital, Denmark Street is the natural home of Chateau Denmark, an uber-sleek hotel that pays homage to the area's unique history. Spread across 16 characterful buildings (keep your eye out for their trademark coiling snake door knockers), the 55 rooms, suites and apartments were inspired by punk, psychedelia and vintage gothic and encompass rich textures, dramatic finishes, bespoke headboards and striking artwork. There's butler service, and some units offer bars stocked pre-arrival with your choice of beverages. For drinks and dining, Thirteen is an opulent all-day hangout and cocktail bar serving Japanese small plates, while Tattu dishes up contemporary Chinese fare.

The Coach

26–28 Ray St St, London EC1R 3DJ

Not all resurgent boozers are equal, and if we're honest very few are a match for The Coach, which serves fabulous food and has four very comfortable rooms upstairs for those wanting to stay the night. And why wouldn't you? It's in a brilliant location, on the fringes of Clerkenwell and Holborn, the rooms are spacious, peaceful and very stylish, and the Modern European food is as good as anything served in this part of London – quite a claim in an area where places to eat are thick on the ground.

The Shangri-La

31 St Thomas St, London SE1 9QU

Very much the hotel for a special occasion, not many places can match the views from this iconic London landmark, whose 200 rooms' floor-to-ceiling windows make the most of its prime location in The Shard. If that's not enough, scoot up to the 52nd floor to enjoy the city's highest infinity pool, spa and gym – and of course a wonderful rooftop bar.

Sunborn London

Royal Victoria Dock, London E16 1AA

Moored in London's Docklands, this 108-metre superyacht has rooms ranging from simple to suites. Anchored opposite ExCel Centre and close to both City Airport and Canary Wharf, it's well-suited to corporate folk, but its appeal to leisure visitors is also easy to see, with a quieter location outside but well connected to the city centre. Oh and the views of the Thames from the onboard rooms are stunning.

Bermonds Lock

Chateau Denmark

The Coach

The Southeast

Kent • Sussex • Surrey • Hampshire • Isle of Wight • Berkshire • Buckinghamshire • Hertfordshire • Bedfordshire • Oxfordshire

London casts a long shadow in South East England, but it's striking how quickly you can be in what feels like the deepest countryside outside the capital. To the north and west of London, Bucks, Berkshire, Hertfordshire and especially Oxfordshire have their moments, with beautiful countryside, riverside towns and historic villages luring jaded Londoners out of the Smoke, while parts of Kent, Surrey, Sussex and Hampshire are as rural as anywhere in England, with the South Downs National Park, Kent coast, New Forest and Isle of Wight offering proper countryside retreats and seaside escapes. Not surprisingly, there is no shortage of great places to stay, and you can soak it all up in a variety of smart country houses, contemporary hotels, cosy pubs and boutique B&Bs.

Montagu Arms, p.64

Fort Road Hotel

A very comfortable Margate boutique hotel with a bar, restaurant and sea-view rooms

Perhaps nowhere sums up resurgent modern Margate quite as much as this former seaside boarding house, originally opened in 1820 and now a funky boutique hotel on the edge of the resort's Old Town. After 30 years of standing idle, Fort Road Hotel was bought in 2018 by a group of local creative entrepreneurs and was re-opened after a full-scale renovation in 2023 – as a hotel and restaurant offering grown-up Margate hospitality that's very much of its time and place.

The hotel's 14 guest rooms, smart restaurant and cool underground bar make for one of the best places to stay in a town that's increasingly full of good options. Views from some of the rooms and the hotel's roof terrace are of the Turner Gallery, Margate's harbour arm and most importantly the sea, while inside things are properly local and right up-to-date, with local Haeckels toiletries in the bathrooms, work by local artists Tracey Emin, Matthew Darbyshire and Hannah Lees in the bar, and photographs of Margate in the hallways. Even the bedtime reading you'll find in the rooms is from and about this stretch of the Kentish coast.

If it's the coast you've come for, you really ought to opt for a sea-view room or suite, but whichever you choose you'll find stylish rooms that have been individually designed with a mid-century aesthetic, including vintage pieces here and there and artworks hung on neutrally-painted walls – which, together with books on shelves and plants in pots, add life to these light and airy spaces. No bed is smaller than a king, no room without a Roberts Bluetooth radio and there are no TVs in all but three of the rooms. It all adds up to a relaxing place to stay that encourages reading, exploration and conversation.

The shared spaces help with that too. The bar, with its exposed brick walls and bare bulbs, is very much part of the local scene, often hosting events, while upstairs the restaurant is more refined but not at all formal and continues to celebrate its location with lots of Kentish produce on the menu. It too attracts lots of non-residents and is well worth eating in at least once while you're here. However, don't by any means forget why you came – nice as Fort Road is, you need to get out and discover what all the fuss is about: the art, the sea, the style, the food and the fun of Margate in the 2020s!

CONTACT 18 Fort Road, Margate, Kent CT9 1HF • 01843 661 313

HOW MUCH? Double rooms from £140 a night.

ROOMS 14 Guest Rooms.

The Albion Rooms

It may occupy a classic seafront Cliftonville location with unforgettable views of the sea and the kiss-me-quick delights of Margate just a short walk away, but that's about as close to a a traditional seaside guesthouse as The Albion Rooms gets. Famously purchased by indie band The Libertines a few years ago, their studio forms an impressive extension to the rear of the property, but it's also a contemporary hotel, with guest rooms that are about as appealing and well-equipped as any you'll find in this part of Kent, with big comfy beds, en-suite bathrooms, B&O Bluetooth speakers, robes and slippers, tea and coffee and complimentary drinks. The band designed the rooms themselves in a theatrical yet cosy style, plastering the walls with a selection of contemporary artworks that is perfectly in tune with the raffish Margate vibe. There's a 24-hour 'cocktail concierge' and the basement bar is also open until a decently late hour.

CONTACT 31 Eastern Esplanade, Cliftonville, Margate, Kent CT9 2HL • 01843 264041
HOW MUCH? Double rooms with breakfast from £130 a night.

7 Longport

7 Longport is about as homely a Canterbury haven as you could find, not only enjoying a great position that's handy for the centre of Canterbury (and stations), but tucked away in a peaceful location opposite the ruins of St Augustine's Abbey. It also offers a great deal more privacy than most B&Bs, with accommodation in a separate one-bedroom cottage in an enclosed garden. On sunny days, saunter out of your cottage and have breakfast in the serene courtyard behind the main house. The cottage is as comfortable as it is private, and is decorated and furnished in a tasteful, contemporary style. The ground-floor sitting room is decked out in soft shades and is home to a wood-burning stove and a modern, mosaic-tiled wetroom with handmade soap and Noble Isle toiletries, while upstairs there's a supremely comfy king-size bed with a handmade mattress. There's all the tech and amenities you need, too: wifi, a DVD player, Bluetooth speaker, flatscreen TV and digital radio.

CONTACT 7 Longport, Canterbury, Kent CT1 1PE • 01227 455 367
HOW MUCH? Double rooms from £110 a night, including breakfast.

Oakside Lodge & Treehouse

The great thing about Oakside Lodge is its location, location, location. We say it three times, because there are at least three location-related reasons that make this guesthouse a fantastic place to stay. Firstly, it's less than three miles from Canterbury. Secondly, despite its proximity to the city, it has a rural setting on the edge of an ancient woodland. And, thirdly, it's easily accessed from the A2, which provides a direct link to London. With just five rooms in a timber-clad lodge building, it has a pleasing intimacy that many places lack. Indeed your hosts Stuart and Georgiana own five acres of this ancient forest and rear pigs among the trees – and their home-reared bacon and sausages feature in the excellent breakfasts you will enjoy each morning. Their touch is present everywhere, from the welcome you'll receive to the fabulous treehouse room in the grounds, which has all the same facilities but a lofty and unique setting. It's one of the quirkiest B&B rooms you'll find anywhere.

CONTACT Upper Harbledown, Canterbury, Kent CT2 9AX • 01227 788 466
HOW MUCH? Double rooms from £89 a night including breakfast. Treehouse from £200 a night.

House of Agnes

This is one of our favourite Canterbury boltholes, an exceptionally well-run, funky and friendly boutique B&B that was featured – and highly praised – on Channel 4's 'Four in a Bed' series. Once a restaurant, and a nightclub before that, it's situated in a Grade II-listed historic house said to be mentioned in 'David Copperfield', with a beautiful (and surprisingly large) walled garden out the back, nine quirky rooms inside and eight in a converted stables. Each bedroom in the main building is individually decorated according to a theme – mostly cities – meaning you can spend the night in the Mumbai, Marrakesh or Tokyo, to name just the most exotic destinations. Stay in romantic Paris and make the most of a huge en-suite with claw-foot bath. They all have wifi, flatscreen TVs, coffee- and tea-making facilities and decent-sized bath or shower rooms. There's an honesty bar and a cosy lounge with books and board games, and the breakfasts are excellent and generous.

CONTACT 71 St Dunstans Street Canterbury CT2 8BN • 01227 472 185
HOW MUCH? Double rooms with breakfast from £85 a night.

Boys Hall

An elegant restaurant with sumptuous rooms in a historic Kent mansion

Stay at Boys Hall in Kent and you won't forget it. That's because this elegant restaurant with rooms offers something for all of your senses. For starters, the sight of this Grade II-listed mansion house is pleasing. Its symmetrical gabled front facade is covered in wisteria which in season smells delicious. Step inside and there's another aroma – a signature scent that's diffused through every room. The sound is similarly ever-present – chilled music quietly playing from vintage-style Roberts radios. There are tactile surfaces everywhere: velveteen upholstery, banisters worn smooth over centuries and gnarly beams over your head. And for taste? That's from the restaurant downstairs. It's seasonal, local and fresh.

For centuries, this place was the family home to the Boys family. Charles I and Samuel Pepys are said to be among those who stayed there. It's only just started welcoming paying overnight guests. As such, Boys Hall provides a level of style and hospitality that's perfectly in keeping with present-day expectations. Alongside the period features, there are plump cushions, modern fabrics, and walls painted in pewter greens and dusky pinks. There are plants in every room and subtle lighting in hallways.

There are just nine guest bedrooms in this Jacobean house, which dates from 1616 and has been renovated in a way that ensures history has been honoured, not lost. Bathrooms are as modern and light as you could wish for, yet many of the bedrooms and communal spaces feature antiques and artwork that reference the age of the place. You feel that most in the master suite, the Bishop's Quarter, where you'll find ornate panelling on the walls and leaded mullion windows looking out to the garden. It also has a generously proportioned bathroom with a rolltop bathtub and spacious walk-in shower. Notably, there are no TVs. This is a place to read a book, sink into a bath and enjoy conversation. Tea, coffee and toiletries are lovely and locally sourced.

Boys Hall - its rooms, restaurant and pub (yes – it has its own watering hole!) is in Ashford – a handy location if you're on the way to the Continent. It's also a terrific place for a weekend stay out of London, about an hour away by road or rail, and also a central spot if you want to explore Kent's vineyards, castles and coast. But of course, you could just stay and enjoy the sounds, scents and unmistakable style of Boys Hall.

CONTACT Boys Hall Road, Ashford, Kent TN24 0LA • 01233 427 727

HOW MUCH? Double rooms from £180 a night.

ROOMS 9 Guest Rooms.

Port Lympne Hotel

A historic country house hotel in the grounds of a Kent safari park

Choose a stay at the Port Lympne Hotel in the Kent countryside and you'll be joining the ranks of some illustrious folk. Winston Churchill, T.E. Lawrence and Charlie Chaplin have all been former guests at this Grade II-listed mansion, and it retains much of the glamour and extravagance of the early 20th century. But the company you'll keep here is slightly different now. Port Lympne has been a wild animal reserve since 1976 and nowadays your neighbours will be upwards of 800 animals, including – yes – lions and tigers and bears!

By staying here you're contributing to their upkeep in a place that aims to ensure the survival of endangered species, and, where possible, to return them to the wild. Stays include entry to the reserve (both during usual opening times and after hours), a safari tour and your own golf buggy to get around in. You're welcome to visit the sister wild animal park, Howletts, too. In fact, even just one night here is not really a hotel stay at all but a weekend's worth of experiences you simply can't get anywhere else.

Set high on a hillside with views across Romney Marsh and the Kent coast, the hotel is one of no fewer than 14 accommodation options at Port Lympne, although its elegant guest rooms, just eight of them in total, are the most grown-up and luxurious. Hotel guests need only pop downstairs to the cosy bar for a drink, and it's just a few steps outside to the excellent Garden Room Restaurant. There's a more casual pizza place and a family-friendly grill too – though for either of those, you'll probably want to jump in your golf buggy, leaving time to stop and look at the animals as you pass.

When the time comes to head to bed, the solid walls and heavy doors of the hotel mean that the roars of lions and whoops of monkeys are kept out as you drift off in a comfortable bed that's made up with quality linen. There are tea- and coffee-making facilities in every room, Nespresso machines in the suites, Smart TVs and wifi, but it's the antique furniture, artwork on the walls and what's beyond the window that makes this such a unique experience – just like being on a real safari, but in Kent! Port Lympne's other accommodation options include the luxury Lion and Tiger Lodges, with windows on the big cat enclosures, the safari tents of Bear Lodge, self catering in the reserve's canopy-level Treehouses, plus more basic cabins and camping.

CONTACT Port Lympne Reserve, Lympne, Near Hythe, Kent CT21 4PD • 01303 234 112

HOW MUCH? Double rooms from £269 a night including breakfast.

ROOMS 8 Guest Rooms.

Alkham Court Farmhouse

There's nothing like staying on a farm, but you'd be hard-pushed to find a B&B like Alkham Court Farmhouse, which is owned and run by Wendy Burrows and her husband Neil. They enjoy sharing the delights of their Kentish farmhouse with other people, and provide a personal welcome on arrival together with a slice of homemade cake. Wendy is always keen to share her favourite walks and cycle rides, and she can even arrange for you to explore on horseback. It's a short walk to the village, where there's a decent pub, and numerous footpaths into the surrounding downs. There's a sauna and hot tub, legendary breakfasts and optional packed lunches and evening snacks. There are just three guest rooms, each individually designed and all equipped with high-quality bed linen, robes and slippers, Nespresso machines, mineral water, TV and DVD, digital radios and mini-fridges, and fresh flowers on arrival. Bathrooms are recently refurbished and have posh toiletries.

CONTACT Meggett Lane, South Alkham, Kent CT15 7DG • 07557 122 713
HOW MUCH? Double rooms with breakfast, £150-£185 a night.

The Jolly Sportsman

Situated in a great position on the edge of the South Downs, this classic Sussex pub with rooms is not only located in a picturesque Downland village, complete with ancient church, a couple of pubs and walks galore, it's also a great place to eat, whether for a special occasion or just a casual lunch. The pub itself is very attractive, with a vintage Sussex clapboard exterior and a comfortable yet quite contemporary set of rooms inside. It's more of a place to eat these days than somewhere you stop by for a pint, with stripped-back tables and cool, crisp art adorning pastel green and rusty red walls. Given the location, we couldn't blame you if you wanted to stay over, and they have three dog-friendly double rooms and a suite where you can do that – simply but very tastefully furnished, with white walls, super-king-size beds with high-quality mattresses, good wifi, flatscreen TVs, and modern and well-appointed en-suite bathrooms with rainfall showers, fluffy towels and toiletries.

CONTACT Chapel Lane, East Chiltington, East Sussex BN7 3BA • 01273 890 400
HOW MUCH? Double rooms from £140 a night, including breakfast.

Tillingham Winery

As you wind your way into Dew Farm, you'll notice ancient woodland, fruit trees and roaming livestock – and of course, carefully planted rows of vines, because it's also home to Tillingham winery. The former hop barn has 11 characterful guest rooms, an on-site restaurant and bar and a striking oast house where grapes are left to ferment. Just a 10-minute drive from Rye, this 70-acre organic farmstead runs tours and tastings after which you can enjoy lunch from a set menu or dinner from the seasonal six-course 'Garden Menu'; they also serve woodfired sourdough pizza in the Dutch barn. Rooms range from Standard to Large to Feature – some have super-king-size beds and free-standing baths, while others have kings or doubles and large walk-in showers. All are uber-stylish, with Roberts radios (no TVs, but you definitely won't mind), vibrant artwork and glorious estate views. If you're up for a more rustic option, go for a high-spec bell tent, with a double bed and wood-burning stove.

CONTACT Dew Farm, Dew Lane, Peasmarsh, East Sussex TN31 6XD • 01797 208 226
HOW MUCH? Double rooms from £175 a night including breakfast.

Leonardslee House

Set in 240 stunning acres near Horsham in West Sussex, to call Leonardslee House a 'restaurant with rooms' underplays its luxurious accommodation and spectacular sculpture-filled grounds. But then again, with a Michelin-starred restaurant, it's understandable that gastronomy takes centre stage. Inside this Grade II-listed Italianate house, 10 comfortable bedrooms boast sweeping views of the grounds and come with king-size beds, flatscreen TVs, Tyneham toiletries, fluffy white bathrobes and Nespresso machines, and a fridge filled with chilled wine from the Leonardslee Estate's own vineyard. The Interlude restaurant is open from Thursday to Sunday (food is available other days at the Clocktower Café in the grounds). With just eight tables, dinner here is designed to be an occasion – many ingredients are foraged directly from the estate's Grade I-listed gardens, while some of the finest local produce in Sussex also plays a starring role.

CONTACT Brighton Rd, Lower Beeding, Horsham, West Sussex RH13 6PP • 0871 873 3363
HOW MUCH? Double rooms from £260 a night, not including breakfast.

Trading Boundaries

Enchanting boutique B&B guest rooms – and much more! – in a lovely part of Sussex

An Indian stone elephant standing out front of a Georgian coaching inn gives some indication of what lies within at Trading Boundaries. Here, in the quintessentially Sussex countryside, where villages cluster around cricket pitches, Trading Boundaries offers a more exotic alternative. Handcrafted Indian furniture, fabrics and collectibles have been sold here for more than 25 years since a former pub at a crossroads was turned into a popular trading post. Its evolution over time has seen more aspects added to the family business – the latest of which are eight lovely guest rooms.

As you might imagine, these boutique rooms are exquisitely furnished with one-off pieces from India. The luxury room, for example, has a seriously cool, beautifully-carved vintage Indian bed, the likes of which you won't find anywhere else. But whichever room you choose — there are dog-friendly rooms, family suites and twins as well as doubles — you can expect something to pique your interest. You can also expect a modern bathroom, good wifi, a Bluetooth speaker, a Smart TV and tea- and coffee-making facilities.

The rooms are all positioned around a courtyard, and are a short stroll from the Trading Boundaries shop, art gallery and café/bar, which is another thriving arm of this family business. It's here you'll have your continental breakfast during your stay. From Wednesday to Sunday, the café and its terrace are open all day too and lunch here is highly recommended. Like your rooms, the dining area combines vintage Indian and contemporary style. There's a real tuk-tuk as part of the decor but the menu focuses on locally-sourced food and drink and includes plenty of English wines. Live music is another integral part of the Trading Boundaries offering, with jazz brunches on Sundays and regular concert nights.

After browsing the shop and taking a peek at Britain's only gallery devoted to the work of 1970s icon Roger Dean (best known for his distinctive prog rock album cover artwork), you can get out to explore the area, which offers plenty to see and do – nearby vineyards, the neighbouring National Trust property, Sheffield Park, or the steam trains of the Bluebell Railway. Trading Boundaries is within the High Weald Area of Outstanding Natural Beauty and on the edge of Ashdown Forest, with lots of walks, good pubs and great cycling. All this and it's just an hour or so from London.

CONTACT Sheffield Green, Fletching, Near Uckfield, East Sussex TN22 3RB • 01825 790 200
HOW MUCH? Double rooms from £125 a night.
ROOMS 8 Guest Rooms.

The Relais Cooden Beach Hotel

A stylish beachside hotel in East Sussex

This stylish seafront hotel mixes the fresh chic of New England decor with the timeless charm of a British holiday by the seaside. The Relais Cooden Beach is a coastal hotel situated in Bexhill, less than two hours' drive south of London – to get here, you drive until the road runs out on the south coast's shingle shores, or perhaps hop on a train from London Victoria to arrive at Cooden Beach station, just a couple of minutes' walk from the hotel. It's easily reached and a perfect destination for a few days, relaxing and recharging to the sound, sight and smell of the sea. And who knows, you might even take a dip in the sea, which is handily located just a few yards from your room!

People have been visiting this quintessential seaside destination since 1928, when the hotel was first opened. But it has most certainly evolved with the times. Its most recent renovation, into a Relais Retreat, has seen all 45 en-suite bedrooms freshly styled with a nod to the beach. That means nautical stripes in gentle sea blues or warm terracotta to emulate the south coast's sunnier days. It also means a contemporary finish and New England-style panelling – all soft and subtly elegant. There are rooms and suites for solo travellers, couples, families and those with reduced mobility. But, whichever room you decide on, we'd recommend a sea view to make the most of the beauty of the seafront location - and even if you don't, everyone can enjoy views of the beach from the communal spaces downstairs. Perhaps the best of these is from the Rally Restaurant, where locally-caught fish is the highlight on a menu of seasonal dishes that can be eaten al fresco on the terrace. Strolling carefree from your comfortable room to a leisurely breakfast, down to the beach and back again is what this place is all about.

The hotel is the second in a growing collection of Relais Retreats (thc first was The Relais Henley), a collection of stylish waterside escapes within two hours of London. There's no denying that being by water, whether it's the sea at Cooden Beach or by the river at Henley, makes for a relaxing environment. The trick of Relais Retreats has been to carry that feeling into the indoor spaces of historic hotels, all with an eye on modern tastes. The result? Quite simply a terrific place to stay. By the water.

CONTACT Cooden Sea Road, Bexhill-on-Sea, East Sussex TN39 4TT • 01424 842 281
HOW MUCH? Double rooms from £156.50 a night; Suites from £173.50. Seaview doubles from £190.50 a night; Seaview suites from £233 a night.
ROOMS 45 Guest Rooms.

Port

A cool seafront hotel, restaurant and bar offering a chic stay in up-and-coming Eastbourne

Looking for a boutique hotel in a cool, south-coast seaside destination, not far from London? No, not Brighton – we're talking about Eastbourne, fast shedding its former staid reputation to emerge as one of the hotter spots for a coastal weekend away in the southeast of England. Port is a classy example of all the good things happening in the town, a thoroughly updated Victorian seafront townhouse just across from the beach with terrific views and a keen sense of what makes for a chic weekend by the sea.

Six of the hotel's stylish rooms overlook the beach and the pier (binoculars are provided, a nice touch), but the rest of the rooms don't let you down either, with muted tones, plenty of natural light and views over the town and the South Downs. The top choice is the Studio Apartment, with its balcony and full-height bay window – you feel like you're almost in the sea – but even the smallest Cabin rooms have king-size beds, smart bathrooms with a walk-in shower, plus a large TV, a bar-fridge, Nespresso machine and USB charging ports. There are two family rooms on the lower ground floor – 'below deck', that is with no sea views. One has bunks, the other a fold-out sofa-bed. And three of the rooms are dog-friendly, if it's beach walkies you're thinking of. The age of the building means that it's not accessible to wheelchair users, but parking is handily available on the road in front of the hotel, using the voucher provided.

The restaurant and bar scene has also picked up in town and you can ask for recommendations, while Port's welcoming seafront restaurant is open for breakfast all week, for lunch and dinner on Fridays and Saturdays, and on Sundays for roasts, sourcing ingredients from Sussex producers. Expect tasty dishes like Wagyu rump of beef, vegetarian Wellington and banoffee pie for dessert. There's also a bar stocked with local wines and beers and artisan spirits that's also open to non-residents.

Port is right on the promenade, with walks up to the pier and along the gardens, with the iconic chalk cliffs of Beachy Head and the Seven Sisters beyond. Or there's the contemporary Towner art gallery, bringing more modern British pizzazz into a seaside town very much on the up.

CONTACT 11–12 Royal Eastbourne Parade, Eastbourne, East Sussex BN22 7AR • 01323 438 526

HOW MUCH? Double rooms from around £89 a night.

ROOMS 19 Guest Rooms.

Bailiffscourt Hotel & Spa

A beautiful West Sussex hotel and spa by the sea

The beautiful Bailiffscourt Hotel is somewhat misleading. What looks like a smattering of ancient, medieval buildings, is in fact an ostentatious 20th-century creation with a genuinely fascinating history of fancy and folly. Sitting on the West Sussex coast just behind Climping's popular pebble beach, roughly midway between Littlehampton and Bognor Regis, this sprawling hotel is all leaded windows, huge wooden doors and crumbling old sandstone.

But none of these old parts really belong here, as Bailiffscourt is a marvel in the art of salvage and restoration, dreamt up by Lady Moyne – wife of Walter Guinness of the famous brewing family – and built by architect, Amyas Phillips, who travelled the country to seek out original medieval features. The result is an incredibly atmospheric, ancient-looking construction with a history dating back just 90-or-so years. There's really nowhere else like it in the country.

The hotel also has plenty to please contemporary visitors. First are the rooms, which, in keeping with the beautiful surroundings, are situated in a series of charming houses and cottages overlooking the grounds and the sea. Each one is different, ranging from medieval-style rooms with four-poster beds to more contemporary designs, but all of them come with lovely en-suite bathrooms with Temple Spa toiletries and fluffy dressing gowns.

The location and facilities are likewise superb. Walks along the coast or among the 30 acres of gardens are a pleasure and you are close to lots of other seaside delights, like West Wittering and Chichester, not to mention the glories of the South Downs and the historic town of Arundel, with its magnificent castle, a few miles inland.

The spa is sublime, with its heated outdoor pool from which you can hear the ocean crashing on the stones nearby, and the restaurant has a trio of excellent menus offering locally sourced produce and exceptionally fresh seafood. Service is seamless, and the warren of lounges throughout the main building are a cosy place to while away an afternoon by the fire. What's more, dogs are welcome too, as with all three hotels in the excellent Historic Sussex Hotels group.

CONTACT Climping Street, Climping, Near Littlehampton, West Sussex BN17 5RW • 01903 723 511

HOW MUCH? Double rooms from £325 a night, including breakfast.

ROOMS 39 Guest Rooms & Suites.

The Bell in Ticehurst

A one-of-a-kind village inn in a beautiful corner of East Sussex, with superb food

Quirkiness, comfort and history prevail in this delightful East Sussex pub. Not only can you drop in for a drink or something delicious to eat, you can also stay over in one of their eccentrically decorated rooms or lodges and appreciate one of the most unusual and welcoming places to stay in the region. It's comfy, contemporary and unique, run by people who've put their stamp on a country inn that dates back to the 16th century but is as full of life as ever.

Above all, The Bell in Ticehurst is a great village pub – cosy and comfortable, with plenty of beams and battered sofas, bare boards and faded rugs, open fires and candlelight. It's mischievous and quirky too, with bowler hat light fittings, coat hooks fashioned from cutlery, a tower of books forming a twisted column by the bar, and even a Banksy in the hall. Have a look too at the tubas in place of urinals in the gents' loos (sadly the ladies' are nowhere near as much fun). The food is whatever you want it to be, with both a pub-style menu and a more refined tasting menu served once a week.

Above the pub, the seven stylish guest rooms are equally eccentric, with rustic king or super-king beds and handmade mattresses. One is a suite on two levels with a sofa bed for extra guests; a couple have deep copper baths, while they all have en-suite bathrooms with bespoke toiletries, homemade cookies, Freeview TVs, good wifi, tea- and coffee-making facilities – and dogs are welcome. In addition to the rooms, the pub also boasts four garden suites with mezzanine floors, huge baths and their own terraces, wood burners and fire pits. The rooms and lodges are so homely and there's so much going on at The Bell that it can be hard to leave – as well as regular live music, they offer painting, calligraphy and crafting courses. The surrounding countryside is beautiful too – easy to explore by bike or on numerous local footpaths – and there are lots of local attractions, including activities at nearby Bedgebury, watersports at Bewl Water and Rudyard Kipling's home at Bateman's.

CONTACT High Street, Ticehurst, East Sussex TN5 7AS • 01580 200 300
HOW MUCH? Double rooms from £125 to £295 a night, not including breakfast.
ROOMS 7 Guest Rooms & 4 Suites.

Ockenden Manor

A beautiful Sussex manor house hotel with swanky spa and an award-winning restaurant

Old meets new at Ockenden Manor in Cuckfield, West Sussex, as this grand old Elizabethan mansion is paired with a beautifully modern spa whose exterior is almost industrial in design. The elegance of the main house isn't diminished, though, as its lavishly decorated bedrooms – think four-poster beds, plush carpets and enormous bathtubs – and classically homely lounges and bars make a wonderful countryside retreat. Well placed within the South Downs, this is the place to come for long walks, fireside G&Ts and long soaks in the heated pool.

Parts of the hotel date back to the 1600s, and its exterior is all golden sandstone, towering chimneys and ivy that glows a fiery red in autumn. The superb spa offers a place to warm up in its heated indoor/outdoor pool, where you can float to views of the lawns and woods beyond. Treatments range from floatation pods to reiki to traditional massages, and there's a 'walk-through' rainforest shower fed by a natural spring.

Guest rooms and suites vary from the more traditional options in the main house to spacious suites in the spa, but they all come with Vispring beds, good wifi, Smart TVs, tea- and coffee-making facilities (including a Nespresso machine) and beautiful en-suite bathrooms with bathtubs, Temple Spa products and robes. The hotel's restaurant is excellent, with local produce transformed by an award-winning chef, and their afternoon teas are an indulgent treat. Dogs are allowed everywhere except the restaurant and spa, and can be left with reception staff while you relax in the pool. Dogs also get a bowl, blanket and biscuits.

The hotel grounds have magnificent views over the South Downs, and it's within easy reach of a clutch of gorgeous Sussex gardens – Wakehurst Place and Sheffield Park amongst them – or, to the south, the pretty village of Ditchling and the South Downs. You could also visit one of a number of nearby vineyards. Whether you'll want to leave the hotel, though, is a different matter.

CONTACT Ockenden Lane, Cuckfield, West Sussex RH17 5LD • 01444 416 111
HOW MUCH? Double rooms from £225 a night, including breakfast.
ROOMS 28 Guest Rooms & Suites.

Saddlers B&B

This West Sussex boutique B&B is a fantastic place to stay near Goodwood, Chichester and West Wittering

Just three miles from Chichester, the elegant rooms of this boutique B&B offer a great base to discover West Sussex. Situated in the rural village of Funtington, Saddlers B&B specializes in warm, home-from-home hospitality. It's a historic property but one in which comfort is thoroughly contemporary and very much the primary focus.

Fresh flowers throughout, homemade treats in the bedrooms, smoothies and garden-fruit compote with yoghurt at breakfast, homemade jams… these are just some of the things that make Saddlers special. Milly, the owner and host, offers a modern take on the time-honoured tradition of B&B accommodation, and goes the extra mile to make sure her guests have the best possible experience. It's a relaxing place to stay that's firmly rooted in its location. Coffee-table books in the shared Snug downstairs celebrate nearby Goodwood along with local attractions and events. Much of the breakfast is locally sourced and even the refillable soaps and shampoos are from West Sussex-based Temple Spa.

The decor throughout is elegant. The interiors are painted in soothing shades and filled with a medley of modern British design, hand-picked antiques and artworks by Milly's family and friends, creating rooms that are inviting and cosy. It's a tasteful feel that extends to the three well-appointed bedrooms, each with a light and spotlessly clean en-suite bathroom and either a king, queen or double bed dressed in Egyptian cotton. They are named after racetracks – and of course Goodwood, which many will be visiting for. But the area has much else to offer – Chichester is just down the road, and Funtington is a great base if you want to walk on the South Downs or relax on the famous sandy beach of West Wittering. The village also has a good pub, a restaurant and a well-stocked farm shop, and a gastro pub, the Horse and Groom, a mile down the road.

CONTACT Funtington Road, Chichester, West Sussex PO18 9LG • 01243 575 029
HOW MUCH? Double rooms with breakfast from £140 a night.
ROOMS 3 Guest Rooms.

Denbies Vineyard Hotel

A relaxed, rural wine retreat with more than a dash of luxury in the gorgeous, rolling Surrey Hills

For the sort of relaxed, rural wine retreat you'd find in France or Italy, you need to head for the gorgeous rolling hills of Surrey – and specifically Denbies winery, England's largest single-estate vineyard. Their vineyard hotel occupies an original 1850s farmhouse and a newly built wing, where 17 en-suite rooms look out over the landscaped grounds and surrounding vines. It's a fabulous, dog-friendly getaway, set on an extensive estate, so apart from the wine attractions, there are country walks, trails and bike rides right from the door.

The rooms are light and contemporary takes on country living – warmly furnished doubles and suites (all with king-size beds), whose windows open onto beautiful views of regimented vines marching off into the distance. Colours throughout pick up the vineyard tones, plus there are Smart TVs, coffee- and tea-making facilities and eco-toiletries in the bathrooms from the French vineyard, Caudalie. Two family rooms (with sofa bed) can be interconnected while five ground-floor rooms in the adjacent annexe are dog-friendly, which means beds, bowls, towels and treats for your four-legged friend. For breakfast and evening meals and drinks, look no further than the Vineyard Restaurant & Bar, which offers classy, orangery-style dining with more of those sumptuous views. There is cabana-seating in the garden, brunch and bubbles options, food and wine pairings and tastings in the Wine Library. Indeed the winery excels as an all-in destination, offering wine-tasting tours, train-rides through the vines between April and October and even a range of classes and treatments, from massages to pilates. Beyond the grounds, you can walk to the local market town of Dorking or head out on to Box Hill for quintessential English country views. And then back for another glass of something crisp or sparkling before the deepest of sleeps in England's premier wine region.

CONTACT London Road, Dorking, Surrey RH5 6AA • 01306 076 777
HOW MUCH? Double rooms from £145 a night including breakfast.
ROOMS 17 Guest Rooms & Suites.

The Percy Arms

Beautifully positioned in the Surrey hamlet of Chilworth, The Percy Arms looks like the quintessential English village pub. Inside, however, things are a little bit different. With energetic South African owners at the helm, this is a classy restaurant with rooms as well as a traditional boozer, and Africa is the theme. Authentic artefacts and the odd animal skin floor-covering create a comfy hunting lodge vibe, and the food is focused around great steaks and a wine list that is a stroll through some of South Africa's best vineyards. The Percy also has five very comfortable bedrooms upstairs, each named after one of the 'Big Five' game animals in Zulu and other African dialects: two super-king en-suite rooms, with gigantic double beds and roll-top slipper baths, two doubles with king-size beds, and a twin – all featuring en-suite bathrooms with organic H2K toiletries, flatscreen TVs, wifi, goosedown duvets, Egyptian cotton linen and a tea tray and coffee machine.

CONTACT 75 Dorking Road, Chilworth, Surrey GU4 8NP • 01483 561 765

HOW MUCH? Double rooms from £115 to £160 a night, including breakfast.

Brooklands Hotel

Celebrate the golden age of motor racing at this stylish hotel where you can kick back in the track-side hot tub and watch cars racing around the historic Brooklands motor-racing circuit. Inside, the hotel is a blend of Art Deco and contemporary styling, with huge windows offering great views of the track. Luxury guest rooms, named after former racing stars and decorated in smart blacks, reds and greys, feature king-size beds, 100 per cent cotton sheets, smart faux-leather headboards, 42-inch TVs and bathrooms with speakers and powerful showers (larger rooms and suites also have baths). The BSpa is a big draw, with its sunlight therapy room, water-beds, sauna, steam room and range of pampering treatments. The two AA-rosette 1907 restaurant dishes up both fine-dining and comforting fish and chips, and a decent vegan menu. Finally, there are the added attractions of Mercedes Benz World and the next door Brooklands Motor Museum where you can also tour the cabin of a Concorde!

CONTACT Brooklands Drive, Weybridge, Surrey KT13 0SL • 01932 335 700

HOW MUCH? Double rooms from £144, including breakfast.

Aviator

Airport hotels tend to be functional and a bit boring, but Aviator is different, a stylish hotel with huge panoramic windows that give you a bird's-eye view of the planes taking off and landing on the runway at Farnborough airport. Not only that, the look and feel of this design-led hotel will really catch your eye, with attention to aeronautical detail even stretching to airplane-shaped jelly babies at reception. Bedrooms are equally luxe, with walnut panelling, Venetian wooden blinds, Egyptian linen and goose-down pillows and duvets on king or super-king beds, and powerful walk-in rain showers that will put plenty of pep in your step. The One Eleven American diner offers a relaxed vibe, while the Sky Bar is a great place to relax with a signature cocktail and those floor-to-ceiling views of the runway. At weekends, you can enjoy treatments, plus there's a fitness studio, complimentary movies and a music library - or why not pop next door to the Farnborough museum?

CONTACT 55 Farnborough Road, Farnborough, Hampshire, GU14 6EL • 01252 555 890
HOW MUCH? Double rooms from £155 a night including breakfast.

The Greyhound on the Test

This 16th-century gastropub in the quaint village of Stockbridge oozes rustic charm and is a fabulous place to stay if you want a break from London, with a cosy bar and 11 dog-friendly rooms. Each one is different but there's a seamless country-style vibe throughout, with half-panelled walls in Farrow & Ball heritage hues, cool mirrors, thick velvet curtains and embossed cushions and bedspreads. Comfortable king-size beds, quality linen and underfloor heating provide a blissful sleep. There's tea and coffee (from a Nespresso machine), an honesty bar of nibbles and drinks and old-fashioned sweets, and bathrooms are stylish and spacious, either with roll-top stand-alone baths or large cubicles with powerful rain showers, natural stone sinks and lush Molton Brown toiletries. The two AA-rosette restaurant dishes up hefty portions of local produce while breakfast is an array of quality hot and cold options, including delicious wild mushrooms with poached eggs.

CONTACT 31 High Street, Stockbridge, Hampshire SO20 6EY • 01264 810 833
HOW MUCH? Double rooms from £175 a night, including breakfast.

Borough Court

Country living at its best – two stunning B&B rooms with period touches in an historic Hampshire manor

When everyone says it's the best, it would be rude not to agree! Borough Court, a Hampshire country house set in 90 acres, and with 15th-century origins, has been lauded as one of Britain's top, luxury B&Bs. And we're not going to argue, because staying here is an absolutely stunning experience. The proof is in the history – only four families have lived in the house since 1480 (the current owners are descendants of Anne Boleyn!) and it's a beautiful building, rich in period detail but updated with 21st-century comforts very much in mind.

There are, in fact, only two double bedrooms, both in the main house and accessed by the impressive main staircase. The Attic Suite sits under eye-catching curved beams from the hull of a large ship, and the bed is a super-king-size French antique. The panelling is original, and the bathroom, with its slipper bath, sits tucked under the eaves and boasts a view of the garden and lake. Alternatively, you can stay in the Chinese Room, the house's original master bedroom, with a super-king-size bed, Chinese wallpaper, high ceilings, a 16th-century fireplace and an impressive bay window. There are his-and-hers sinks and a roll-top bath in the room, plus a separate walk-in wet room and shower. You really couldn't wish for two more idiosyncratic but wonderfully comfortable rooms with the wow-factor – the only sadness is that you have to choose just one!

Breakfast includes locally farmed sausages and bacon, free-range eggs and homegrown tomatoes, as well as pancakes, homemade preserves and freshly baked croissants. It's served in the dining room, another glorious space with a large fireplace. One point to note is that the age of the house precludes TVs and kettles in the rooms, but you're invited to think of yourselves as house guests with the run of the property, so coffee, tea and a drinks tray are available in the drawing room, where you can help yourself and sit down with a G&T in front of the fire.

You're also welcome to stroll the grounds and woods or head out to nearby villages for age-old pubs and agreeable restaurants. Towns like Basingstoke, Reading and Newbury are within half an hour, the North Hampshire Downs are nearby, and central London is within an hour by car, making this a terrific weekend-away option for anyone who'd like to step back in time for a taste of high-class country living.

CONTACT Borough Court Road, Hartley Wintney, Hampshire RG27 8JA • 07710 056 086
HOW MUCH? Double rooms from £130 a night, including breakfast.
ROOMS 2 Guest Rooms.

The Red Lion, Odiham

As stylish and historic a place for a short break from London as you could wish for

Less than an hour southwest of London and just off the M3 near Hook and Basingstoke, The Red Lion in Odiham is a stylish, historic pub with a buzzy vibe, impressive accommodation and a menu to match. The building dates back to the 17th century, and owners New Dawn Pubs serve cracking locally-sourced food to overnight guests and locals. There are also seven beautiful boutique bedrooms to entice you for an overnight stay.

Upstairs, elegantly understated decor blends seamlessly with Tudor beams and a rustic charm that reveals its coaching inn heritage. Dogs are welcome in all rooms, and receive bowls, a cushion and gluten-free treats baked locally. Spacious rainfall showers, ESPA toiletries, reliable wifi, Smart TVs, tea trays and coffee machines come as standard. Extra touches like blackout blinds, earplugs and retro Roberts radios are testament to the thoughtful consideration of your hosts.

Hungry guests need not venture far. The bar-restaurant downstairs boasts excellent service and an eclectic menu that's consciously local, seasonal and beautifully presented. Pub grub classics like fish and chips, homemade burgers and a pie-of-the-day all feature, alongside a good choice of specials and a good array of gluten-free options. Drinks-wise, beers on draught include Hogs Back and Tilford, brewed down the road in Farnham, while the wine list includes Hampshire sparkling varieties alongside locally distilled gins.

Beyond the cosy confines of the pub, Odiham's vibrant high street is peppered with quaint chocolate-box buildings and indy retailers, and the town itself is brimming with history. Its ruined castle, accessed via a pleasant stroll along the Basingstoke canal, was once home to King John, who set off from here en route to seal the Magna Carta at Runnymede in 1215.

CONTACT 102 High Street, Odiham, Hampshire RG29 1LP • 01256 701 145

HOW MUCH? Double rooms from £90 a night, including continental breakfast weekdays, cooked breakfasts at weekends.

ROOMS 7 Guest Rooms & Suites.

The Hare & Hounds

Handsome village coaching inn, pub and restaurant on the edge of the North Wessex Downs

Newbury in Berkshire is a horse-racing town, so it's no surprise to find an old coaching inn with an equestrian vibe nearby. But following a chic renovation, the 17th-century Hare & Hounds, on the edge of town in the village of Speen, has brought a whole lot more to the table, from classy rooms to superior dining.

There are thirty guest rooms spread across four adjacent buildings, from stables to a former coach house, and all have been given a rather chic country makeover. Expect muted, painted panelling and pretty bed throws, but also a horse picture here and an antler light fitting there, and you won't go too far wrong. Styles, size and aspect vary according to location, but they are all very handsome, with coordinated colours and furnishings, quality king-size beds and en-suite wet rooms. Deluxe rooms have bigger, super-king-size beds and a tad more space, while there are two suites in the coach house (one in the attic) where you also get a roll-top copper bath. Biggest of all is the Bridle Suite in one of the lodges, with copper bath, walk-in rain shower, his-and-hers sinks and your own built-in bar. Ground-floor rooms are dog-friendly – they'll put a dog bed, bowl and treat box in the room for your pet. One of the ground floor rooms is fully accessible with a lower bed and wet room bathroom.

That's only the half of it, though, because the pub and barn dining room are also really comfortable – and while there's a rustic elegance and a horsey vibe, it's not at all formal or fancy: just good, locally sourced food and drink, from artisan cheeses to craft ales. There's fish and chips, or chicken and ham pie, but also anything from a flat-iron steak to a plant-based burger. Saturday brunch is one for family and friends, and a lounge around with the newspapers, or you could stop off for Sunday lunch after a stroll – sorry, canter – in the nearby North Wessex Downs.

CONTACT Bath Road, Speen, Newbury, Berkshire RG14 1QY • 01635 521 152
HOW MUCH? Double rooms from £175 a night.
ROOMS 30 Guest Rooms & Suites.

Montagu Arms

A lovely New Forest country retreat with a very special restaurant

Part of the same group that owns the nearby Careys Manor spa, the Montagu Arms is a bit of a Cool Places favourite, mainly because it ticks all the boxes we usually look for in a good country hotel. It's in a fabulous location, right in Beaulieu village in the heart of the New Forest. It occupies a nice old building with lovely gardens that feels a bit special while still being relaxed and informal. And it has an excellent restaurant, so you don't have to stray very far in search of sustenance.

In fact, the nice thing about the Montagu Arms is that you can leave your car keys in your pocket while you're here, venturing out into the forest on long walks and cycle rides during the day – the walk along the river to Buckler's Hard is a popular one – and collapsing into the arms of the hotel in the evening, where the cosy bar and very highly-rated Terrace Restaurant will take care of you. The hotel's 22 rooms in the main house are all of a good size and are very comfortable: traditional but not fussy in style; some are dog-friendly, a couple have four-posters and all have spacious en-suite bathrooms with robes and White Company toiletries and Smart TVs. There are also two Hayloft Suites and nine Garden Rooms that are if anything more luxurious, some of them with free-standing baths as well as a rainfall shower. All rooms also come with a complimentary decanter of gin! The Terrace restaurant is very much a destination in its own right, offering Modern British dining that makes the most of the nearby forest and coast, as well as the hotel's own kitchen garden. The restaurant itself is full of character and charm – much like the hotel – with traditional wood-panelled decor that's complemented by the quality of service, which is friendly and relaxed. If you would rather something more informal, try the hotel's alternative eatery, Monty's Inn, next door – equally good but serving simpler fare for both lunch and dinner.

CONTACT Beaulieu, Hampshire SO42 7ZL • 01590 612 324

HOW MUCH? Double rooms with breakfast from £224 a night.

ROOMS 33 Guest Rooms & Suites.

Cottage Lodge Hotel

Rustic chic and home comforts in the heart of the New Forest National Park

Located in the heart of the National Park, on the edge of the lively town of Brockenhurst, this family-run hotel couldn't be better suited to a short break in the New Forest – a unique and quirky place to stay that feels almost as if it has been crafted out of the surrounding woodland. Not only is much of the furniture handmade using nearby trees, the owners make a point of using mainly local suppliers, with the aim of becoming the first fully sustainable New Forest hotel. They won the New Forest's 'Sustainable Business' award in 2022, and Boutique Hotelier's 'Sustainable Achievement' award the year before, and it's a thoroughly eco-friendly property in almost every way (although the room that was powered by its own exercise bike is sadly no more).

The hotel is also very comfortable and relaxed throughout, something most manifest in its 16 rustic-chic, individually designed guest bedrooms, each of which has good fast wifi, TVs with Freeview and good-sized en-suite bathrooms, mostly with bath-showers combined and eco-friendly refillable toiletries; they also have tea- and coffee-making facilities and there's homemade cake on hand whenever you want it. Around half the rooms are furnished with amazing four-poster beds that look as if they crept in from the forest outside (one is carved from a single, fallen oak tree, another from a single ash, while a third is a grouping of silver birch trunks). There is also a family room with its own garden and three dog-friendly rooms at the rear of the property with their own patios.

There's an honesty bar downstairs and a breakfast room which serves a terrific breakfast each morning. The same room turns into the separately run 'White Tails' restaurant most evenings, serving a good-value menu of delicious crowd-pleasing classics – just what you need after a day in the forest!

CONTACT Sway Rd, Brockenhurst, Hampshire SO42 7SH • 01590 622 296
HOW MUCH? Double or twin rooms from £110 a night in low season, £140 a night in peak season, always including breakfast.
ROOMS 16 Guest Rooms.

Luccombe Manor & Hall

Beautifully situated Victorian-era Isle of Wight hotel with fantastic sea views

If you've got one superbly sited Isle of Wight clifftop hotel, it makes perfect sense to buy another next door – and here's Luccombe Manor to prove the point, under the same ownership as the adjacent Luccombe Hall (and the nearby Shanklin Villa Apartments), and just as alluring. There is a slightly different vibe here – a bit smaller in scale, with a touch of true Victorian clifftop, seaside splendour – but the same excellent qualities are all in place, from the slick, can-do service to the comfortable rooms with their breathtaking sea views.

There are 23 rooms in all, charmingly decorated in light seaside colours, as well as a high-spec, three-bedroom self-catering apartment. Unlike a lot of places on the island, dogs are welcome in most of the rooms, and there are gardens opposite for daily dog walks. However, many visitors say that it's the choice of facilities that marks out Luccombe Manor. There's an outdoor hot tub and summer spa pool, a private garden and games room, but as all guests also have access to neighbouring Luccombe Hall, there's a whole lot more to your stay than that – from two more pools and a sauna to a well-equipped children's play area and more garden space with amazing sea views. There's a very good breakfast included in the room rate while for other meals you can walk over to Luccombe Hall and make the most of their excellent restaurant and bar. Otherwise, you're right on the edge of charming Shanklin Old Village, with its thatched buildings, pubs and tea rooms. Meanwhile, the coastal path runs north to Sandown and south to Ventnor, for easy walks straight from the hotel. Book a seasonal walking break, and they'll throw in a map, guide and other supplies to get you on the right track.

As for Luccombe Hall, it too has a contemporary seaside vibe in its bright guest rooms, which come with Smart TVs, hairdryers and tea- and coffee-making facilities, plus interconnecting and bunk-style rooms for families. Neighbouring Shanklin Villa Apartments has a choice of eight super-stylish apartments. Four of them are luxurious three–four-bed apartments with sea views, hot tubs and private patios or roof terraces. The other four are bijou one-beds and studios for couples, but they all have access to a communal garden, where there's a hot tub to share.

CONTACT Popham Road, Shanklin, Isle of Wight PO37 6RG • 01983 869 000

HOW MUCH? Double rooms from around £100 a night, including breakfast.

ROOMS 23 Guest Rooms in Luccombe Manor, 29 Guest Rooms in Luccombe Hall, 8 Apartments in Shanklin Villa.

The Loch & The Tyne

A thoroughly modern eco-friendly pub, serving outstanding food and with two indulgent rooms

Based not far from the Thames in the large village of Old Windsor, The Loch & The Tyne is the latest offering from the talented British chef and restauranteur Adam Handling. It's his contemporary take on a traditional British pub, and serves food that is a notch above most pub grub and also has a couple of luxurious guest rooms for overnight stays. Their motto is 'sustainable British luxury', which is a nice strapline but these guys really mean it, with solar panels, a recycled water system and their own kitchen garden out the back, making it not only a candidate for an easy break-out weekend from London but one that you can feel quite smug about, too.

The pub has won several awards and among other things was named 'Best Pub for Food' in the Great British Pub Awards 2023. But The Loch & The Tyne is about much more than food, and has two guest rooms for those who want to make a night of it. One of these is really a suite, furnished with a comfy super-king-size bed, a free-standing bath tub in the living area and a swanky en-suite bathroom; the other room is much the same but everything is scaled down, with a king-size bed and no living area. Each room has a Smart TV, coffee- and tea-making facilities and the bathrooms include high-end toiletries. Rates also include a superb breakfast and the chance to take their 'Nespresso Velosophy' bike for a spin around the beautiful Berkshire countryside (it's made out of recycled Nespresso capsules).

Meanwhile, the pub has the pleasing feel of a modern inn, a place to drink but mainly to eat, from a seasonal menu that is deliberately British in tone and ingredients. They do a terrific selection of bar snacks – cheese doughnuts, anyone? – while starters and main courses take in everything from beef tartare with pickled mushrooms and crispbread to pub staples like fish and chips or macaroni cheese. On Sundays they offer roasts – beef Wellington, pork belly, roast chicken or a fish and veggie option – at the centre of a two- or three-course menu.

CONTACT 10 Crimp Hill, Old Windsor, Berkshire SL4 2QY • 01753 851 470
HOW MUCH? £150–£250 a night.
ROOMS 1 Guest Room, 1 Guest Suite.

Goswell House

Modern hotel rooms in the very heart of royal Windsor

Tucked down a cobbled pedestrianized street, Goswell House could hardly be in a better location if you're visiting to see the sights of Windsor. The hotel has 17 guest rooms that occupy the top three storeys of a historic building in the centre of town. The entrance, tucked down a side street, offers a subtle welcome via a small lobby, that is manned during business hours, after which there's a convenient self check-in system. Upstairs, the rooms are more comfortably furnished than you might expect from the no-fuss arrival, with plush upholstery, plump pillows and Hypnos beds.

There are family rooms as well as doubles and twins, all with clean, modern en-suite bathrooms. Each has tea- and coffee-making facilities, a TV, a hairdryer, an iron and board; standard stuff for a town-centre hotel that will be used as a base for exploring. With that in mind, the hotel doesn't offer sociable spaces beyond its small breakfast room. There's an option, if booked in advance, for a very reasonably-priced continental breakfast, which is handy if you've got somewhere to be. But if you're on a leisurely break, take advantage of what's outside the front door and take your pick from the eateries in the town.

Goswell House is also a good car-free place to stay: Windsor Central Station is even closer to the hotel than it is to the castle and one of the best restaurants in town – Sebastian's – is right next door. For something more fancy, head over the river to Gilbey's in Eton. It's likely that you've come to Windsor for the castle and that alone will take a full day to explore but the town also offers boat trips on the Thames, Windsor Great Park, the Theatre Royal and shopping – all of it within walking distance.

CONTACT Goswell Hill, 135 Peascod Street, Windsor, Berkshire SL4 1DS • 01753 444 444
HOW MUCH? Double rooms from £115 a night.
ROOMS 17 Guest Rooms.

The Farmhouse at Redcoats

A very homely, yet stylish hotel, restaurant and wedding venue in the heart of Hertfordshire

Situated in the hamlet of Redcoats Green, Hertfordshire, The Farmhouse at Redcoats is somewhere we've always had a soft spot for – a perfect place to escape to for a weekend or short break in the countryside near London. Parts of the building date back to the 15th century and it boasts four acres of gardens with lovely views across the rolling Hertfordshire countryside.

Perhaps the nicest thing about The Farmhouse at Redcoats, though, is that it doesn't feel as if it's near anywhere much. But it's in fact just a few miles from Hitchin, just off the A1, so is extremely easy to get to. Its country location and good bar and restaurant mean you don't have to do much once you're here other than stroll around the gardens or stride off across the fields in your wellies. And they give you a handy map on arrival just in case you want to do just that.

The hotel has 27 guest rooms – five in the main farmhouse, seven in the old stables and a further 15 in the reconstructed barn. Two ground-floor barn rooms offer walk-in showers, and the courtyard rooms are dog-friendly. The rooms in the main house have been refurbished but retain characterful features like oak beams and fireplaces; the courtyard rooms outside are more contemporary with cleaner lines and bolder colours; while the barn rooms are the most modern, set across three floors with spacious bathrooms with powerful showers – the ones at the top are cleverly squeezed in amongst the eaves and beams. All have tea- and coffee-making facilities, complimentary mineral water, TVs, phones and super-fast wifi, and are air-conditioned, too.

The rest of the hotel revolves around the cosy bar and Orangery restaurant, where they serve a delicious, contemporary British menu based around seasonal and local ingredients – produce from the garden, oysters and seafood from North Norfolk, local game and pork, Hereford steaks and a trio of roasts on Sundays.

CONTACT Redcoats Green, Hitchin, Hertfordshire SG4 7JR • 01438 729 500

HOW MUCH? Double rooms with breakfast from £135 a night.

ROOMS 27 Guest Rooms & Suites.

Artist Residence Oxfordshire

A cosy – and contemporary – country inn that's a convenient base for Oxford and the Cotswolds

Nestled in the Oxfordshire countryside, just a few miles west of Oxford on the eastern fringes of the Cotswolds, Artist Residence Oxfordshire is the ultimate country inn – with 15 bedrooms tucked away in the eaves, outbuildings and garden, plus excellent food and drink served in their pub, The Mason Arms.

The rooms really set this place apart, equipped with large, comfy beds, powerful showers and the sort of vintage-tinged but contemporary decor we've come to expect from the quirky Artist Residence group (which has sister properties in London, Brighton, Bristol, and Penzance). Rooms all have free wifi, flatscreen Freeview TVs, digital radios, Nespresso coffee machines, and mini-fridges stocked with local goodies – and there are Bramley toiletries in the bathrooms, some of which have rolltop baths. The rooms range in size, from the compact Rabbit Hole through the more spacious Farmhouse Loft rooms (which are dog-friendly) to the lovely Farmhouse Suite, which has a lovely copper bathtub in the room itself, a separate bathroom with shower and an adjoining seating area. Rooms in the outbuildings include the spacious Stable Suite, a luxurious take on the bohemian countryside retreat; Stable, with its private terrace; and Barn Suite, which comes complete with a four-poster. Fancy something a bit different? Overlooking the herb garden there's a homely Shepherd's Hut to hunker down in, while other options range from the small but perfectly formed Burrows to the Potting Shed, with its own entrance.

Back in the tavern, enjoy an open fire, local ales, armchairs to lounge about in, and homemade bar snacks. They also serve a full menu in the dining room that hits all the right buttons – local, seasonal produce, beautifully cooked and presented. All in all it's a contemporary yet traditional approach to comfort, service and food that will certainly have you coming back for more.

CONTACT Station Road, South Leigh, Oxfordshire OX29 6XN • 01993 656 22
HOW MUCH? Double rooms from £125 a night, not including breakfast.
ROOMS 15 Guest Rooms.

The Double Red Duke

A heavenly rural retreat in an idyllic corner of Oxfordshire

Despite being within an hour or so of London, the appealing and ancient Oxfordshire village of Clanfield, with its two village greens, babbling brooks and partly Norman church, is about as close to the idyll of rural England as it's possible to get. The village of Bampton, where much of TV series 'Downton Abbey' was filmed, is close by, as is the village of Kelmscott, whose manor William Morris described as 'heaven on earth' when he moved there in 1871. But the best bit is that you can stay here too – at The Double Red Duke, a 17th-century Cotswolds honey-stone coaching inn. It's a thoroughly contemporary country hotel, with 19 beautiful bedrooms, cosy public spaces with roaring log fires, a snug and intimate bar and a restaurant that serves excellent seasonal and local food. The rooms are a contemporary, high-end mix of antiques and modern features, and all come with either super-king-size or 'emperor' beds, tea- and coffee-making facilities, Roberts radios, wifi, Smart TVs, air-con and en-suite bathrooms provided with 100 Acres toiletries. Some rooms are dog-friendly, and a couple have direct access to the garden.

Run by an ex-Hawksmoor chef, the restaurant revolves around its open fire, with a focus on simple grilled meats and local veg that you can enjoy either in the main dining area or the newer, lighter garden room, or out on the adjacent terrace during summer, where there are beautiful mature gardens that are perfect for an after-dinner wander. You can also eat in the bar, at a 14-cover kitchen counter or in the hotel's designated 12-seater 'feasting room'.

Once you've eaten your fill and slept like a baby in one of the hotel's oversized beds, there's plenty to do nearby too – you can stroll around Clanfield itself and visit Bampton and Kelmscott Manor, and you're also very close to the historic market town of Witney, ancient Minster Lovell and the riverside nature reserve at Chimney Meadows. You really couldn't be better – or more comfortably – placed for a weekend break in the country.

CONTACT Bourton Road, Clanfield, Bampton, Oxfordshire OX18 2RB • 01367 810 222
HOW MUCH? Double rooms from £120 to £300 a night, including continental breakfast.
ROOMS 19 Guest Rooms.

The Greyhound Inn

A proper village pub with comfy rooms and top-quality food on the edge of the Berkshire Downs

Set in Letcombe Regis, a pretty village in South Oxfordshire, The Greyhound serves top-notch food and has eight tastefully decorated bedrooms and was quite rightly one of CAMRA's 'Country Pubs of the Year' not so long ago. It's a relaxed place for a drink, while the rooms upstairs are en-suite, individually decorated, and come complete with a pocket spring mattress, flatscreen TV, homemade biscuits and Bramley bath products. Some rooms are dog-friendly, with a dog bed, towel for muddy paws, treats, water bowl and poo bags, and they also have a couple of family suites.

Much importance is placed on food at The Greyhound, something they're deservedly recognised for: in 2023, they were awarded two rosettes by the AA and retained their place in the Michelin Guide. The regularly changing menu features an array of locally sourced produce, with imaginative dishes such as twice-baked cheddar soufflé (a popular mainstay) and rabbit boudin with warm lentil and tarragon salad alongside pub classics like beer-battered haddock with chips, homemade sauce and mushy peas and burgers with bacon jam, smoked cheddar and fries.

To work up an appetite, just get out on the Ridgeway National Trail, which is close by, or the nearby Thames Path. The pub's staff are more than happy to help with walking routes – they have several mapped out for guests of varying lengths and difficulties.

CONTACT Main Street, Letcombe Regis, Oxfordshire OX12 9JY • 01235 771 969
HOW MUCH? Double rooms from £105 to £140 a night, including breakfast. Family suites from £180 a night.
ROOMS 8 Guest Rooms & Suites.

Bull

There are quite a few renovated coaching inns in the Cotswolds, but none quite like Bull, a historic pub that has been totally reimagined by PR guru Matthew Freud. Some of his art collection hangs here, which means originals by Bacon, Dali and Damien Hirst, while guest rooms are a very comfortable mix of rustic and contemporary. Arguably, though, what really distinguishes Bull is the dizzying array of activities on offer, from ceramics, meditation and choir practice in the old chapel to beekeeping and even the odd poker lesson later on. This fosters a collegiate air between guests, who can compare notes on the day's classes while choosing between Bull's unique choice of three separate restaurants. Stay here for a long weekend and you can try all three: Wild, where food is grilled on open flames; Horn, where a changing set menu is paired with wine; and finally Hiro, a Japanese omakase restaurant, where ex-Nobu chef Hiromi helps you choose from the 10-course menu. There's also a help-yourself pantry for all-day snacking.

CONTACT 105 High St, Burford, Oxfordshire OX18 4RG • 01993 822 220
HOW MUCH? Double rooms from £385 a night.

The Kingham Plough

This 17th-century Oxfordshire pub with rooms has undergone quite a makeover in the last 10 years or so. Not that long ago you couldn't get so much as a cheese roll in what was a typical village boozer. Nowadays it's a terrific contemporary village inn serving really good food and with some very comfortable rooms upstairs. It's welcoming and relaxed while making a big effort to ensure guests have an extra-special stay. Having worked with the likes of Raymond Blanc and Fergus Henderson, owners Matt and Katie continue to source local, seasonal ingredients for both pub classics and more adventurous British dishes. All but one of the rooms has super-king-size beds, with high-quality linen, tea- and coffee-making facilities and minibars with fresh milk, good wifi and large Smart TVs. Bathrooms have baths with showers (two have roll-top baths) and locally made Bramley toiletries. Two rooms are dog-friendly and come with a bed, bowl, treats and a towel for muddy paws.

CONTACT The Green, Kingham, Chipping Norton, Oxfordshire OX7 6YD • 01608 658 327
HOW MUCH? Double rooms with breakfast from £145 a night.

The Old Crown

Nestled on the edge of the Cotswolds, The Old Crown Coaching Inn is home to a four-star hotel and a two-AA-rosette restaurant, plus a set of very comfortable guest rooms that have recently been restored to their former glory. Dating back to 1550, the property provides a little slice of history and is the ideal base for those wanting to explore this scenic corner of Oxfordshire. They've preserved the traditional main bar with its original inglenook fireplace, but at the same time elevated the hotel's game when it comes to food, both in the bar and in the excellent Ballroom restaurant. There are 14 guest rooms, each one individually furnished with flair and style, from the flagship Courtroom suite, featuring a super-king-size four-poster, to regular doubles with king or super-king beds with uber-comfortable mattresses. Whichever room you opt for, you'll be greeted by wifi, large flatscreen TVs, tea-making facilities and en-suite bathrooms with toiletries and fluffy towels.

CONTACT 25 Market Place, Faringdon, Oxfordshire SN7 7HU • 01367 242 744
HOW MUCH? Double rooms from £85 a night.

The Relais Henley

An hour outside London, overlooking the River Thames, The Relais Henley is a historic hotel that has been carefully reimagined to suit modern guests. But it's all been done with the utmost respect for the past and its riverside location. Add to this a superb spot in the centre of this well-to-do riverside town, and you have the makings of a weekend getaway to remember – the train station is a five-minute walk away so it's also a location that works well without a car. Bedrooms range from the antique-dressed Heritage Rooms to the light, airy and accessible Courtyard Rooms and the yacht-inspired Riverside Rooms. Whichever you choose, they all have comfy beds, Algotherm toiletries, Illy coffee machines and all the usual inclusions. The menu in the hotel's Clipper Restaurant is brimming with fresh, seasonal dishes, accentuated by its carefully-chosen wine list, so when you're wondering where to go for dinner, look no further than just downstairs.

CONTACT Hart Street, Henley-on-Thames, Oxfordshire RG9 2AR • 01491 523 288
HOW MUCH? Double rooms from £168 a night.

Lucky Dip

No 42

42 High St, Margate, Kent CT9 1DS

Situated in the heart of Margate's Old Town, this 19-bedroom hotel occupies a prime position overlooking the resort's magnificent beach. With its fabulous Mediterranean-style rooftop bar, Pearly Cow restaurant – where you can enjoy steaks and seafood on an outdoor terrace – and funky seafront café, it's the epitome of modern Margate. The rooms are dog-friendly and vogueishly on-point throughout, with Smart TVs and vinyl record players, tea- and coffee-making facilites, Roberts radios and robes all as standard. All have en-suite bathrooms with showers while the more expensive rooms have baths and sea views to enjoy from your own balcony. It's a good car-free place to stay too – ask nicely and they'll transport your luggage from the station!

Artist Residence Brighton

34 Regency Square, Brighton, East Sussex BH1 2FJ

This quirky hotel has 23 individually designed rooms and apartments and makes a wonderfully informal base for Brighton. It's at once homely and eclectic, with an eccentric mix of vintage furnishings alongside quirky pop-art prints and touches of retro, and has an all-day restaurant serving breakfast, brunch and cocktails.

Careys Manor Hotel

Lyndhurst Road, Brockenhurst, Hampshire SO42 7RH

This comfy country hotel is is the sister of the nearby Montagu Arms (p.64) and couldn't be better placed for exploring the New Forest. It also has a superb spa with pool (the perfect end to a hard day's hiking through the woods), three restaurants and 70-odd spacious and comfortable rooms. For a proper splurge try the Thai-inspired Rosewood Suite, which is handy for the spa and has a seven-foot-wide bed.

The Crown Inn Dial Post

Worthing Rd, Dial Post, West Sussex RH13 8NH

Occupying an almost impossibly desirable position overlooking this Sussex village green, The Crown Inn is a cosy country pub, with a well deserved reputation for its food, which is pretty much exclusively based around locally farmed and foraged produce. They also have four comfy and beautifully appointed guest rooms, plus a self-catering cottage. All the rooms have fast wifi, Smart TVs, mini-fridges, Nespresso machines, complimentary water and homemade biscuits, high-quality vintage beds and bedding and en-suite bathrooms with walk-in showers and toiletries. Very handy for visiting the rewilding project at the nearby Knepp Estate.

The Gallivant

New Lydd Road, Camber Sands, Rye,
East Sussex TN31 7RB

Right opposite the beach and dunes at Camber Sands, this cool clapboard-style hotel and restaurant is the closest you'll get in England to a weekend in The Hamptons. Along with a good restaurant, there are 20 double rooms with king or super-king beds, all with en-suite facilities and some with both bath and power showers.

The Kings Arms

5-6 High St, Egham, Surrey TW20 9EA

For a slice of 'Surrey chic', the lovely Kings Arms in Egham makes for a terrific weekend away in the well-heeled countryside near the grounds and meadows of historic Runnymede. Named after the barons who forced King John to sign Magna Carta, the rooms are sumptuous quarters, with striking colour tones and coordinated artwork, wood panelling, big beds, padded headboards and luxury perks like Roberts radios and Nespresso machines. If it's boutique upstairs, it's very definitely gastro downstairs in the bar and restaurant, with inviting tables and a Modern British take on a bistro menu.

The Gallivant

Careys Manor Hotel

The Swan at Streatley

Streatley-On-Thames, Berkshire RG8 9HR

Sitting pretty on the River Thames, this riverside hotel is an idyllic escape for a weekend – a smart, contemporary property with sociable downstairs spaces that are great places to relax and make the most of the river. The best rooms have river views, and there are also a couple of family suites with space for two adults and two children. On the ground floor, there's a café-bar opening out to a manicured lawn, and waterside dining at the excellent Coppa Club restaurant. The hotel is also dog-friendly, and has everything a pampered pooch could want for.

The Swan at Streatley

The Southwest

Gloucestershire • Wiltshire • Somerset • Dorset • Devon • Cornwall • Isles of Scilly

England's South West is different from the rest of the country – not so much historic as 'pre-historic', a mystical land that's the home of myths and legends, romance and standing stones. It also has the longest coastline of any English region and a holiday industry to go with it. It's not exactly undiscovered. But from Cornwall's fabled coastline to the moorlands of Devon – a county that is home to not one but two national parks – the green rolling hills of Somerset to the Jurassic Coast of Dorset, it is perhaps England's most compelling and diverse region. And its well-developed tourist infrastructure is not necessarily a bad thing, ensuring as it does that it is home to some terrific places to stay, from clifftop hotels to cosy boutique B&Bs. No wonder people come back every year.

Old Bell Hotel, p.90

Calcot & Spa

A high-end country house hotel with loads of facilities that's great for both kids and grown-ups

We love a country house hotel, and the great thing about Calcot & Spa is that it delivers everything you would expect without standing on ceremony – and doesn't expect you to do so either. So, while it occupies around 200 acres of prime Cotswolds countryside and has 35 beautiful guest rooms filled with all manner of luxury items, you don't have to be on your best behaviour to enjoy it. Plus they positively encourage families, and have all sorts of things for kids to enjoy. We like that – it reminds us that we live in the 21st century while spending the weekend acting up as landed gentry.

The rooms themselves are very stylish indeed – airy, spacious and well equipped, with ultra-comfy beds, satellite TV, fruit and snacks, and bathrooms with powerful modern showers, fluffy robes and slippers, Aromatherapy Associates products and sometimes a free-standing bath too. Twelve adult-only bedrooms are located in the main building, the remainder – including family rooms – can be found in the grounds.

The hotel also has a beautiful spa, with a great indoor pool, gym, a steam room and sauna and any number of treatments to enjoy – and lots of packages if you're after a thoroughly pampered weekend away. While you're doing that the kids can enjoy the Playzone (for little ones) or The Mez, which has XBoxes, PlayStations and other activities for older ones, while there's also an outdoor pool, bikes and horse-riding on offer for more outdoors types. Celebrating a big birthday? The Barn is the ideal spot to host a bash, a rustic chic space complete with a pretty courtyard and fire pit. Choose from a number of areas that cater for a variety of group sizes. The Shed seats 16 while The Loft has a capacity of 150.

At the end of the day there's also the excellent Brasserie restaurant, which serves lunch, dinner and afternoon tea and is a lovely light and airy space overlooking the hotel grounds. They also have a very stylish lounge and bar, The Hive, which serves food all day, including brunch and afternoon tea, and transforms itself into a cocktail bar in the evening. It's a handy place to lounge about at any time of day, with lots of cosy nooks and corners, whether you want a cup of tea or an after-dinner nightcap. So you never need leave the womblike confines of Calcot & Spa at all – unless it's to visit their sister hotel The Painswick (p.84). Or why not visit their northern cousin, the Lord Crewe Arms (p.217).

CONTACT Tetbury, Gloucestershire GL8 8YJ • 01666 890 391

HOW MUCH? Double rooms with breakfast from £229 a night.

ROOMS 35 Guest Rooms & Suites.

Wild Thyme & Honey

Stunning boutique rooms and suites in a honey-coloured stone Cotswolds village inn

If you know the Cotswolds, you'll be able to picture the honey-coloured villages with their quaint stone buildings and ancient inns – that quintessential England of rolling green fields and dreamy landscapes. These things all come together at the charmingly named Wild Thyme & Honey, a boutique collection of rooms and suites overlooking the peaceful brook in Ampney Crucis, a few miles outside Cirencester. And the wild thyme? It grows between the Cotswold stone and in the verges of this most cherished of English country regions.

The need-to-know here is that Wild Thyme & Honey is in fact part of a beautiful 16th-century village pub, The Crown, with both parts of the venue lovingly restored and just across the courtyard from each other, linked by the reception and lounge areas. The 24 rooms and suites have been given a serious boutique makeover – think exposed stone walls, original beams, natural wood floors and calming colours but with a burst of urban, loft-style chic. Bathrooms throughout are excellent, with thumping rain showers, while little luxuries are commonplace, so whichever room you choose you can expect a Nespresso machine, a calming pillow spray and a decanter of sloe gin on arrival. As for your accommodation, there are king-sized double bedrooms with views over the neighbouring farms and hills, or larger suites that overlook the trout-filled river. Most eye-catching of all is a very special apartment with a private terrace, hot tub and sauna, a free-standing copper tub in the bathroom, and an amazing bespoke bed fashioned from silver birch.

It's 'posh country' all right, but you are invited to tramp around the gorgeous countryside too – there's storage for muddy walking gear in all the rooms, and if you've forgotten your wellies they'll lend you a pair of Hunters. Breakfast, plus reviving drinks and meals are across at The Crown, with its open kitchen, fancy grill and locally sourced farm-to-table ethos. The menus are wide-ranging enough that you can stick with a Caesar salad or cheese souffle or splash out on a rib-eye steak with all the trimmings, and the bartenders know their way around the cocktail list. Everything, as you might expect, is just so, and for a special-occasion stay in the heart of England's green and pleasant land, it's hard to beat this luxurious overnight serving of wild thyme and honey.

CONTACT Ampney Crucis, Cirencester, Gloucestershire GL7 5RS • 01285 851 806
HOW MUCH? Double rooms from £170 a night.
ROOMS 24 Guest Rooms & Suites.

The Painswick

Stylish boutique hotel with 16 bedrooms in a Cotswolds manor house

Nestled into one of the South Cotswolds' most delightful small towns, this magnificent manor house is a stylish and luxurious country house hotel, part of the same group as the nearby Calcot (p.80). Midway between Stroud and Gloucester, its 16 bedrooms are all individually designed, and range from smaller rooms up in the eaves of the house through larger rooms in the Garden and Chapel wings right up to the full-blown 'George's' suite, complete with four-poster bed and private balcony. Whichever you plump for, all the rooms are airy, contemporary and spacious, and excellently equipped with ultra-comfy beds and bathrooms with powerful modern showers, posh bath products and fluffy robes – some have free-standing baths too.

Food is taken very seriously at The Painswick, with an ever-evolving menu of contemporary cuisine that is well-priced and always imaginative – not least breakfasts, where you can opt for a 'Full Elvis' with waffles, banana, peanut-butter ice cream and crispy bacon alongside classic full English or continental options. They serve a great lunch menu that varies from light bites – Scotch Eggs, Piazza Bianco – to more substantial fare, and the dinner menu includes Cornish lobster, steaks and a great selection of seasonal dishes with a twist.

All of this is in excellent counterpoint to the hotel's treatment rooms, which offer massages, facials, pedicures and everything in between. If we're honest, it's difficult to leave what is a very comfortable place to just hang about and do not very much at all, but if you do manage to drag yourself away, you'll find that the charming town of Painswick is worth a look (and hosts the popular 'Art-Couture' festival every summer), and Gloucester and Cheltenham are also both within striking distance. The property also has impressive views down to the Slad Valley, where there are ample walking opportunities. All in all a fabulous place to stay, in a terrific location.

CONTACT Kemps Lane, Painswick, Gloucestershire GL6 6YB • 01452 813 688

HOW MUCH? Double rooms from £169 a night.

ROOMS 16 Guest Rooms and a Suite.

The Crown & Anchor

This Wiltshire village inn ticks all the boxes a 21st century pub should – with good food and some very comfortable upstairs rooms

Situated in a pretty Wiltshire village on the edge of the North Wessex Downs AONB, local pubs don't get much better than Ham's Crown & Anchor, which ticks all the boxes a proper 21st century inn should – welcoming dogs, walkers and cyclists and serving local ales and excellent food; it even has some cosy rooms upstairs to collapse into at the end of the evening.

Recently refurbished, it's quite as cosy as a village inn should be, with flagstone floors scattered with antique carpets, a curved wooden bar, a fireplace with a wood-burner and oak panelled walls. Artworks range from old photographs to contemporary pieces by local artists and are surrounded by the sort of comfortable mismatched furniture that urges you to take the weight off, while on hot summer days the terrace at the back beckons.

They offer a good selection of local ales, including their own locally brewed bitter, and the short, moderately priced menu is a perfect blend of local, seasonal and above all British dishes but with a modern twist – spicy Scotch Eggs, Brixham crab and shrimp ravioli, lovely local partridge and venison along with classics like fish and chips. There are five individually furnished, en-suite bedrooms and a three-bedroom Stable for families. Each room is equipped with a Hypnos mattress and good quality linen, Freeview TVs, tea- and coffee-making facilities, fresh milk and water and good wifi. The newly refurbished bathrooms are simple and elegant, with reclaimed wooden doors and decent showers (only one has a bath), and are provided with 100 Acre toiletries in eco-friendly sizes. Dogs are allowed in all rooms and get treats, a blanket and a dog bowl.

Finally the location, which is the West Country, but only just, midway between Newbury and Marlborough and well placed for visiting Avebury, Stonehenge and the Vale of Pewsey. It's also a perfect location for enjoying country walks, with three long-distance footpaths nearby and a great cycle route too.

CONTACT Ham, Wiltshire, SN8 3RB • 01488 503 040
HOW MUCH? Double rooms wih breakfast £110–£130 a night.
ROOMS 5 Guest Rooms & a 3-bed Stable.

Ingleside House

Sumptuous rooms with dramatic flair in the capital of the Cotswolds

Bold colours, striking designs and an exuberant style set Ingleside House apart from many other hotels in the Cotswolds. Set in a Grade II-listed building in Cirencester, the exterior may share the honey-coloured hues that'll be familiar to anyone who's spent time exploring this pretty part of the world, but step inside and the honey turns to gold. There's a deliberate Gatsby-esque style to this boutique hotel that makes it less twee and more ta-dah.

This super-stylish place has 11 guest rooms ranging from the relatively simple king rooms to the lavish four-poster suite. But, as we say, the simplicity is relative here. Although the king rooms are the most compact, they still share the drama of the rest of the hotel with colours, textures, prints and lighting all contributing to a sumptuous feel. Step up to a super-king room for more space and choose 'deluxe' for a free-standing bath in your room. Whichever you opt for, the quality of the place is told in the room inclusions: a radio from Roberts, coffee from a Nespresso machine and toiletries from Molton Brown.

All the drama of the rooms is amplified downstairs, where there's a residents' lounge, restaurant, piano bar and an associated theatre next door. More on that later, but for now there's the important business of dinner and cocktails. These can be taken inside in the main Téatro restaurant, where pre-theatre and main menus are served to gold-topped tables, or outside on the heated terrace where a slightly simpler menu is on offer. On Fridays and Saturdays the place is brought to life with live music, but the plush velveteen upholstery, statement wallpaper and quirky objets d'art mean that it's never dull in here.

A few steps from the front door, the 200-seater Barn Theatre hosts performances from touring theatre groups on a regular basis. Take a look at their own website for details and tickets. In addition, the shops, eateries and museums of Cirencester are five minutes' walk away and beyond that, there's all of the Cotswolds to explore. Country walks, cute villages and long pub lunches await within a short drive. These are the lovely days of a classic Cotswolds holiday – but they come with the promise of a return to something rather more luxe and lavish at Ingleside House.

CONTACT 5 Beeches Road, Cirencester, Gloucestershire GL7 1BN • 01285 648 230
HOW MUCH? Double rooms from £126.50 to £287.50 a night, not including breakfast.
ROOMS 11 Guest Rooms.

Whatley Manor

A Cotswolds country house hotel with a Michelin-starred restaurant

A Michelin-starred restaurant, a spa and 12 acres of beautiful gardens make Whatley Manor a rather special place to stay – particularly if it's a celebratory occasion. To really make the most of this country house hotel in the Cotswolds, don't just book a room or a suite. Make sure you add treatments to your time in the spa, indulge in an afternoon tea on the terrace, book a table at The Dining Room, and why not add a wine flight for good measure?

You approach Whatley Manor up a long, tree-lined drive. At the top, you'll find a Grade II-listed mansion that houses 26 guest suites and rooms. Each has been individually designed and all are equally elegant, with understated colours and a sophisticated style. Whether you choose a Classic Room or a Deluxe Suite, you'll find a supremely comfortable king-size bed and underfloor heating in your en-suite bathroom. Robes and slippers are eco-friendly, wifi is reliable, tea and coffee carefully sourced, and cookies are handmade.

This, as you may have guessed, is a five-star retreat – in fact, it has the AA's highest accolade, five red stars. But those aren't the awards this place shouts loudest about. Its proudest achievements are green ones: it's won an Award for 'Best Green Practices' and has been named the 'Best Eco-Conscious Spa'. Even its restaurant's Michelin star is green, recognising a kitchen that uses produce from its own no-dig garden and meat from the farm next door. It's this commitment to sustainability that makes the luxury here all the more appealing, and it stretches from the on-site recycling centre to the Molton Brown toiletries in refillable bottles that are provided in your room.

Although this country pad has only 26 guest rooms, you'll find ones that are dog-friendly and others suitable for a family (children over 12 years are allowed). It also has a choice of two restaurants, with Grey's offering a relaxed alternative to the fine dining of The Dining Room. The gardens are beautifully kept and offer a place to wander and while away the hours – and if it rains, there's even a private cinema that you can hire to watch a film of your choice. All this, and you're also perfectly poised for exploring the Cotswolds. The Westonbirt Arboretum in Gloucestershire is close by, not to mention the attractive market town of Malmesbury.

CONTACT Easton Grey, Malmesbury, Wiltshire SN16 0RB • 01666 822 888

HOW MUCH? Double rooms from £318 a night.

ROOMS 26 Guest Rooms.

Old Bell Hotel

A historic Wiltshire hotel with contemporary rooms and an excellent restaurant

For a hotel that's rumoured to be one of England's oldest, The Old Bell does a good job of catering to modern tastes. It's got a coffee bar in reception, a refined restaurant boasting an indulgent tasting menu, and 34 individually designed guest rooms – all with wifi and Smart TVs. But don't let the amenities fool you into thinking that this place has lost its historic charm. That's still here in spades. You'll see it in the Grade I-listed walls, the 13th-century fireplace in the bar and the exposed beams of some of the bedrooms. A full-scale design-led renovation may have introduced quirks, colour and bold patterns, but all are somehow at ease with the 800 years of hospitality that came before. And that's really saying something, when a giraffe in the entrance hall is one of the first things you see when you get here.

All the communal spaces and bedrooms at The Old Bell are designed and dressed with similar confidence and flair. Characterful heritage features sit alongside a mixture of antiques, modern pieces and designer wallpaper, with warm lighting that sets it all aglow. Everywhere is inviting and interesting, from the three cosy guest lounges to your private en-suite room.

As might be expected from a building that has evolved over several centuries, there's no standard size or shape to the bedrooms. Instead, you have a wide choice, from the spacious Junior Master Suites overlooking neighbouring Malmesbury Abbey to the Cosy Rooms of the Coach House. They also have four Townhouse suites nearby, which can sleep two to five guests, and in which you can self-cater if you prefer. Back in the main hotel, there are single rooms, family rooms and even dogs are welcome. Whichever you choose, you'll find Bramley toiletries, Wiltshire-roasted coffee for your cafetiere and a Dyson hairdryer – a company that is, incidentally, based right here in Malmesbury.

This commitment to quality continues in the hotel's Abbey Row Restaurant, which serves a tasty breakfast and has menus featuring local produce for lunch, afternoon tea and dinner. If you're here for a night, there's no need to go anywhere else. Stay for longer, and you may want to try elsewhere in town. That won't take long, because you're in the heart of it. The hotel was originally built for visitors to Malmesbury Abbey, which stands next door and houses the tomb of England's first king, Athelstan, while outside town, Highgrove Gardens, Westonbirt Arboretum and the Cotswolds Water Park are all within 10 miles.

CONTACT Abbey Row, Malmesbury, Wiltshire SN16 0BW • 01666 822 344
HOW MUCH? Double rooms from £195 a night.
ROOMS 34 Guest Rooms & Suites.

Royal Crescent Hotel & Spa

Location, location, location: period splendour in a prime spot in the centre of Bath

If you're going to do Bath, you may as well do it properly – and that means staying in the city's iconic Royal Crescent. This sweeping arc of terraced Georgian townhouses is a UNESCO World Heritage Site and Grade I-listed. At its centre, numbers 15 and 16 have been combined to form the Royal Crescent Hotel and Spa, which offers just what you might expect from such a grand address: outstanding hospitality and service, valet car parking, a concierge service and an elegant restaurant and bar. But it also proffers some surprises, including an acre of gardens, a modern spa, and family-friendly and even dog-friendly rooms.

The Royal Crescent has been the most desirable address in Bath since the 18th century, and the accommodation here helps to maintain that reputation. Step inside and the elegance of the crescent's facade is mirrored by the public spaces inside. The history is part of the attraction, but you won't find anything tired or old-fashioned here. A recent renovation has brought a fresh elegance to the place that's been carefully balanced with its many period features. There's the lobby with its open fire, the drawing room with its plush sofas and high ceilings, chandeliers and large windows everywhere. Perhaps the star of the show is Montagu's Mews restaurant and bar. It's mentioned in the Michelin Guide and has three AA Rosettes. Choose the tasting menu or opt for á la carte, and you can take your meal inside or out on the heated terrace, which opens to peaceful gardens beyond.

Guest rooms also blend contemporary comfort with character features. At one end of the scale, Deluxe rooms are a perfect base for a couple who want a taste of this elegant address but intend to spend days out exploring the city. At the other end, Master Suites are big and grand enough to relax in all day, with a seating area with sofas, views of the Royal Crescent lawn or gardens and a four-poster bed. Whichever room you opt for, all have at least a queen-size bed dressed with high-quality linens, and bathrooms with fluffy towels, robes and Noble Island toiletries.

The hotel's spa is across the garden, home to a pool, sauna, steam room and treatment rooms. Booking yourself in here, in the original spa town, seems an appropriate way to while away a few hours, but of course there's plenty more to explore. See where the Romans relaxed at The Roman Bath House and find out about Bath's most famous resident at the Jane Austen Centre. All of it is within walking distance of Bath's most desirable address.

CONTACT 16 Royal Crescent, Bath, Somerset BA1 2LS • 01225 823 333
HOW MUCH? Double rooms from £405 a night, including breakfast.
ROOMS 45 Guest Rooms & Suites.

Brooks Guesthouse Bath

A contemporary and welcoming boutique guesthouse within easy reach of Bath city centre

The word 'guesthouse' does Brooks a bit of a disservice. This independently owned 22-room hotel on the edge of Bath city centre is a slickly run establishment with an eye very firmly on its boutique credentials. The rooms are cleverly in tune with the Victorian building, yet cool and contemporary at the same time, with large fireplaces, jazzy wallpaper, curvy period furniture and florid rococo styling. All are well-equipped with high-quality bed linen and goose-down duvets, digital radios and iPod docking stations, flatscreen TVs and DVD players. There's free wifi throughout and bathrooms have been handsomely refurbished in a modern style and kitted out with designer toiletries. You can choose from smallish but great value Standard rooms with queen-size beds and larger Superior rooms with king-size beds, as well as a handful of family suites that can comfortably accommodate two adults and two children. Breakfast is delicious, with lots of alternatives on offer if you don't want their excellent Full English. There's also a downstairs honesty bar and lounge.

As for the location, it's on a busy road so the rooms at the back are quieter, but it's just a few minutes' walk from everything you might want to see in Bath. It's also worth knowing that they offer great midweek packages that include two-hour sessions at the excellent nearby Thermae Bath Spa – one of our favourite things to do in the city.

CONTACT 1 Crescent Gardens, Upper Bristol Road, Bath, Somerset BA1 2NA • 01225 425 543
HOW MUCH? Double rooms from £80 to £150 a night. Family Rooms £120–£160.
ROOMS 22 Guest Rooms.

Berwick Lodge

A unique boutique country house hotel on the outskirts of Bristol

Statement furniture, chandeliers and mosaic-floored bathrooms give an elegant and exotic edge to the guest rooms at Berwick Lodge, a boutique country house hotel on the outskirts of Bristol that has all the hallmarks of Old England, but inside displays the colour and flair of Turkey. Fabric, furnishings and artefacts from Istanbul decorate the guest rooms and complement the building's original character and features. This marriage of styles from east and west is a reflection of the English-Turkish roots of the hotel's owners who have spent over a decade creating this luxury retreat.

Each of the 14 rooms at Berwick Lodge has its own character and style; there's nothing homogeneous here. You certainly won't find another bed like the one in Troya, which was created from the carved wooden pulpit of an old church, with steps leading up to each side and a flatscreen TV rising from the foot of the bed. A number of other rooms have four-poster or sleigh beds and there are roll-top baths and mosaic floors in the most luxurious bathrooms. Whichever room you choose, an en-suite bathroom, TV and tea- and coffee-making facilities come as standard – even though the decoration is anything but.

The hotel's restaurant, Hattusa, has a similarly sumptuous style, serving up Modern British cuisine for breakfast, lunch and dinner – not to mention afternoon tea, which in good weather can be taken in the garden. From the hotel, you can see all the way to Wales, thanks to the hotel's location northwest of Bristol. This means that it's easy to reach from the M5 and Severn crossing, and is an ideal base from which to explore this part of the southwest. You couldn't get much closer to Bristol's surfing lagoon, The Wave, and the city centre isn't far away either. Whether you want to explore the city or escape it, this country-style hotel beyond the suburbs is a very enticing retreat.

CONTACT Berwick Drive, Bristol BS10 7TD • 0117 958 1590
HOW MUCH? Double rooms from £109-£179 a night; Superior Suites £189-£209; Deluxe Suites £219-£259.
ROOMS 14 Guest Rooms.

Brooks Guesthouse Bristol

Fab city centre boutique bolthole – with a glamping option on the roof

There's a lot that's surprising about Bristol's Brooks Guesthouse. First of all it's much more than just a guesthouse, with fewer than 23 rooms, a boutique chic vibe, and a fabulous location bang in the heart of Bristol, right by the St Nicholas Markets, just a few minutes' walk from the waterfront.

Set around a quiet, secluded courtyard, its rooms are furnished in contemporary style with retro furniture, funky wallpaper and Shaker-style wood panelling, and generously equipped with goose-down duvets and high-end bed linen. The cheaper ones are smaller, with smaller beds, but all have Freeview TVs, DVDs and free wifi and you will be extremely comfortable in any of them.

Just in case you fancy something different, though, it's worth knowing that they also have a fleet of four retro-style Airstream caravans with en-suite bathrooms on the roof – that's right, rooftop glamping right in the middle of Bristol! The caravans, which are all handmade British affairs, range from a 16ft Rocket with a small double bed to a 20ft Rocket with a regular double and room for two little ones, and all have predictably great views over the city and beyond. Each has a small and very ingenious bathroom, low-energy heating and lighting and Roberts radios. Whether you're glamping or playing it safe in one of the downstairs bedrooms, breakfast is fab, with a choice of eggs multiple ways, crepes and French toast or the Full English. They also have an honesty bar and some comfy chairs for sitting around and planning your day, as well as seating in the courtyard outside. You may also be interested to know that the same people have another city property in nearby Bath (see p.94), though, sadly, it doesn't have a caravan on the roof... Yet.

CONTACT St Nicholas Street, Bristol BS1 1UB • 0117 930 0066
HOW MUCH? Double rooms from £90 a night.
ROOMS 23 Guest Rooms & 4 Airstreams.

Artist Residence Bristol

One of Bristol's most unique and comfortable places to stay, full of cool, shabby-chic charm

Based in a former boot factory overlooking Portland Square in the nowadays funky and desirable Bristol neighbourhood of St Pauls, Artist Residence Bristol is one of the city's most unique and comfortable places to stay, with all the cool, shabby-chic charm that we have come to expect from the Artist Residence group. Once a squat, it was rescued from dereliction about five years ago and has 23 guest bedrooms, including several suites, each decorated with the characteristic style of the other hotels in the group – vintage furniture mixed with a bit of industrial archeology, contemporary furniture, luxury bathrooms, the odd free-standing bathtub and works by local artists. Above all it's an extremely comfortable place to spend the night: all rooms have good wifi and Smart TVs, Roberts radios and Nespresso machines – and most importantly good quality linen and comfy beds. There's also a wide range of room types, from budget Shoebox rooms to larger Boot Rooms a two-level apartment, The Lookout, which has a balcony with views over the city, and the top-of-the-range Artist Suite and Club Suite, which look out over the square. Some rooms are dog-friendly and dogs are welcome in all public areas.

Breakfast is served in the main restaurant, which is an appealing place to hang out all day if you so choose. Like the group's other properties, Artist Residence aims to be much more than just a hotel, with a buzzy bar and restaurant and a relaxed vibe that encourages plenty of non-resident activity. Interestingly, some of the people who used to live here come by from time to time, while, for visitors, Bristol is on your doorstep and yours to explore. In St Pauls and adjacent Stokes Croft you're based in Bristol's most famously creative neighbourhoods, yet the sights and shops of the city centre are also just a short walk away, making this an ideal spot for a city break.

CONTACT 28 Portland Square, St Paul's, Bristol BS2 8SA • 0117 428 8440
HOW MUCH? Double rooms £125–£295 a night. Loft rooms and suites £285–£435 a night.
ROOMS 23 Guest Rooms.

The Swan at Wedmore

A quintessential West Country pub with rooms in a lovely Somerset village

Anyone seeking a quintessential Somerset pub in a quintessential Somerset village need look no further than the lovely Swan at Wedmore – a handsome contemporary coaching inn that is currently in great hands. Its seven rooms consist of one small, two medium and three large rooms as well as a restful second-floor loft room, all decorated in elegant greys with splashes of bright colours courtesy of scatter cushions and throws, pictures and posters, and hummingbird print wallpaper. Furnishings are mostly French vintage style: mirrored dressers, bedside tables, armchairs and window shutters – all very chic. Fresh milk is provided, along with scrummy biscuits, Nespresso machines and Teapigs teabags, and Bramley bath products in the bathrooms.

Downstairs, locals and visitors happily rub along together in the spacious bar – part lounge, part snug – beyond which is a slightly more formal dining area, the only part of the pub in which dogs (otherwise welcome) are not allowed. The food is local and seasonal and much of it is homemade – bread and cakes, home-cured ham and bacon – on a simple menu focused around local lamb, fish and veggie dishes, and a selection of roasts on Sundays. They offer a kids' menu or smaller portions to little ones, and they also serve sandwiches and snacks all day in case you're peckish. You can eat in the bar or restaurant and in summer both drinkers and diners move out to the stone terrace and immaculate lawned garden.

Finally, Wedmore itself is a pleasant village on the edge of the Somerset Levels, which offers wonderful sanctuary along with some of Britain's finest birdwatching. The peaks and gorges of the Mendip Hills are also just a few miles to the north.

CONTACT Cheddar Road, Wedmore, Somerset BS28 4EQ • 01934 710 337
HOW MUCH? Double rooms £85–£195 a night.
ROOMS 7 Guest Rooms.

The Sheppey

A pub set in glorious isolation with views of Glastonbury Tor and music on Fridays

Secreted away in rural isolation at the heart of the magical Somerset Levels, you wouldn't give this unprepossessing roadside pub a second glance. But step inside, and any preconceptions are immediately dispelled – The Sheppey is fun and funky, from the cool-as-a-cucumber bar to the retro furnishings.

It's actually a converted dairy farm, and accommodation comes in the form of three rooms above the pub: modestly-sized spaces that are artfully decorated with paisley-style wallpaper plus music- and film-themed pictures and posters – the best room is the one with the reclaimed vintage telephone doors and copper bath, while another boasts a balcony perched above the river, albeit with drinkers supping away below. Bathrooms, meanwhile, come with free-standing tubs and jumbo-sized rain showers, plus organic toiletries and fresh flowers thrown in for good measure. Included is a breakfast consisting of organic local cereals, yoghurt and fruits served in your room.

While here, it'd be remiss not to sample the pub's awesome food. The menu is suitably eclectic – they don't do boring – with everything from Sri Lankan curry and beer-battered jackfruit, to a cracking Sunday roast. What's more, there's a fine selection of local Somerset beers on offer, like the Amber Ale from the Gert Lush microbrewery down the road. It's the perfect accompaniment to a bowl of the pub's signature fish stew – snag a spot on the riverside terrace to complete the experience. Glastonbury is nearby so it'll come as no surprise that they host regular live music and DJ nights. For those who prefer the soothing sounds of nature, there's a cluster of tranquil nature reserves in easy reach: Westhay Moor, Avalon Marshes and RSPB Ham Wall to name a few. Glastonbury Tor is also just 15 minutes away.

CONTACT Lower Godney, Glastonbury, Somerset BA5 1RZ • 01458 831 594
HOW MUCH? Double rooms £120–£140 a night.
ROOMS 3 Guest Rooms.

Bossington Hall

A luxury Exmoor B&B with sumptuous grounds and sensational views

There are posh B&Bs, and then there is Bossington Hall: a luxury Somerset bed & breakfast that not only enjoys a marvellous location, with eight acres of grounds, gardens and leisure facilities, but is also home to nine extremely comfortable, spacious guest rooms, most with wonderful views out to sea or over the moors and woodland behind. Based just outside the popular seaside village of Porlock Weir, on the edge of the mighty Exmoor National Park, there are plenty of B&Bs in the area, but we have to say that none can match the personable luxury of Bossington Hall, not to mention the glorious views. Come here once and we guarantee you'll return.

Formerly known simply as Lynch House, the house was built in the early 20th century by a local shipping magnate, in a 'sunny spot' just a stone's throw from the sea. All the rooms are different, but they're all very generous sizes, especially the massive Greenaleigh Suite (which can accommodate four in double and twin bedrooms). All the other rooms are regular but spacious doubles, and because of the way the house is configured, only four have en-suite bathrooms (the other five each have private bathrooms). Again all the bathrooms are spacious and well-equipped, with towels, robes and toiletries, and a couple feature roll-top baths. Beds are king-size or super-king-size, with comfortable, high-quality mattresses, and all the rooms have good wifi, Smart TVs, tea- and coffee-making facilities and a complimentary hospitality tray. Two of the six rooms allow dogs, and two can inter-connect, making them perfect for a family with slightly older children (young children are not allowed). Breakfasts, meanwhile, are legendary, with a choice of Full English or continental, and packed lunches can be provided for hungry walkers.

Bossington Hall also has a more than the average crop of B&B facilities, including an EV car charging point, an honesty bar complete with a fabulous selection of cheese, a room with a large cinema screen, a tennis court, the oldest private squash court in the country, plus a river, pond and acres of informal gardens. There is also a sauna and wellness/massage suite for holistic relaxation.

You also couldn't be better placed for exploring Exmoor, and Porlock is only a mile away, with plenty of options for drinks and dinner. Very much a place to relax and explore both the stunning coastline and national park.

CONTACT Porlock, Somerset TA24 8HJ • 01643 862 800

HOW MUCH? Double rooms from £135 a night.

ROOMS 9 Guest Rooms.

The Mole Resort

A glorious family-friendly, dog-friendly North Devon resort with lodges and rooms

If countryside is always 'rolling', then in the amazing grounds of The Mole Resort it also tumbles, spreads, unfurls and uncurls. This is North Devon at its most glorious, where the lodges and rooms of this sumptuous family resort make a fantastic base for a fun-filled country activity holiday, just a half an hour drive from Barnstaple and the coast.

There are guest rooms in and around the original manor house at the heart of the estate – in categories that range from Snug to Suite. Think hotel comforts, contemporary country design, and some of those sweeping countryside views, especially from the larger rooms. But to put yourself right in the picture, plump for one of the resort's luxurious, elevated self-catering lodges, spread right across the grounds and each with either meadow or valley views. They sleep four to eight people (in two to four bedrooms), and all have amazing outlooks, a private hot tub and a spacious, decked balcony with outdoor dining (Devon weather permitting!). They are stylish, open-plan, designer spaces, with plenty of natural light, excellent kitchens and bathrooms – and at least one en-suite master bedroom in each lodge. It's the well-thought-out extras that make them even better: all are dog-friendly, and there's also a pooch and bike-wash point at each lodge, plus cycle racks, umbrellas, torches, and even safety glassware for the hot tubs.

The resort's Cellars Pub offers local ales and microbrews, with their very own ale taking centre stage, and serves pub grub like Devon-caught haddock and chips, Devon-raised Ruby red beef burgers and homemade shepherd's pie. The Devon View Restaurant, winner of two AA Rosettes, offers everything from breakfast and cream teas to dinner, again with plentiful local fare, and takeaways and barbecue packs are available for lodge guests. There's also an on-site farm shop, with an emphasis on locally sourced ingredients and seasonal produce.

The extensive facilities include impressive outdoor and indoor heated swimming pools, a sauna, steam room, Jacuzzi and gym, and daily exercise classes. They've got all-weather tennis and pickleball courts, a croquet lawn and a five-a-side pitch – they even have their own parkland golf course. Other activities include archery and laser-clay shooting, and walks and cycle trails start right from the doorstep (rental bikes are available). The helpful resort staff can point you in the right direction, with mapped routes for all abilities.

CONTACT Chittlehamholt, Umberleigh, Devon EX37 9HD • 01769 540 561
HOW MUCH? Double rooms from around £115 a night, lodges from £269 a night.
ROOMS 35 Guest Rooms & 58 Lodges.

Saunton Sands Hotel

A very comfortable family-friendly hotel – with one of the best coastal views in the UK

This family-friendly beachside hotel has one of the best coastal views in the UK. The gorgeous, wide and long stretch of Saunton beach and its dunes are visible from all the public spaces, as well as from the expansive outdoor terrace and pool area and many of the rooms. It's a landmark building, and one of the most comfortable places to stay along this iconic stretch of the North Devon coast, especially if you're surfing or walking in the area, with excellent service, rooms, food and other facilities.

Saunton Sands' Art Deco premises are quite simply fantastic, and the building retains many original features together with a vibe that is as relaxed and family-friendly as you could wish for (as you might expect in a hotel that was recently voted one of the 'Top 100 Family Hotels in the UK'). There are vases of fragrant freshly cut flowers all over the place, and spacious guest rooms that come in all shapes and sizes – both cosy and deluxe doubles, family rooms and so-called 'Living Suites' and fully-fledged apartments. They also have a number of inter-connecting rooms that are perfect for families with older children.

All the rooms have large and comfy beds, flatscreen Freeview TVs with Sky Sports thrown in, plus tea and coffee, Temple Spa toiletries and wifi. The more contemporary Living Suites have a Bose sound system and a fridge, and offer an early check-in. Parents will also be pleased that they can book the kids into the beautifully equipped creche for up to two hours each day and treat themselves to a relaxing massage or beauty treatment in one of several classy black and white treatment rooms.

There's an indoor and an outdoor pool, a sauna and gym, tennis, squash and croquet – and a fine-dining restaurant that's among the best in the area, serving a regularly changing, locally sourced seasonal menu featuring local delicacies like Brixham crab, venison from Exmoor and an amazing selection of UK cheeses. There's also a simpler restaurant, the Terrace Lounge, which serves lunch, afternoon tea and dinner.

But the hotel's greatest asset is perhaps the beach and dunes, where they also run the Beachside Grill, whose wooden deck is a great place to watch the surf while having lunch or just nursing a drink or snack. Overall it really is family – and seaside – heaven.

CONTACT Saunton, Near Braunton, Devon EX33 1LQ • 01271 890 212
HOW MUCH? Double rooms from £105 to £250 a night.
ROOMS 77 Guest Rooms & 10 Apartments.

Weeke Barton

The ultimate Dartmoor escape for jaded city types

Weeke Barton is the ultimate Londoners' escape from the big city, since that's exactly what its owners, Sam and Jo, did several years ago, when they threw it all in and moved down here from East London. It's a long way from Hackney, for sure, a thick-walled longhouse that has been here 500 years and they hope will be here for 500 more, still providing the kind of place any London escapee would be happy to pitch up at.

You can rent the whole house if you want and it's a great place for group bookings and special occasions, but Weeke Barton is also a thoroughly contemporary and comfortable B&B. There's a studied naturalness to the place that almost enforces relaxation – stylishly decorated rooms with big comfy beds and natural stone en-suite bathrooms with locally made posh toiletries, fluffy towels and robes; and a lounge with squishy sofas, a wood-burning stove and books and magazines. The dining room has slate-topped tables where they serve breakfast at civilized hours (with their own award-winning granola) and excellent home-cooked dinners four nights a week from spring to autumn (Monday and Friday in winter), with plenty of ingredients sourced locally. There's wifi throughout, and a cosy snug with an honesty bar offering everything from sparkling wine from the vineyard next door to local gins and Dorset vodka! Sam and Jo will also direct you to the best local pubs, such as the Horse in Moretonhampstead or the Teign House Inn.

The property is set in its own five acres of grounds so there is plenty of room to properly relax and enjoy the amazing night skies. On sunny days you can breakfast on the patio before strolling the grounds. There is good wifi and Sonos music systems, but interestingly no TV reception – just flatscreen TVs on which you can watch a choice of DVDs from their extensive library. Dogs are welcome in all rooms if you can manage to keep them clean and off the beds. All in all, it's a fabulous place from which to explore Dartmoor or to just kick back and relax.

CONTACT Dunsford, Devon EX6 7HH • 01647 253 505

HOW MUCH? Double rooms £165–£190 a night, including breakfast.

ROOMS 6 Guest Rooms.

The Old Rectory Hotel

A stylish boutique hotel tucked away in a quiet corner of Exmoor National Park

Boutique hotels are two-a-penny these days, but Huw Rees and Sam Prosser got it right when they took over the Old Rectory around 15 years ago – not only is its location second-to-none, idyllically sitting in Exmoor National Park with spectacular views across the Bristol Channel towards Wales, but the thoughtfulness with which they went about the whole project is impressive. The result is ten very comfortable rooms furnished in a contemporary style, decked out with fresh flowers, large bathrooms, wifi and everything else you could possibly need.

Beyond the rooms the hotel fosters the atmosphere of a convivial country house party, with afternoon tea in the comfy downstairs sitting room, early evening canapes and an excellent dinner served in the dining room. Native North Devonian Thomas Frost is at the helm in the kitchen and his motto is 'local all the way', with fish from day boats, meat from nearby Heale Farm and fruit and veg from their kitchen garden. How does Ilfracombe crab, lime and avocado cocktail followed by fillet of Ruby Red Devon beef sound?

Outside, the location couldn't be more peaceful, and there are lovely gardens in which to enjoy it; for the more energetic the steep wooded valleys and high cliffs of Exmoor National Park are on your doorstep – you're just 500 metres from the South West Coast Path. Beyond lies the coastal resort of Lynton and Lynmouth – take a ride on the Cliff Railway that joins them, the highest and the steepest totally water-powered railway in the world. In the other direction, you'll find the gorgeous and rightly renowned beaches of North Devon – Woolacombe, Croyde, Saunton are just a short drive away. Not bad in terms of local attractions then, but above all the Old Rectory is a lovely country house retreat to come back to at the end of the day.

CONTACT Martinhoe, Devon EX31 4QT • 01598 763 368

HOW MUCH? Double rooms with breakfast from £210 a night.

ROOMS 10 Guest Rooms.

The 25 Boutique B&B

An ultra-stylish Torquay guesthouse that was voted the 'The World's Best B&B'!

The 25, run by hospitality gurus Andy and Julian, is like no B&B you have ever stayed in: an adults-only, boutique-style luxury guesthouse that is helping to drag Torquay into the 21st century by pure style. It was recently declared the 'World's Best B&B' on Tripadvisor and has been Visit England's B&B of the Year two years running!

These accolades are well-deserved. Andy and Julian used to run a country house hotel in North Wales, and their experience and attention to detail shows in everything they do – from the high standard of design throughout to the cleanliness of the rooms but above all in the warmth of the welcome and the nothing-is-too-much-trouble attitude they demonstrate to their guests. Breakfast is fabulous – a real award-winning highlight – with everything from kippers to eggs Benedict, and the scrambled eggs come courtesy of a closely guarded family recipe.

There are six rooms in all, each a different size and styled with a different colour palette. The large Torre suite is decorated with a zebra theme; the mood in the Broadsands room is purple; while the Oddicombe is decorated with a fabulous large mural of an orange gerbera. All the rooms have Netflix, Amazon Echos and ultra-fast wifi – and fresh milk for your tea and coffee. The four luxury rooms have super-king-size beds – the rest have king-size beds – and all rooms have complimentary iPads and Nespresso machines. Each room also has a contemporary en-suite bathroom equipped with posh Elemis toiletries, power showers and fluffy bathrobes and slippers. However, although they personally love dogs, sadly they're unable to accept them at their B&B.

As for the location, The 25 B&B is situated in a busy area of Torquay close to Torre Abbey, which is a short – and, for Torquay, a relatively flat – walk from the seafront and very handy for the town's shops, restaurants and public transport. And Torquay itself? Well, it retains much of its faux-Mediterranean charm, and more than repays a two- or three-night visit, plus it's a good base for all manner of attractions nearby. Andy and Julian are big fans of the town and indeed the Torbay area in general, and their enthusiasm is catching. There's nothing they don't know about Torquay and its environs, and they're always happy to share their tips for days out, places to eat and drink and much more.

CONTACT 25 Avenue Road, Torquay, Devon TQ2 5LB • 01803 297 517

HOW MUCH? Double rooms from £129 a night.

ROOMS 6 Guest Rooms.

Cary Arms & Spa

Perhaps the perfect Devon seaside inn, reinvented as a sumptuous boutique hotel

Tucked away on scenic Babbacombe Bay, Cary Arms couldn't have asked for a much better location. Perched delicately on the rocks above the pebble beach, at the bottom of a slightly hair-raising descent down a single-track road, this secret seaside inn brilliantly combines traditional Devon delights with all the style and comfort you expect from a contemporary boutique hotel.

Winner of a 2023 award for 'Best Waterside Hotel', Cary Arms has 10 rooms and suites, plus six quirky huts and two beach suites. It was famously visited by Queen Victoria and Prince Albert, who were apparently rowed ashore here for a cream tea when visiting Torquay, and it remains at heart a coastal inn but with a feel that is more New England than English Riviera. The rooms and suites have fabulous sea views and their own terraces, along with king-size beds with good-quality linen, Smart TVs, tea- and coffee-making facilities, complimentary bottled water and a decanter of sloe gin, and White Company toiletries and waffle bathrobes in the en-suite bathrooms. Two of the ground-floor rooms welcome dogs

What with the beach, the local ale in the beamed dog-friendly bar, the sunsets and the hotel's excellent restaurant, this seaside capsule of comfort can be hard to leave (especially considering the hike up the hill!) The moderately priced restaurant serves good simple gastropub food centred on local beef and lamb, and of course the freshest fish and seafood, and they also do a great-value set lunch menu. There's a comfy lounge and billiard room, along with a spa and gym. There's also a decked sun terrace with an outdoor fire and boxes of blankets for winter days.

It is worth leaving occasionally, however, if only to experience Babbacombe proper via the 1920s funicular railway. Known for its model village, which is one of the best-known attractions in the area, Babbacombe is a charming seaside Devon town, with some fine fish and chips, and from here you can explore the nearby bays of Oddicombe and Petitor Downs along the coastal path.

CONTACT Babbacombe Beach, Devon TQ1 3LX • 01803 327 110

HOW MUCH? Double rooms from £205 a night, beach huts & suites from £285 a night.

ROOMS 10 Guest Rooms & Suites + 12 Beach Suites & Huts.

The Lamb Inn

A proper village pub with rooms and great food in the green heart of Devon

There are some pubs that get just about everything right, and The Lamb Inn, just outside Crediton, bang in the middle of the green heart of Devon, comes pretty close. It's a proper village pub, for a start, with plenty of locals popping by just for a drink, but it serves excellent food too and has a handful of rooms upstairs to tempt you into staying overnight. No surprise, then, that it has featured in the Daily Mail's '20 Best British Country Pubs', has won 'Best Devon Pub' and was voted the i Newspaper's 'Best UK Summer Pub' a couple of years ago.

The Lamb is actually a 16th-century coaching inn at heart, but its eight guest rooms are not by any means stuck in the past – they're crisply refurbished in a contemporary style, with luxurious king-size beds, flatscreen TVs with Freeview, good wifi, tea- and fresh coffee-making facilities and complimentary water, and recently updated bathrooms, some of which have giant baths to luxuriate in. There's a scattering of newspapers in the bar downstairs to make you feel at home, and overall the feel is both cosy and comfortable, but with the sort of service and facilities you expect from a decent hotel.

The pub itself is furnished in a traditional style, with a roaring fire in winter and a pleasant beer garden to enjoy in summer. The food is excellent – a short and fairly traditional menu but with innovative touches and really good cooking; there's plenty for vegetarians and their Sunday roasts are superb. Like all good pubs, The Lamb is also dog-friendly, with dogs welcome throughout the pub and in all guest rooms.

Finally, The Lamb is an easy place to reach – just outside the small Devon market town of Crediton, not far from the M5 and just off the main north–south Exeter to Barnstaple route. Dartmoor is a short drive away, as is Exeter and the coast beyond. All in all, it's a terrific place for a a short but indulgent countryside break.

CONTACT The Square Sandford, Crediton, Devon EX17 4LW • 01363 773 676

HOW MUCH? Double rooms from £59 to £155 a night, not including breakfast.

ROOMS 7 Guest Rooms & 1 Suite.

The Cotley Inn

A classy, quintessential English country inn on the edge of the Blackdown Hills in Somerset

When England does things right, it really does things right – and the classy Cotley Inn, on the edge of the Blackdown Hills in Somerset, is Exhibit A. This stone farmhouse, now a boutique inn, dates back to the 17th century and is the quintessential English country pub with rooms, set in rolling farmland amid chocolate-box villages. It's run with a highly personal touch by the latest custodians, Ben and Maddie, who have put heart and soul into making the pub a sustainable part of the community, from sourcing produce from the local estate to growing their own greens and herbs and smoking meat and fish on the premises.

Four, super-stylish, en-suite B&B rooms have been carved out of the former stables, and all are luxuriously turned out, from high-thread-count cotton linen and goose-down duvets to Smart TVs and Nespresso machines. The Holt is the largest room, set across two floors, with a king-sized bed, roll-top bath and separate living area. As with the other larger room, The Den, the sofa bed can accommodate kids if you're en-famille. The other two rooms are 'dinky doubles', perfect for couples on a romantic break, while dogs are welcome in the larger rooms.

Over in the inn, food and drink is similarly exceptional, with 'food miles' down to bare yards with doorstep-sourced produce and kitchen-garden ingredients. Menus are seasonal, whether it's seafood from the local coast or game from the estate, with both fancy versions of pub classics and beautifully presented fine-dining dishes. Everything is relaxed and unhurried, while warm weather sees the inn's lawns and lavender-edged terrace come into their own. Just note that the inn is closed a couple of days a week, so those nights are room-only. Out and about, you're on the edge of the Blackdown Hills AONB, and just half-an-hour's drive from Lyme Regis and the Jurassic Coast. They'll even pick you up from the nearest station in Axminster.

CONTACT Wambrook, Near Chard, Somerset TA20 3EN • 01460 623 48

HOW MUCH? Double rooms from £150 a night.

ROOMS 4 double rooms.

The Horn of Plenty

A beautifully located dog-friendly boutique hotel overlooking the Tamar Valley

Bang on the Devon-Cornwall border, high above the Tamar Valley, The Horn of Plenty looks like the house of your richest friend – and if you don't have a pal like that, then you still get to stay in this splendid country manor, enjoying its impeccable service and attention to detail. Built in 1866, it was the former crib of a local mine-owner, later converted into a restaurant in the 1960s, when its then owner became the first British woman to be awarded a Michelin star. It's now been a hotel for thirty years, and the individually designed guest rooms have more than kept pace with the times – they are spacious and well-equipped, with high-quality beds, sleek bathrooms with all the luxuries you would expect and sweeping views too (most of the rooms have balconies) – indeed the hotel was the Good Hotel Guide's editor's choice for UK 'Rooms with a View' recently and one of The Times 'Top 40 Places to Stay in Britain' a few years ago. The rooms vary in size but all offer Freeview TVs, coffee- and tea-making facilities, bottled water, fresh milk and a mini bar, luxury bathrobes, hair dryer, TV and wifi. The six rooms in the main house retain their high ceilings, large windows and original fireplaces; the 10 rooms in the coach house conversions are larger with a contemporary country feel. All of the coach house rooms are dog-friendly, and you get a dog bowl and dinner. There are also five acres of grounds for walkies, as well as loads of walks into the countryside beyond, either in the valley below or further afield to Dartmoor.

Other facilities include on-site spa treatments and massages, afternoon teas in the drawing room, the library or on the patio and lovely outdoor weddings in the gardens if the weather is kind. The food too is bang up-to-date, with admirably executed and perfectly formed lunch and dinner menus that are full of delicious, original choices, from local wood pigeon and wild rabbit to Brixham mackerel and Dartmoor lamb.

CONTACT Gulworthy, Tavistock, Devon PL19 8JD • 01822 832 528

HOW MUCH? Double rooms with breakfast £130- £295.

ROOMS 16 Guest Rooms.

Bovey Castle

A luxurious Devon country house hotel in vast grounds with a spa and golf course

Hidden from view by its front gardens and entrance, Bovey Castle is a country house hotel that saves its grandest views for its esteemed guests. Whether strolling through the grounds, tee-ing off on the golf course, or heading down to the tennis courts, the imposing neo-Victorian facade watches over you from its elevated position on a 275-acre estate within Dartmoor National Park. Actually, Bovey Castle is more of a stately home than a castle, with grounds that luxuriate in stunning Dartmoor surroundings – think Downton Abbey, with you as the Master of the House!

The hotel has a spa, restaurant and cocktail bar, along with 60 bedrooms and suites ranging from the relatively modest Mews Bedrooms to Grand State Rooms with dining tables and roll-top baths. The rooms are suited to a wide range of guests from honeymoon couples to those with children or dogs. All rooms come with coffee- and tea-making facilities (including Nespresso machines), and of course the finest fluffy robes and slippers. And if you prefer the flexibility of self-catering but crave the facilities of a top-notch hotel, you can stay in one of Bovey Castle's 22 lodges, which sleep up to eight people in the utmost comfort.

Outside, the plus-foured outdoor staff can be seen warming up the Land Rovers for clay-pigeon shooting trips, a bit of off-road adventure on Dartmoor, or a spot of falconry. They'll also park your car for you when you arrive. Other offerings include a horse and carriage ride to the nearby chocolate-box village of North Bovey and its Ring of Bells country pub, more footpaths than you can count, and there's croquet on the lawns, of course. When the Dartmoor weather closes in, you can avail yourself of the spa facilities, whether in the form of a treatment, a dip in the whirlpool or a few lengths in the swimming pool. And of course, you can eat and drink: head for Smith's Brasserie for Mediterranean dishes or the three-AA-Rosette Great Western Grill for elegant á la carte cuisine. And after a hike on the Moors, you can collapse in front of the fire in the grand common room with one of Devon's finest afternoon teas.

Hotels don't get much better than Bovey Castle, and service is superb throughout. But don't just take our word for it – it has five AA red stars, which means that it's the best of the best, one of around 50 UK hotels to hold this prestigious rating. Oozing style in that mythological English country house sense, it's a slice of pure Devon luxury.

CONTACT North Bovey, Devon TQ13 8RE • 01647 445 000
HOW MUCH? Double rooms from £229 a night. Lodges from £629 a night.
ROOMS 60 Guest Rooms & Suites.

Hotel Endsleigh

A lavish yet homely country residence, courtesy of hotelier Olga Polizzi

Quite literally situated on the border between Devon and Cornwall in the glorious Tamar Valley, the fairytale Endsleigh Hotel is the country cousin of the excellent waterside Tresanton in Cornwall, both owned by the renowned designer and hotelier, Olga Polizzi. Occupying a 19th-century hunting lodge that was the rural retreat of the Duke of Bedford, the hotel's grounds were designed 200 years ago by Sir Humphrey Repton and cover 100 picture-perfect acres of gardens, streams, woodlands, follies and grottoes. It is, as gardener Alan Titchmarsh described it, 'a hotel built in paradise'.

Despite having restored the house from a virtual ruin, Polizzi has done very little to change the structure. The original fireplaces, doors, windows and shutters ensure that the hotel has the feel of the country residence of your richest most stylish and perhaps most eccentric aunt. Its 18 rooms and suites range from Classic through the more spacious Repton and Bedford rooms to a number of well-appointed suites. All are artfully and individually decorated, with a stylish mix of old and new furniture, wooden floors, hand-painted wallpapers, roll-top baths and book-lined shelves. Touches of modern luxury include walk-in showers and big comfortable beds – and, in the family suites, separate sitting rooms and tongue-and-groove cabins with built-in bunk beds for little ones, plus their own TV in the wall. There's also a further suite in the former gatekeeper's lodge with a private garden and wood-burning stove. and a new suite with a double shower and seating for two. Each room is like entering another tale of wonder, each with its own story and uniquely curated with the closest attention to detail.

All rooms are dog-friendly and have stunning views over the gardens and grounds, which you must get out and explore: numerous footpaths meander around the rolling moorland. You can of course hang out on the vine-covered terrace and do not very much at all, but for the more energetic there are lots of activities on offer, including falconry, shooting, fishing, horse-riding and cycling along the new Drakes Trail to Plymouth. Above all, the hotel is a lovely place to return to after a hard's day's yomping through the woods, with its cosy lounge and a restaurant that serves very good, well-priced and unpretentious food. They also do a good afternoon tea. In short, Endsleigh is exactly what it was always meant to be – a fabulous country bolthole, and perfect weekend escape.

CONTACT Milton Abbot, Devon PL19 0PQ • 01822 870 000

HOW MUCH? Double rooms from £270 a night, not including breakfast a night.

ROOMS 18 Guest Rooms & Suites.

St Michaels Resort

A superb beachside resort hotel with spa, fitness centre, tennis and more – plus it's dog-friendly!

Located a stone's throw from Gyllyngvase beach in Falmouth, St Michaels Resort is inspired by its surroundings – the calming sea blues and sandy hues that flow across the interiors of the hotel. The nautical-themed design emphasizes the hotel's focus on tranquillity, coupled with the notion that your stay here will be as hassle-free and indulgent as you desire.

Having won various awards for its hospitality and spa, the hotel has a plethora of activities and foodie options to enjoy on-site before you'd even think of exploring the town. They have a health club (with spinning room, gig-rowing area, spacious gym and pool) and a world-class spa, making it much more than just a place to stay, although the guest rooms are particularly well-appointed, with high-quality beds and linen, wifi and flatscreen TVs, tea- and coffee-making facilities and en-suite bathrooms with Elemis toiletries. Some have sea views, super-king-size beds, Smart TVs and floor-to-ceiling windows with their own terrace, whiel the Spa Garden Lodges sit amid sub-tropical gardens and have poutdoor bathtubs. The hotel also has some gorgeous apartments that can accommodate two to eight people. With huge windows and spacious sea-facing balconies, they give you all the benefits of self-catering while enjoying all the facilities of the hotel. St Michaels is also particularly dog-friendly, with dogs welcome pretty much everywhere – in the rooms, the casual dining Garden Kitchen and even the main restaurant, Brasserie on the Bay.

The hotel is right by 'Gylly Beach', a Blue Flag beach with clear, almost Mediterranean waters and lots of watersports activities, including paddleboarding, kayaking and snorkelling. You're also right on the South West Coast Path, and the hotel recommends a number of delightful circular walks.

CONTACT Gyllyngvase Beach, Falmouth, Cornwall TR11 4NB • 01326 369 767
HOW MUCH? Double rooms from £150 a night, apartments £114–£585 a night.
ROOMS 92 Guest Rooms & Suites.

Talland Bay Hotel

A quirky and luxurious hotel tucked into an idyllic bay between Looe and Polperro

Bang on the South West Coast path, the Talland Bay Hotel is all about pure relaxation. Forget the trappings of spa treatments, indoor pools and sports facilities – here the focus is on glorious sea views, sub-tropical gardens, fine Cornish cuisine and lounging around in a quirky but luxurious environment.

The hotel's guest rooms and suites have been individually decorated – there's an airy seaside feel throughout, a roll-top bath in one, a sleigh bed in another – and many have gorgeous sea views and direct access to patio, terrace or garden. The hotel also has a number of separate cottages and a self-catering bungalow if you want that bit more flexibility while still being able to enjoy the facilities of the hotel. There's also a pretty big collection of local and international artwork, both in the rooms and dotted around the gardens. They have two places to eat – the main restaurant and the sea-view conservatory where they serve an à la carte menu at lunch and dinner and also offer the option of a tasting menu in the evening. There's a very comfy bar too, which is a perfect place to sip a G&T made with their own Talland Bay gin, and like the rest of the hotel it's dog-friendly. Just as well: this is prime territory for strolling with your faithful hound, a short walk away from glistening Talland Bay – childhood haunt of Dame Judi Dench – from where the South West Coast Path runs east to Looe (3.5 miles) and west to Polperro (2 miles).

Sweeping up a grand tally of awards, including 'Best Small Hotel in Cornwall' and 'Best South West Restaurant' a few years ago, this former family home proves that location, style and cuisine are all you need to relax and embrace the natural beauty and lifestyle this part of the world offers. The fab clifftop location and ocean backdrop would also look pretty good in wedding photos...just saying!

CONTACT Porthallow, Cornwall PL13 2JB • 01503 272 667

HOW MUCH? Double rooms with breakfast from £160 to £250.

ROOMS 19 Guest Rooms & 4 Suites.

The Greenbank Hotel

Charming historic hotel perched on the edge of Falmouth harbour with a great restaurant

On the water's edge at Falmouth harbour, The Greenbank is a real crowd-pleaser with class. Originally built in 1640, it's the town's oldest hotel, with uninterrupted panoramic views from both rooms and restaurant – perfect for a relaxing coastal break. The location could hardly be better and they have a range of guest rooms from Classic to Deluxe (some of which are dog-friendly), and the best rooms make the most of it – not just sea views and ocean-inspired colour schemes, but king-size beds, balconies, decent bathrooms and – in the Florence Suite at least – harbour views from your roll-top bath. It's just fabulous to draw back the curtains for another glistening view of Falmouth's magnificent harbour in the morning. Service is superb – confident and personable, with nothing too much trouble.

The restaurant looks over the water, so you can also feast on the views of Falmouth harbour before tucking into sumptuous food from the two-AA-Rosette menu, on which fish and seafood feature highly. The restaurant flows through to a comfy and rather stylish bar, and the hotel also has its own pub – The Working Boat – which has outside tables by the water and serves bar meals and Sunday lunches. The Greenbank is only footsteps from Falmouth town, so all in all it's the perfect place from which to explore Cornwall's most historic resort and port. It is also the only hotel in the southwest to boast its own quay, meaning that if you simply have to travel here on your own yacht you'll be fine.

CONTACT Harbourside, Falmouth, Cornwall TR11 2SR • 01326 312 440
HOW MUCH? Double rooms from £120 a night.
ROOMS 60 Guest Rooms.

Budock Vean Hotel

A beautifully situated, very well-equipped South Cornwall hotel, spa and resort

Set on a splendid private estate of lawns, mature woodland and a private nine-hole golf course above the lovely Helford River, this is not simply an engagingly traditional country house hotel. With a huge swimming pool and intimate spa, it's a good place for both romantic couples and families, and also has a number of self-catering cottages and holiday homes available.

Above all it's a place where you can quickly feel at home. We love the way you can choose between sitting by an open fire, in the conservatory or even on an outdoor terrace; and the variety of public spaces (several lounges, a cocktail bar and a snooker room) mean there's plenty of room for everyone, even on a wet day. We also adore the huge pool, which is another great place to while away a wet afternoon; it also has an open fire and sauna, as well as a little terrace with a hot tub. If that's not your thing, head to the small yet cosy spa, where you can indulge in a variety of holistic and beauty treatments.

The hotel offers Standard bedrooms with a traditional feel, and Signature'rooms that have been updated in a more contemporary country house hotel style, with lush bathrooms and walk-in showers. If you really want to push the boat out, opt for a spacious suite, complete with garden and golf course views. Breakfasts are abundant, with hot dishes cooked to order, and lunch and dinner can be either a formal occasion in the restaurant, or a more casual one in the cocktail bar. There's also a children's tea, daily at 5.30pm. The hotel also offers self-catering options in traditional cottages – all child- and dog-friendly and with encosed gardens – and super-chic Scandinavian-style houses, with open-plan living spaces on the first floor to make the most of the views and featuring wood-burners and floor-to-ceiling windows.

CONTACT Mawnan Smith, Falmouth, Cornwall TR11 5LG • 01326 252 100
HOW MUCH? Double rooms from £168 to around £400 a night. Cottages & Lodges from around £1600 a week.
ROOMS 49 Rooms & 7 Cottages.

The Old Coastguard

This Mousehole hotel is the last word in relaxation and good food, Cornish-style

The folk behind this hotel cut their teeth on the excellent Gurnard's Head near Zennor and the two places have plenty in common, not least a glorious scenic location, great food and a determinedly laid-back vibe that is infectious. Situated in the picturesque seaside village of Mousehole, near Penzance, The Old Coastguard is a supremely relaxing place to stay, with 14 comfy guest rooms, all of which have some sort of view over the sea. The same group's third hotel, the excellent Felin Fach Griffin, is also well worth a visit if you're in that part of the world.

Downstairs too the easy-going atmosphere of the hotel is evident throughout: rows of sofas look seaward, children and dogs get a hearty welcome, and there's often live music in the restaurant alongside Sunday lunch. As with its sister hotel, the emphasis throughout is on comfort, good food and relaxation, with big comfy beds in spacious rooms equipped with Roberts radios and posh toiletries, high-quality tea and coffee, and lots of books to browse. Some rooms have balconies, and most have baths, but all are that little bit different. Whichever you choose you'll be so cosy you may not want to leave, but luckily there is plenty to tempt you downstairs, not least the hotel's lovely gardens, which stretch all the way down to the sea. There's also a wood-panelled bar and of course a very high quality restaurant, which serves a deliberately local menu – à la carte at lunchtime, when you can feast on Cornish mussels, fish stew and various other regularly revolving dishes, and fixed two- and three-course options at what they call Supper: once again made up of comforting but imaginative dishes based on the best local produce. They also do a terrific Sunday lunch.

As for Mousehole itself, it's an archteypal Cornish harbour village, albeit with a contemporary patina of cafés, restaurants and galleries. Beyond, you can take to the coastal path (St Michael's Mount and the Lizard Peninsula are on your doorstep), take in a performance at the nearby Minack Theatre, or just go to the beach – in which case you'll be delighted to be fairly close to wonderful Sennen Cove, which is a grand place for both lounging and more high-adrenaline activities like surfing.

CONTACT The Parade, Mousehole, Penzance, Cornwall TR19 6PR • 01736 731 222

HOW MUCH? Double rooms with breakfast from £185 a night.

ROOMS 14 Guest Rooms.

Watergate Bay Hotel

Taking the concept of luxury beachfront hotel to a new level

An extension of the relaxing beach life bang on the doorstep, Watergate Bay Hotel invites you straight off the sand into stylish accommodation. Not only do many of the rooms and living areas benefit from dazzling views over the two-mile stretch of Watergate Bay's sandy beach, but all the beach activities you could dream up can be arranged at the click of your fingers.

There is an emphasis on luxury and comfort without pretension and a liking for the outdoor life, dogs and families, making it the perfect place to chill out and relax, safe in the knowledge that you will be well fed and that nothing is too much trouble. There's a 25-metre indoor infinity pool overlooking the sea; an outdoor hot tub and loungers on the terrace and beach-facing boardwalk; their take on a spa, gym and Finnish sauna; and finishing touches such as outdoor showers and a surf-in/surf-out kit area where your wetsuit can be dried overnight. There's also an Ofsted-registered Kids' zone and brilliant facilities for teens, as well as a Forest-School-inspired 'Beach School'. Dogs are also welcome – as they are, crucially, on the beach itself.

With no fewer than 73 guest rooms, including four Village family apartments with open-plan living spaces and seven beach lofts right next to the water, you're sure to find something to suit you: rooms range from Standard to Best along with beach loft and family suites (the latter with double bed and a separate space with bunks). All rooms have en-suite bath or shower rooms with bathrobes and toiletries, plus tea- and coffee-making facilities, flatscreen TVs, Bluetooth speakers, wifi and hairdryers. In most rooms, they can add a cot or small child's bed too so you don't have to opt for a family suite or apartment. All are available with or without sea views and apart from that the main difference between categories is simply size.

There are three stunning restaurants at Watergate Bay; The Living Space – one of Cornwall's coolest sea-view lounges for food and cocktails; Zacry's on the sea wall, which serves a seasonally changing three-course menu; and the Beach Hut, which serves burgers and grills and is situated (you guessed it!) on the beach itself (dogs are allowed everywhere except Zacry's restaurant).

If there is a better beachfront hotel in Cornwall, then we have yet to find it.

CONTACT On the Beach, Watergate Bay, Cornwall TR8 4AA • 01637 860 543
HOW MUCH? Double rooms £200–£700 a night; apartments from £600 a night, beach lofts from £460 a night.
ROOMS 80 Guest Rooms, Suites & Apartments.

Artist Residence Penzance

A quirky boutique hotel with individually designed rooms and a curated art collection

It would have been all to easy to buy up this Georgian mansion and run a traditional hotel with bragging rights about its top location smack bang in the middle of Penzance. Not so for the Artist Residence Penzance, where time and effort has gone into a unique boutique design that stands out from the crowds. The elegant townhouse exterior conceals 19 rooms, stylishly decorated, with limited edition prints, plus there's a three-bedroom cottage, complete with log burner and copper roll-top bath.

Part of the Artist Residence group, which has four other UK locations, the hotel is tucked away on historic Chapel Street, and brings a slice of eccentric charm to the dreamy lanes of this historic seaside town. With 16 eclectically decorated bedrooms, three fabulous suites and a cosy three-bedroom cottage that is the perfect seaside retreat for a family, the key word throughout is comfort. The rooms have en-suite bathrooms with eco-friendly toiletries, flatscreen TVs and wifi, while the cottage has an open-plan living room and kitchenette with log burner, and a luxurious bathroom with copper roll-top bath and walk-in rainfall shower. Most of the roomsoffer a warm welcome to dogs, as does the cottage and all the public spaces, and it isn't unusual to see some of the staff's dogs chilling out by the fire too. Old railway sleepers and leather armchairs maintain the charm of Cornwall in a different era, while following the hotel's unique style in the details.

Breakfast is served in the ground-floor restaurant using fresh local produce, and the restaurant is also open for lunch and dinner, providing a selection of small plates and meat and fish dishes from the smoker. There is a large beer garden complete with table football, ping pong, fully stocked bar and BBQ for summer days, and an indoor bar-lounge with log burner and a focus on local ales and cocktails crafted using Cornish spirits.

It all adds up to a stunning hotel with unique design, delicious food and a thoroughly laid back atmosphere – topped off by that central location that, yes, they should still brag about! It is a refreshingly vibrant place for a break away for a couple or small family, especially as it's only a five-minute walk to the Isles of Scilly ferry.

CONTACT 20 Chapel Street, Penzance, Cornwall, TR18 4AW • 01736 365 664
HOW MUCH? Double rooms from £125 a night.
ROOMS 16 Guest Rooms, 3 Suites & a 3-bed cottage.

Soar Mill Cove Hotel

This South Hams seaside hotel has been owned by the Makepeace family for three generations, and the welcome is warm and the service and hospitality genuine and old-fashioned. But there's nothing old-school about the Soar Mill itself, whose rooms are well furnished and thoughtfully equipped, with big bathrooms, wifi, books and games, and even binoculars for enjoying the spectacular views (and maybe spotting a dolphin or two). You can almost hear the waves, and the coastline is just a step or two away. Accommodation is spread across several options – all with beautiful views across the rolling hills or down to the cove. Some larger rooms and suites are ideal for families, whilst those looking for a little more privacy can stay in one of the self-catering retreats. Activities are right on hand – there's an indoor heated swimming pool, a spa and gym, tennis and pitch-and putt, and a games room with snooker and table tennis. Pet-lovers will be pleased to know that it's also dog -friendly!

CONTACT Near Salcombe, Devon TQ7 3DS • 01548 561 566
HOW MUCH? Double rooms from £159 a night. Family rooms & suites from £209.

Blue Hayes

Nothing is too much trouble at this grand, white aristocratic residence, high on a clifftop just outside St Ives. With panoramic sea views, there's a Mediterranean feel when the sun is shining, especially when you drift out onto the balustraded terrace to view the bay with its pines and palms and well-tended gardens. There are just five double suites and a smaller single suite – all very spacious and sumptuous, decorated in cool off-whites and creams, with high-quality mattresses and goose-down pillows, tea- and coffee-making facilities and Smart TVs. Well-proportioned bathrooms feature body-jet showers and Molton Brown toiletries. Half the rooms have sea views, and two have large private outdoor spaces. There's a convivial bar and dining room and room-service is available in case you fancy breakfast in bed. From the garden gate, you're on the downhill path to the beach and only a short walk from town, but for those who would rather stay in, the hotel serves light suppers on request.

CONTACT Trelyon Avenue, St Ives, Cornwall TR26 2AD • 01736 797 129
HOW MUCH? Suites from £310 a night.

Gurnard's Head

A short walk inland from one of the most wild and rugged sections of the South West Coast Path, The Gurnard's Head is the sort of place you can kick off your muddy boots by the roaring fire and sip a glass of wine while the dog snoozes at your feet. A glance at the art on the granite walls tells you that, despite rustic appearances, this is the sort of place with an eye for the finer things in life. Downstairs there's a menu serving seasonal, locally sourced dishes from wild rabbit and wood pigeon to pig's head and pollock. All this before you've even padded upstairs to find a Vi-spring bed draped with Welsh wool blankets, a Roberts radio and shelves stacked with novels to distract you from the moorland views. The briny air and hearty food encourage such a deep sleep that you might not stir until the cows pass to be milked in the morning. But don't stress, breakfast is a lazy affair and you won't be in a hurry to leave. Dogs and children are welcome, with cots and dog treats provided.

CONTACT Near Zennor, St Ives, Cornwall TR26 3DE • 01736 796 928
HOW MUCH? Double rooms with breakfast from £155 a night.

The Alverton

The Alverton began life as a Victorian manor house belonging to a local banker – until he went bankrupt in 1874, following the collapse of the Cornish tin-mining industry. It was later occupied by nuns and their neo-Gothic chapel makes The Alverton a fabulous venue for a party or a wedding. It became a hotel in 1984 and is nowadays part of a small Cornish hotel group that also owns the Greenbank in Falmouth (see p.120). We reckon it's the best place to stay in the Cornish capital, especially since the opening of its new Courtyard rooms, painted in Farrow & Ball heritage grey, with bespoke Ralph Lauren textiles and magnificent bathrooms. All have fast free wifi and flatscreen TVs with Freeview, and the the two Junior Suites come with a burnished roll-top bathtub in the bedroom. There's also a relaxed brasserie-restaurant that serves a delectable Modern British menu using locally sourced ingredients, with a pleasant terrace overlooking well-tended private gardens.

CONTACT Tregolls Road, Truro, Cornwall TR1 1ZQ • 01872 276 633
HOW MUCH? Double rooms from £89 to £139 a night.

Lucky Dip

Bristol Harbour Hotel

49/55 Corn Street, Bristol, Somerset BS1 1HT

This contemporary boutique hotel occupies two former bank buildings in the heart of Bristol city centre and has a mixture of grand spaces, comfortable contemporary bedrooms, an excellent restaurant and a small spa. Guest rooms are spacious and well-appointed, enjoying the views across the city centre, and with big, comfy beds, en-suite bathrooms with rainfall showers and White Company toiletries. Downstairs, the. Harbour Kitchen is a crisp and contemporary place for dinner, and afterwards you can retire to the funky Gold Bar for cocktails and occasional DJs, in between admiring the fabulous Sansovino Room: without question one of the city centre's most spectacular interiors.

The Cricket Inn

Beesands, Kingsbridge, Devon TQ7 2EN

Tucked away in the pretty coastal village of Beesands, just seven miles from Kingsbridge, this is a beautiful seaside spot by any standards, and this quaint old fishing inn has been reinvented as a light and spacious gastropub with rooms. Variously named after cricket grounds and cricketers, they come with en-suite bathrooms, Smart TV's, Nespresso coffee machines and extremely comfortable king-size beds, while in the morning their mighty (and award-winning) Devonshire breakfast is a fabulous way to start any day.

Fowey Hall Hotel

Hanson Drive, Fowey, Cornwall PL23 1ET

Believed by some to be the inspiration for Toad Hall in Wind in the Willows, this is a fantastic location for the whole family to explore the rugged coastline, preferably with a dog or two in tow. Whether you choose to sink into a plump sofa with the newspaper, relax under the spell of a massage in the spa, take a dip in the pool, or loosen your purse strings in Fowey's waterside boutiques, Fowey Hall Hotel is all about giving parents a chance to chill out.

The Idle Rocks

Harbourside St, Mawes, Cornwall, TR2 5AN

Housed in a beautiful Edwardian waterfront building in the centre of St Mawes, this is a bright and contemporary hotel with a touch of escapism and seaside romance about it. Once voted one of the best 50 beach hotels in Europe, the stripped-down charm of the guest rooms and the unabashed comfort of the public areas make it the perfect place to spend the weekend doing, well, not very much at all.

The Rosevine

Portscatho, Cornwall TR2 5EW

This family-friendly Cornish country house by the sea combines the comforts of a luxury hotel with the freedom of having your own studio or apartment. Set in two acres of gardens above the sandy cove of Porthcurnick, the hotel is in a brilliant location for walks along the South West Coast Path as well as for the best bucket- and-spade beach days. Apartments are comfy, most have sea views and balconies or terraces, and there is plenty to do for adults and kids alike!

The Scarlet

Tredragon Road, Mawgan Porth, Cornwall TR8 4DQ

A sustainably-minded, adults-only hotel that features all sorts of wow-factor facilities – designer rooms, cliff top hot tubs, a solar-heated pool and state-of-the-art spa, plus a swanky restaurant serving only the freshest local produce. It's extremely pet-friendly, too, and dog-friendly rooms come with bowls, blankets, poo bags and homemade treats for your hound.

Westleigh B&B

Fore St, Beer, Seaton, Devon EX12 3EQ

This cute-as-a-button stone cottage just a couple of minutes' walk from the beach and harbour of the picture-postcard village of Beer is a wonderful dog-friendly B&B. They really do walk the doggy walk here: no extra charges, access to all rooms, dog beds, baths and towels, treats and toys, and even free dog food if required, and there are dog-sitting and dog-walking services available too. Not only that, its owner is a 'Cordon Bleu' chef, so breakfasts are fab and dinners – ordered in advance – even better.

The Scarlet

Westleigh B & B

The Idle Rocks

East Anglia

Cambridgeshire • Essex • Suffolk • Norfolk

Despite being one of England's most accessible regions, East Anglia is in some ways also one of its least-known. Essex has a thoroughly undeserved reputation as little more than an extension of northeast London, although this in some way works to its benefit, making it ideal territory for good hotels with great food to tempt jaded Londoners out for a weekend in the country. Further afield, Norfolk and Suffolk are predominantly rural counties whose attractions vary from the glories of the North Norfolk coast to the historic wool towns of Suffolk. This is perhaps England's most historic corner, and as such home not only to some of the country's longest-standing pubs and inns but also some of its best boutique hotels and B&Bs – many of them situated in locations that would adorn any picture postcard.

The Maids Head, p.151

Piglets Boutique Country Stay

This uniquely comfortable Essex B&B is an indulgent and easily accessible place for short breaks from London and around

Housed in an ingeniously renovated piggery with a large and airy brand-new timber-clad extension that forms part of Chrissie and Max Parker's Essex home, Piglets is the result of a lot of nights in hotels and B&Bs. Years of travelling and an enthusiasm for eating out gave Max and Chrissie the idea of creating the ultimate luxury B&B, and that's exactly what they've done, in what is an unusual – and unusually comfortable – Essex home-from-home. Indeed, they deservedly won the 'Best B&B and Guest House' award at the 2023 Visit England Excellence Awards.

The B&B has five guest rooms, all beautifully kitted out with an impeccable eye for detail and a level of comfort that would put quite a few luxury hotels to shame. Rooms are contemporary in style and have super-king-size beds, air-conditioning, flatscreen TVs, Netflix, ultra-fast wifi, DAB radio with Bluetooth, tea- and coffee-making facilities that include Lavazza espresso machines and fresh milk, plus en-suite bathrooms with power showers, bathrobes and Ferragamo toiletries! There are lots of little extras like an ironing board and iron, a high-speed hairdryer and lots of USB charging points for all your devices. The ground-floor bedrooms have private entrances, one of the first-floor rooms has a private balcony, and the other overlooks the Mediterranean patio area. Probably the most unique feature of the property, however, is its large natural swimming pond, whose decked surrounds are a perfect place for a spot of summer sunbathing.

Chrissie and Max place a real emphasis on food and drink, and serve an excellent Full English and lots more besides, including great locally sourced sausage and bacon, plus smoked salmon, eggs all styles, and veggie and vegan options. They also offer various sharing platters for lunch and dinner or you can just make the most of their well-stocked honesty bar with its stupendous display of gins! There's a comfy guest lounge with books and board games (Max's other business) and a separate TV room. Location-wise, it's a hop, skip and a jump from London, and just a short drive from Cambridge, yet rural enough to feel like a real escape. Their adults-only policy makes it a unique place for grown-ups to relax, whether it's in the natural swimming pond, checking out the small but well-equipped gym and games room or by making the most of the multiple walks you can do from the doorstep.

CONTACT Piglets Corner, Top Road, Upper Green, Wimbish Village, Saffron Walden, Essex • 01799 599 800

HOW MUCH? Double rooms from £200 a night.

ROOMS 5 Guest Rooms.

White Hart Inn

A welcoming Essex gastropub with cracking food and luxurious guestrooms

Situated at the mouth of the Blackwater Estuary, Mersea is the most easterly inhabited island in the British Isles, and perhaps one of England's under-discovered gems. Only accessible via The Strood – a skinny Saxon causeway that floods twice daily – it has a relative isolation that is refreshingly different to the 'kiss-me-quick' amusements of other towns on the Essex coast. Instead, its dramatic landscape and myriad surrounding creeks and salt marshes give it a remote and desolate beauty.

It also has a terrific place to stay in the White Hart Inn, a welcoming gastropub that blends chic decor, mouthwatering food and six comfy guest rooms. From the outside, the weatherboard cladding exudes coastal charm, yet inside it's a masterful study in contemporary cool, with a spacious restaurant, snug lounge and an outside terrace that is a real suntrap. Like its sister pub, The Sun in Dedham (p.177), the bar is well stocked with a range of East Anglian ales and British wines and the food menu is a pleasing blend of creative casual dishes alongside fancier mains, including giant ribeye for two and of course those famous Mersea oysters. For those staying over, the six double guest rooms are vibrant and luxurious. Some have sea views, others overlook the village green. Thoughtfully designed, they feature super-king-size beds and lavish 4000 pocket sprung mattresses and Egyptian cotton linens. Freeview TVs, wifi, hairdryers and tea and coffee facilities come as standard and three rooms are dog-friendly. Works by local artists adorn the walls and the spacious bathrooms, boasting walk-in showers, are finished with trendy metro tiles. Lots of little extra touches elevate this place from a simple pub with rooms to the level of a boutique hotel – things like Bramley Bath products and comfy bathrobes. There are even complimentary bikes for guests and the ever-helpful staff are happy to plot you a route around the island.

CONTACT 1 High Street, West Mersea, Essex CO5 8QD • 01206 583 212

HOW MUCH? Double rooms £150–£175 a night.

ROOMS 6 Guest Rooms.

Talliston House

This unique Essex B&B is undoubtedly the most astounding place you will ever stay!

Talliston House & Gardens seems a rather grand name for a three-bedroomed semi in Essex. But then things are not always as they seem. Beyond the front door of this bed and breakfast are a series of extraordinary rooms, each designed and decorated with so much commitment to their wildly different themes that you'll feel like you're exploring another world. There's the futuristic Japanese Tea Room, a 1920s New York study, the Victorian watchtower and the New Orleans kitchen. Of the 13 rooms in total, three are guest bedrooms, but during your stay, you'll explore them all.

The guest rooms are similarly unique, with decorations straight out of visionary owner-cum-storyteller John Tallow's incredible imagination. Take the 'Haunted Bedroom' – decorated to represent the bedroom of a Scottish Edwardian child, complete with a dark wood sleigh bed, heavy fabrics, period wallpaper and appropriately creepy toys. For something a little lighter, the 'Room of Dreams' recreates a Moorish bedchamber, with artefacts from around the world, a soundscape of Spanish wildlife and the scent of orange blossom. The third option is a Canadian Trapper's Cabin – like all the rooms, set not only in a specific location but in a specific era too. This one transports you to 1940s Saskatchewan: the scents are woody and the sounds are bluesy music.

Great Dunmow is a pleasant market town just six miles from Stansted airport, making Talliston a handy location if you have a flight to catch, but really, it's more than a place to stop over. All guests get a short introduction from John, but to really appreciate the property, you should also book the full house and gardens tour, which takes you through the 25-year journey that has transformed this ordinary house into the most extraordinary B&B you've ever come across. The more time you spend here, the more you'll discover – and the more you'll want to come back!

CONTACT Talliston, Newton Green, Great Dunmow, Essex CM6 1DU • 07760 171 100
HOW MUCH? Double rooms from £145 a night including continental breakfast.
ROOMS 3 Guest Rooms.

The Pier at Harwich

A stylish seaside boutique hotel that evokes the maritime spirit of Harwich

Harwich isn't perhaps the obvious location for a boutique hotel and a fancyish restaurant, but that's one of the things we love about this place, which is part of the excellent, Essex-based Milsoms group of hotels. They recently spent a large sum of money of revamping this wonderful old building, right on the harbour in Harwich, and have turned it into a boutique hotel with an all-day dining restaurant that is as chic and stylish a place to stay as you'll find anywhere on the east coast. Perhaps the best thing about the renovation is the way it references Harwich's seafaring past, with both its bar and restaurant and 14 upstairs bedrooms designed to make the most of the stunning sunsets and glorious harbour views.

All the bedrooms are equipped with flatscreen satellite TVs, complimentary soft drinks and posh aromatherapy toiletries, and there's wifi throughout. There's a restaurant on the first floor that opens out onto the building's elegant period wrought-iron balcony and serves fish and seafood (among other things) fresh from the harbour, while downstairs the NAVYÄRD bar is a stripped-back and cool space with estuary views from every table, a good choice of ales and cocktails and a bar menu inspired by the town's Scandinavian roots – open sandwiches, sharing platters and great oysters. We love it when any old building is brought up-to-date and given a bit of overdue love and care, and when it's done this well, and with this much respect to its location, we like it even more. In short, The Pier is a great stop-off if you're catching an early Holland- or Belgium-bound ferry, but why stop there? At less than two hours from London, it's the perfect weekend escape.

CONTACT The Quay, Harwich, Essex CO12 3HH • 01255 241 212
HOW MUCH? Double rooms from £145 a night.
ROOMS 14 Guest Rooms.

Talbooth House & Spa

Lovely boutique spa hotel in Dedham with a pool and a sister fine dining restaurant

The Talbooth House & Spa is an agreeable country house in 'Constable Country', overlooking a lovely rolling green landscape punctured by spires and red roofs. Just outside the lovely village of Dedham, it has just 12 gorgeously styled guest rooms, each deliberately different and named after a renowned poet. Shakespeare and Keats are the main suites while the other mix of superior and deluxe rooms come in various styles and sizes. All come with excellent beds, and with bathrooms supplied with Elemis toiletries, and a range of other goodies and expected services such as complimentary soft drinks and snacks, satellite HD TVs and free wifi. There's a deliberately homely vibe throughout, with an informal flagstoned reception area and a lounge that leads through to a Garden Room and outdoor terrace looking out over manicured lawns and gardens. Beyond here, things get nice and chilled – maybe some tennis or a plunge in the outdoor heated pool (usable in winter too) and hot tub, or downtime in the pool house with its satellite TV, honesty bar, robes and open fire. When the time comes for dinner, their nearby fine dining restaurant, Le Talbooth is just two minutes away, and has a lovely location by the River Stour and a fab terrace to enjoy it from during summer. Otherwise, it's breakfast, lunch and dinner at the excellent all-day restaurant of their nearby sister hotel Milsoms. Talbooth Spa specialises in an array of spa treatments and therapies, and offers brilliant spa packages too, such as whole day, half day or after-hours. The complex appears to have a micro climate of its own, so feel free to use the pool, indulge and relax on the sun loungers any month of the year.

CONTACT Stratford Road, Dedham, Essex CO7 6HN • 01206 322 367
HOW MUCH? Double rooms £215–£275 a night. Suites £335.
ROOMS 12 Guest Rooms & Suites.

The Suffolk

There's no better spot for a Suffolk seaside break than this fabulous Aldeburgh restaurant with rooms

Originally a beachside pop-up of a well-known London restaurant, The Suffolk is a high-quality yet relaxed restaurant with a cool bar for drinks and cocktails and a handful of rooms upstairs for those who want to stay over. And why wouldn't you? You're bang in the centre of Aldeburgh, right above one of the best fish and seafood joints on the Suffolk coast. The town is, quite literally, your oyster!

The Suffolk is more of a restaurant with rooms than a hotel. There's no lobby or reception: you walk straight into the bar and wait for someone to come and help. The bar is a cool space in the front of the building where they encourage people to drop by just for a drink. There's a brilliant roof terrace up top, with views over the sea, and six simply but stylishly decorated guest rooms, two of which have sea views. Decorated in shades of blue, white and grey that evoke the hotel's seaside location, they all have good-sized beds with colourful headboards, a mix of antique and contemporary furniture, and compact en-suite bathrooms with toiletries. Rather than clutter up your room, guests have access to a pantry down the hall where you can help yourself to tea and coffee, water and drinks, and even cold meats, crackers and local cheeses. There's good wifi but no TV, the thinking being that there's plenty to do in Aldeburgh without watching telly. In any case, if you want to watch Netflix, that's what your laptop is for.

Finally there's the restaurant, which is a bright, slightly Scandinavian space where they primarily serve local fish and seafood, including fabulous local oysters from Butley, crab and lobster and the freshest fish from the North Sea. They also serve meat and veggie dishes, and roasts on Sundays, and if you don't fancy a full meal you can opt for that bar menu out the front, which includes yummy hunger-quenchers like smoked mussels, chilli prawns, super local pork belly and of course those delicious oysters!

CONTACT 152 High Street, Aldeburgh, Suffolk IP15 5AQ • 07831 601 411
HOW MUCH? Double rooms with breakfast from £180 to £240 a night.
ROOMS 6 Guest Rooms.

The Crown & Castle

Lovely dog-friendly restaurant with rooms in a prime position on the main square in Orford

Originally founded by the TV hotel inspector Ruth Watson and now part of the local Hotel Folk group, The Crown & Castle is an outstanding place to stay in a terrific location, right on the square in sleepy Orford, Suffolk. It bills itself as a 'restaurant with rooms', and food is very much to the fore here. But the property recently won 'Small Hotel of the Year' in the East of England awards, and its spick-and-span guest rooms are just the ticket for a stay on the Suffolk Coast.

There are 21 guest rooms, seven in the main building and the rest outside, split between a row of Garden rooms – most of which are dog-friendly – Terrace rooms which have private patios and large bathrooms, and a large suite with its own terrace. All the rooms are bright and contemporary and recently refurbished, and all come with Smart TVs, good wifi, king-size beds, complimentary water and tea and coffee; a couple of the rooms in the main building also have sea views, and most of the bathrooms have a bath/shower combined. They're thoughtful too – with electric bikes to rent if you want to explore – although there are numerous great walks nearby.

As for the food, the emphasis is on local ingredients and service that is a perfect blend of attentive and relaxed. What you eat depends on the time of year, but there's usually a good selection of fish and seafood – crab, skate wing, Butley oysters, smoked salmon and other goodies from Pinneys' nearby fish shop and smokery, along with bread from the Pump Street Bakery across the square and Blythburgh pork and local lamb. It's all deliberately understated; plus you can sit outside in the garden, either to eat or to enjoy a pre-dinner aperitif. Dog owners can eat the same menu in the bar or of course outside in the garden.

CONTACT Market Hill, Orford, Suffolk IP12 2LJ • 01394 450 205
HOW MUCH? Double rooms from £165 a night including breakfast.
ROOMS 21 Guest Rooms.

Five Acre Barn

A contemporary Aldeburgh B&B that's ideal for exploring the Suffolk Coast

Housed in an award-winning barn conversion, set slightly back from the coast midway between Aldeburgh and Thorpeness, Five Acre Barn makes a lovely base for seeing the best of the Suffolk coast – a boutique B&B par excellence, with jagged roofs, cedar-cladding and soaring ceilings that reflect the county's modern-day role as a destination for tired Londoners looking for both temporary and permanent respite from the cares of the capital.

Peckham refugees David and Bruce are two such people, and their contemporary B&B is great-value, with prices that compare extremely well with other options in what can be a pricey area. It has five guest rooms, four of which are suites really, with separate sitting rooms and mezzanine floors with king-size beds with cotton sheets and duvets. You can enjoy the soaring ceilings of each room's cool, crisp living area, equipped with Freeview TVs and good wifi, and later on climb the stairs and lie on your bed and gaze at the big Suffolk skies through the large roof lights, drawing the solar-powered blinds once it's time to go to sleep. Bathrooms are small but well-thought-out, two with wet rooms and showers, two with baths, and equipped with Bramley toiletries.

Outside, each room has its own stretch of decking with access to the large garden and woodland, where you can spot rabbits, lots of birds and even the odd muntjac deer. The fifth room – the Garden Room – fills one storey on its own and is accessible for wheelchair users or people who prefer to do without stairs. It has a fully accessible shower and a luxurious bathroom, plus an ottoman which expands to a single bed for an additional guest. Dogs are welcome in some of the rooms but they don't accept children under 12.

Breakfast is a relaxed and sociable affair, with a choice of Full English, smoked salmon and scrambled eggs, waffles, latkes and omelettes made to order. You could, if you wished, chill out for the rest of the day in the Barn, and it's tempting – there's a Sonos music system, games and books and a wood-burner that will make you almost wish for a rainy day. That said, there are plenty of good walks and other attractions – Aldeburgh itself is perhaps Suffolk's premier seaside resort: the home of Benjamin Britten, The Red House, is virtually within walking distance, and the sea at Thorpeness, just over a mile away, is easily reached on foot through the woods.

CONTACT Aldeburgh Road, Aldringham, Aldeburgh, Suffolk IP16 4QH • 07788 424 642
HOW MUCH? Double rooms with breakfast from £125 to £185 a night.
ROOMS 5 Guest Rooms.

Salthouse Harbour Hotel

A cool and contemporary boutique hotel at the heart of Ipswich's resurgent Waterfront district

At the heart of the resurgent Waterfront district, housed in an imaginatively converted warehouse, the Salthouse Harbour is Ipswich at its boutique best, mixing up the town's maritime legacy with a unique modern style that succeeds on every level, from its brilliant location to the classy rooms, restaurant and service.

The style of the hotel is full-on contemporary, with bags of personality and public spaces enlivened by quirky modern sculptures and contemporary art along with ethnic items picked up on the owners' travels. The service is relaxed, confident and attentive but never overbearing, there's a good restaurant that's popular with non-residents, 24-hour room service and parking.

Spread across several floors are 70 large, sharply designed rooms, the topmost of which have floor-to-ceiling windows that look out over the marina and free-standing baths from which to enjoy the views. Squint, and on a sunny day you could be in Antibes. The public areas are classy but never dull, with eccentrically modern furniture and splashes of colour that soften the stark lines, including lots of edgy contemporary art, while the rooms blend the building's maritime legacy with a quirky, modern look and feel. Options range from Contemporary and Salthouse rooms to Marina suites with a balcony and a copper bath positioned to make the most of the view. Bathrooms are large and well-appointed, with power showers, there's free wifi, good coffee and tea, complimentary biscuits and mineral water, air-conditioning, flatscreen TVs, and high-end toiletries and robes.

Finally, there's the ground-floor Eaterie, which is one of the best places to eat in Ipswich, serving great-value set menus and light dishes at lunchtime, and more ambitious fare in the evening. Whatever you choose to eat, try to be here on a sunny summer day at lunchtime or evening when they open the patio doors to the tables on the quayside.

We reckon the Salthouse Harbour is worth the trip to Ipswich on its own, but while here make sure you see something of the town as well, which has a compact centre that is well worth exploring, especially Christchurch Mansion, with its collection of Constables and Gainsboroughs. You're also well placed to see the best of nearby 'Constable Country', including Dedham and Flatford Mill.

CONTACT Neptune Quay, Ipswich, Suffolk IP4 1AX • 01473 226 789

HOW MUCH? Double rooms from £175 a night.

ROOMS 70 Guest Rooms & Suites.

The Bell Hotel

A venerable yet contemporary Suffolk coaching inn with a busy bar and restaurant

The small Suffolk town of Saxmundham often gets rather overlooked in favour of the more obvious tourist honeypots of the nearby coast, which is a shame because it has a terrific place to stay (and to eat) in The Bell. A classic coaching inn in every sense, this has recently received a much-deserved makeover by new owners Beales – a family firm that's been in the hospitality trade for over 250 years. The Bell is one of multiple hotels they've owned since their first purchase back in 1945, so they have plenty of experience.

First of all the location, which is great. Saxmundham is a pleasant small town with two superpowers: it's home to a mainline station and is a brilliant base for the delights of Aldeburgh, Minsmere and the nearby Suffolk coast. The station is only a two-minute walk from the hotel, so The Bell is also an excellent choice if you prefer to leave the car at home.

The hotel has 10 guest rooms of various shapes and sizes, ranged across the two upper floors: all have generously sized beds with Hypnos mattresses, Smart TVs, tea- and coffee-making facilities and complimentary biscuits and water. Some also have mini-fridges and Nespresso machines. Named after local towns and villages, the rooms are decorated in a contemporary style that evokes the nearby sea, and they divide into four categories – Cosy, Classic, Spacious and Deluxe – although the main differences between them are floor space and bathrooms. Cosy and Classic doubles have walk-in showers, Spacious bedrooms have showers over a bath or a wet room for accessibility, while Deluxe rooms have roll-top baths and walk-in showers. The hotel has a lift, going to the first floor (but not the upper levels), and Orford is a dual-aspect accessible room, with an extra-wide doorway, wet room and grab rails.

Dogs are welcome in some rooms, and have the run of the downstairs public spaces except the restaurant, which serves a menu focused on local ingredients, including Blythburgh pork and fresh fish and seafood from the nearby coast. On the other side of the flagstoned lobby, you can also eat in the Coast Lounge or in the popular River Bar, which is a cool and comfy place for an early evening drink. Overall, the hotel couldn't be more comfortable, an old-fashioned sort of place with excellent, understated service and a quirky, contemporary vibe that makes it an ideal base for seeing both the Suffolk countryside and coast.

CONTACT 31 High Street, Saxmundham, Suffolk IP17 1AF • 01728 602 331
HOW MUCH? Double rooms with breakfast from £130 a night.
ROOMS 10 Guest Rooms.

Retreat East

Jaded city dwellers will think they have died and gone to country heaven at this unique Suffolk hotel

Arriving at this former dairy farm, deep in the wilds of the Suffolk countryside, tired city folk may think they have died and gone to country heaven. Made up of a series of self-contained barns, a self-catering farmhouse and a handful of luxury shepherds huts, generously spaced among gorgeous grounds, it's like a deconstructed country house hotel. At its centre lies the purpose-built Great Barn, whose bar and restaurant anchor a complex that is drenched in peace and tranquillity. Indeed it's hard to think of anything they have got wrong at Retreat East. Not only are the barns decked out with flair and taste, and the location about as peaceful as you'll find, the business is run with a keen eye on the environment. As well as charging points for your car, the hotel has its own bore-hole for water and an efficient and sustainable waste system, power comes from solar panels, and many ingredients for the restaurant come from their own kitchen garden. Perhaps not surprisingly, Retreat East was voted a 'Sustainable Hotel of the Year' in the recent East of England awards, and 'Romantic Hotel of the Year' by The Times, which tells you pretty much everything you need to know! It's also barely an hour and a half from London.

There are 29 barns in total, each containing one or two bedrooms: the original Dairy Barns have been beautifully converted, with open-plan kitchens and living spaces with TVs and Bluetooth speakers, private terraces and large bathrooms with powerful walk-in showers and separate bathtubs; coffee and tea facilities are provided, along with fresh milk and other basics. All stays include a continental breakfast, use of the spa and free bike hire. Further afield, there are the equally luxurious, purpose-built Field Barns, beyond which are five beautiful shepherds huts, which boast similar levels of comfort. There's also the original farmhouse, which sleeps eight people and has a private garden. Most of the barns are dog-friendly.

It's the sort of place where it's easy to do nothing much, undertaking undemanding country walks (of which there are plenty). Breakfast is served every day in the Great Barn, as are lunch and dinner, and the food is delicious, locally sourced and seasonal. The Great Barn also houses the hotel's spa, which has a sauna, steam room and treatment rooms, and the hotel has a small gym and hosts regular outdoor events and yoga classes and other wellness workshops.

CONTACT Brick Kiln Farm, Sandy Lane, Hemingstone, Near Ipswich, Suffolk IP6 9QE • 01449 760 480
HOW MUCH? Field Barns from £172 a night, Dairy Barns from £272, Shepherd Huts from £126. The Farmhouse costs from £533 a night and sleeps 8.
ROOMS 27 Barns & 5 Shepherds Huts.

Milsoms Kesgrave Hall

A country house hotel with a cool but relaxed boutique feel

Situated on the eastern edge of Ipswich, this rather grand building used to be a school and was also once owned by the local Tolly Cobbold brewing dynasty, but nowadays Kesgrave Hall is a country house retreat that's part of the small but perfectly formed East Anglian boutique hotel group, Milsoms.

It sits in expansive grounds, and has just 27 rooms and suites, around half of which are in the main house, with the rest in the former headmaster's quarters and various outbuildings. Rooms are sumptuous and on the glam side, even in the smaller, standard rooms, with sound systems, satellite TV, free superfast wifi, and complimentary soft drinks and snacks. Upgrade to the so-called Top Rooms and expect a bit more woo and wow – we're talking massive beds, free-standing bath-tubs in the room, walk-in showers and plenty of space to lounge.

Downstairs there's a bar and lounge that are relaxed rather than stuffy, and the brasserie is deliberately accessible (no reservations, no dress code), staying open all day and featuring stripped pine tables, an open kitchen and a quirky way of ordering – just write what you want on the pad provided. The food is terrific, with a menu that features chargrilled steaks and chops, good fish and seafood and local lamb and pork. Brunch isn't just for weekends at Kesgrave Hall, while summer means drinks on the outdoor terrace, a read of your book and a stroll in the grounds, making sure you're back in time for a proper afternoon tea. Like we said, cool, relaxed and boutique, and super-friendly too.

There is a spa in the grounds, with treatment rooms and a sauna, sunbeds and a large hot tub and log-burning fire on a south-facing deck. Check out also The Hangar, a large space that hosts regular events, weddings and family occasions. The location makes it both handy for Ipswich and some of the highlights of the Suffolk coast – Woodbridge is nearby, as is Sutton Hoo and the coastal backwater of Orford further on.

CONTACT Hall Road, Kesgrave, Ipswich, Suffolk IP5 2PU • 01473 333 741

HOW MUCH? Double rooms from around £125 a night.

ROOMS 27 Guest Rooms & Suites.

Maids Head Hotel

A cosy and comfortable place to stay in the heart of the fascinating historic city of Norwich

This ancient hotel claims to be the oldest in the country, dating back to the 1100s, and without question it enjoys one of Norwich city centre's best positions: right by the cathedral on the edge of the city's most atmospheric quarter, and very handy indeed for its shops, restaurants and pubs. It has also recently refurbished all of its 84 rooms, and really is a unique place to stay, rightly winning the 'Large Hotel' award in the 2022 East of England Tourism Awards.

There's no getting around the fact that The Maids Head occupies an ancient building which has been extended several times over the years, but that's part of its charm. There's a warren of corridors on different levels, made up of the original coaching inn and a 1960s extension at the back of the main building. The guest rooms have been re-fashioned with flair and style and are very comfortable, with tea-and coffee facilities, good wifi, Freeview flatscreen TVs and an in-room iPad. They also have good-sized en-suite bathrooms with either separate showers or shower-baths combined, and all feature a different but stunning image of Norwich on the tiles. Feature rooms and suites tend to have both walk-in showers and separate roll-top baths, sometimes in the room itself. They also have several rooms that are dog-friendly.

Service in the hotel is excellent and they make a point of going the extra mile for their guests – for example with two vintage Bentleys that offer complimentary spins around the city to guests as well as a selection of 'Bobbin Bikes' that guests can use to plan their own adventures. There's private parking, and they have an excellent two-AA-Rosette restaurant in the WinePress, nestled in the heart of the hotel, not to mention the oak-panelled Jacobean Bar that was a popular haunt for US servicemen during World War II.

CONTACT 20 Tombland, Norwich, Norfolk NR3 1LB • 01603 209 955

HOW MUCH? Double rooms from £138 a night including breakfast.

ROOMS 84 Guest Rooms & Suites.

The Angel Hotel

Situated right opposite the abbey in Bury St Edmunds, this ivy-swathed Georgian coaching inn is a historic hotel that was once frequented by Dickens, among others. But although the outside of the building would still be familiar to him, he'd struggle to recognize the interior, especially the guest rooms, which combine calm Georgian elegance with a touch of contemporary flamboyance and boast all sorts of thoughtful and stylish modern comforts – flatscreen TVs, large bathrooms, some with giant free-standing baths, classy toiletries, free water and biscuits and good-quality tea- and coffee-making facilities. Choose a room at the front of the building so you can sip your tea and gaze at the abbey ruins opposite, and then float down to the excellent Eaterie on the ground floor, which offers lunch, afternoon tea and dinner every day. The bar on the other side of the entrance continues the classic-meets-contemporary decor, and serves good bespoke cocktails.

CONTACT 3 Angel Hill, Bury St Edmunds, Suffolk IP33 1LT • 01284 714 000
HOW MUCH? Double rooms from around £140 a night.

The Weeping Willow

Around eight miles west of Bury St Edmunds, Barrow is a thriving but thoroughly rural Suffolk village. Of its two pubs, The Weeping Willow has recently been restored and expanded. A cosy, pubby sort of place, it's child- and dog-friendly and has a menu with a little bit of everything, from sharing boards and bar snacks to steaks, burgers and more adventurous fare, all based on local ingredients. Uniquely, the rooms are located in a set of lodges behind the pub, each with its own parking space and electric charger. Some lodges come with a king-size bed and a sofa bed, making them suitable for up to four guests; they also have a desk and workspace, good wifi, tea- and coffee-making facilities (including an Illy machine) and en-suite bathrooms with a bathtub, rainfall shower and Bramley toiletries. Others have all of the above as well as a wood-fired hot tub outside, while there are also family lodges with both a king-size bed and built-in bunk beds.

CONTACT 39 Bury Rd, Barrow Hill, Barrow, Suffolk IP29 5AB • 01284 771 881
HOW MUCH? Lodges from around £120 a night, not including breakfast.

The Swan at Lavenham

At the centre of this old Suffolk wool town, The Swan is a Lavenham institution, but it has done a good job of reinventing itself over the years. Its rooms come in all shapes and sizes but most blend a modern sensibility with the heritage of the building pretty well, with contemporary headboards and splashes of colour that fit nicely with the ancient beams. Almost all of the rooms have baths (with showers), and all have Freeview TVs, tea and coffee, water and biscuits; all except the lowest categories have super-king-size beds and a couple have four-posters if you want to properly get into the character of the building. Some rooms are dog friendly, and pooches get a bowl and treat on arrival. Other facilities include two restaurants – the atmospheric Gallery, which serves a fine-dining menu, and the Brasserie, which is more informal – plus the next-door spa, whose sparkling facilities offer the chance to time-travel forward several centuries as you leave the creaky corridors of the main hotel.

CONTACT High Street, Lavenham, Suffolk CO10 9QA • 01787 247 477

HOW MUCH? Double rooms with breakfast from £190 a night.

The Black Lion

A small Georgian coaching inn that's been updated beautifully: wooden floors throughout, artfully mismatched furniture and a comfy lounge with armchairs and newspapers all combine to suggest a comfortable house in the country at which you are one of the most important guests. There are 10 guest rooms in all, most of which overlook the village green. Apart from a couple of cheaper 'Snug' rooms, all are spacious, and come with king-size beds, good wifi, flatscreen televisions with Freeview, tea- and coffee-making facilities (with Nespresso machines), homemade biscuits and two kinds of mineral water. All rooms have en-suite bathrooms with tubs and Noble Isle toiletries (one room also has a standalone shower), and there's a suite with an additional room with bunk beds if you're looking for somewhere big enough for a family. In all, there are five Luxury rooms, three Snug rooms, a family room and a suite.

CONTACT The Green, Long Melford, Suffolk CO10 9DN • 01787 312 356

HOW MUCH? Double rooms with breakfast from £155 a night.

The Grove Cromer

Very comfortable family-run hotel on the North Norfolk coast in a great seaside location

The Grove is the sort of hotel we really like at Cool Places. It's family-run and has been for years; it occupies a lovely historic building that exudes a lived-in and appealing comfortableness that is hard to find – and even harder to fake; and it is run by enterprising people who are always looking to make the most of their property, and to go the extra mile for their guests, who tend to return again and again. Indeed, the feeling of peace that you get as you drive through The Grove's gates, whether it's your first or your tenth visit is always welcome, and the grounds have an almost womb-like appeal.

The hotel has 16 guest rooms, spread between the main house – very comfortable and provided with all amenities – and a timber-framed building in the garden, where the five Orchard Rooms are a bit more contemporary in style. The style of all the rooms is simple, understated and homely, with a mixture of antique and up-to-date furnishings and well-appointed en-suite bathrooms; all the rooms have Smart TVs, good wifi and tea- and coffee-making facilities, and there are four rooms which are perfect for families (one with a record deck and stock of vinyl for dads and teens!).

The sumptuous grounds and gardens of the hotel are home to a heated indoor swimming pool, along with a handful of dog-friendly self-catering cottages, plus a shepherds hut and five yurts for glamping. Nearby, the impressive kitchen garden provides ingredients for the hotel's two-AA-Rosette restaurant as well as its unique Sundowner Café in the grounds, which dispenses excellent pizzas and 'Norfolk tapas' throughout the summer – both are as much of a draw for non-residents as for hotel guests. There's also a cosy bar in the main house, with patio tables outside.

Finally, there's the location, which is something special. A footpath leads from the grounds through the woods to the cliffs and the beach below, and it's also a short stroll into the busy resort of Cromer in one direction, with its pier and nationally renowned chippies, or a slightly longer one to the nearby village of Overstrand, where the sand is lovely and there are crabs and lobsters for sale and a good clifftop beach café. The Grove is basically North Norfolk heaven – for couples, families, or really anyone!

CONTACT 95 Overstrand Road, Cromer, Norfolk NR27 0DJ • 01263 512 412
HOW MUCH? Double rooms from £130 to £200 a night. Family rooms £200–£235.
ROOMS 16 Guest Rooms + Yurts & Cottages.

Titchwell Manor

A tremendous North Norfolk coast country boutique hotel with great food

Looking out over the coastal salt marshes, Titchwell Manor is about as comfortable and stylish a place to enjoy the North Norfolk coast as you will find. Fashioned out of a large red-brick Victorian farmhouse, it ticks all the right boxes for a short break, with 26 boutique rooms and a reputation for food that puts it head and shoulders above its competitors on a coast that's not exactly short of good places to eat.

There are nine rooms in the main building and four in a cottage annexe, with the rest arranged around the U-shaped stable block herb garden courtyard behind. They're all individually styled, with retro furniture, clean, crisp lines and a bold colour palette that makes you think of the sea. Price-wise, they range from the cheapest Good doubles through Better and Best up to the largest Signature rooms and two shepherds huts. Good rooms tend to be in the main house and cottage annexe and are slightly smaller, with king-size beds; 'Better' rooms are a bit more contemporary, with king-size beds and sometimes sea views as well. Best rooms all feature super-king-size beds; some have private patio areas and others have freestanding baths and separate showers, while Signature are naturally the largest and have complimentary soft drinks and Bluetooth speakers – and a couple have their own terraces with private hot tubs. The shepherds huts are double-bedded with a small living area with sofa and wood burner. These rooms have a shower room and large partially covered decking area with Jacuzzi and views over nearby farmland. All the rooms have good wifi, flatscreen Smart TVs, hairdryers and robes, tea- and coffee-making facilities, Nespresso coffee machines and spacious en-suite bathrooms with White Company toiletries. Around a third of the rooms are dog-friendly, and dogs are greeted on arrival with their own bed, towel, biscuits and a map detailing the excellent walks. And for humans who come back to their room tired and sore, then the hotel has the perfect antidote – in-room massages and holistic therapies that will have you in dreamland.

As for the rest of the hotel, it's bright and contemporary, with a sunny coastal feel that's perfectly in tune with its seaside location. There are two options for dining: fine dining or a more relaxed bistro menu, both served with flair and flavours that have consistently earned three AA rosettes since 2013.

CONTACT Titchwell, Near Brancaster, Norfolk PE31 8BB • 01485 210 221
HOW MUCH? Double rooms £165-£235 a night; Signature rooms and Shepherds Huts £260–£425 a night. All rates include breakfast.
ROOMS 26 Guest Rooms + 2 Shepherds Huts.

The Ironmongers Aylsham

Terrific Norfolk boutique accommodation in a historic building overlooking Aylsham's marketplace

Located in a historic Elizabethan townhouse at the heart of the small North Norfolk market town of Aylsham, The Ironmongers – or 'Clarkes' as it's known by locals – is the kind of boutique accommodation we love: a gorgeously refurbished old building that makes a respectful nod to the past while being firmly rooted in the traditions of modern-day hospitality. Its beamed and characterful rooms are stylishly finished and very comfortable, with all possible modern comforts and lots of sustainable, eco-friendly touches.

Overlooking Aylsham's triangular market square, The Ironmongers is basically a B&B without the 'B', a beautiful, 17th-century property where you pay for your room and source your breakfast at one of the many options nearby; there's no reception, just codes for the main entrance and your room. It's like arriving at your own holiday home in the country. Each of the eight rooms has been individually designed in a manner inspired by the town's historic tradesfolk – as well as ironmongery, the building has hosted a wine merchant, tailor's shop, and all sorts of different businesses over the years. The large Haberdashery room has a four-poster and lots of fancy silks and satins (it also has a small adjoining room with bunks); The Ostlers sits above the old stables and is all beams and brick, and The Cobblers plays host to all sorts of shoe-related paraphernalia. All of the rooms are spacious and light, but cosy at the same time, with heating under solid oak floors, Smart TVs, good wifi, tea- and coffee-making facilities and treats on arrival, and en-suite bathrooms provided with ample-sized showers, fluffy towels and toiletries. You can also feel smug about staying here – heat and hot water are provided by air-source heat pumps – and dogs are welcome in two of the rooms.

The location, too, is terrific. Aylsham is a friendly little town with an ancient church and a couple of good pubs, one of which – The Black Boys – is a good spot for a slap-up breakfast (as is the fabulous Bread Source bakery downstairs). It's also only a five-minute drive from the Jacobean splendour of Blickling Hall (where there's another pub, The Bucks Arms, and the Blickling estate stretches for miles). The Bure river is popular canoeing territory and Aylsham is at the end of the Bure Valley Railway line, which runs to Wroxham in the heart of the Broads. You're also just 20 minutes or so from both the ancient city of Norwich and the glories of the North Norfolk coast at Blakeney and Cley.

CONTACT 30 The Marketplace, Aylsham, Norfolk NR11 6EN • 07770 928 567
HOW MUCH? Double rooms from £154 a night.
ROOMS 8 Guest Rooms.

Congham Hall

This boutique country house hotel has all the makings of a perfect Norfolk weekend

Surrounded by the fields and meadows of the northwest Norfolk countryside, Congham Hall is an elegant, very peaceful and rather homely boutique country house hotel that's just 10 minutes' drive from King's Lynn and a short drive from Norfolk's fabulous sandy beaches, but feels a million miles from anywhere, which is exactly the point. The hotel retains a relaxed, weekend-in-the-country feel, but the rooms are top-notch, and it's a wonderful place to relax, with spacious grounds, an excellent spa and other leisure facilities, and lots of comfy ground-floor lounges to plonk yourself in if you fancy doing nothing in particular.

A handsome Georgian manor house, Congham Hall was a private home until 1982, when it became a hotel. Its last decade or so has arguably been its best, when under the stewardship of Nicholas and Ruth Dickinson, it has refined its offering and expanded. It now has 31 rooms and suites – 15 in the main house, 11 Garden rooms and five magnificent Orchard cabins. All the rooms are spacious and very comfortable, equipped with wifi, Smart TVs, tea- and coffee-making facilities and fresh milk, and still and sparkling water in mini-fridges. They all come with spacious en-suite bathrooms with separate baths and walk-in showers apart from the standard House rooms, which have baths with overhead showers. The Best Garden rooms can sleep a family of four if desired, while the Orchard Cabins are well-named, each with a private terrace overlooking Congham's orchards and complete with an outside bathtub for a spot of 'star-bathing'. Inside, they are sleek and spacious contemporary spaces with king-size beds, comfy armchairs and sumptuous bathrooms, each with a bath and large separate shower.

As for other facilities, the spa has a good-sized pool with big windows that let the outside in, a steam room, sauna, experience showers, a foot spa and a hot tub on the terrace, plus a selection of upstairs treatment rooms. There's a tennis court (you can borrow racquets and balls) and croquet, and staff can provide details of a number of easy circular countryside walks in the local area, so you really can leave your car keys in your room while you're here. The restaurant and bar are bright and contemporary, serving a simple yet refined two AA-rosette menu based on ingredients from the kitchen garden and local area wherever possible.

CONTACT Lynn Rd, Congham, King's Lynn, Norfolk PE32 1AH • 01485 600 250
HOW MUCH? Double rooms with breakfast and dinner from £280 a night for two people.
ROOMS 31 Guest Rooms & Suites.

Sculthorpe Mill

This North Norfolk watermill is a tranquil haven, with contemporary rooms and first-rate food

Look out for the colourful roadside sign before driving down a long narrow lane to Sculthorpe Mill, a top spot for pub lovers and foodies that was once a working watermill. Taken over in 2021 by restauranteurs Siobhan and Caitriona Peyton, the former Greene King boozer is now a stylish yet homely destination to eat, drink and stay.

Named the Sunday Times' 'Best Hotel in East Anglia' in 2021 and featured among their '100 Best Places to Stay in Britain for 2023', Sculthorpe Mill is set in the bucolic Norfolk countryside, a five-minute drive from the market town of Fakenham and a quarter of an hour from the coast at Wells-next-the-Sea and Holkham Beach.

It's a supremely peaceful spot, overlooking the gently babbling River Wensum and with a gorgeous garden that's perfect for summertime eating and imbibing. Home to seven en-suite bedrooms, splashes of colour are seen throughout, whether it's yellow floors, red curtains or patterned rugs. Choose from cosy doubles, spacious super-kings or dog-friendly offerings – some overlook the river and its graceful weeping willows, others the capacious, well-kept garden. Whichever you opt for, you'll find a comfy bed fitted with crisp white sheets and a bathroom with a big walk-in rain shower. Thoughtful touches include Nespresso machines, fresh milk, Roberts speakers and Norfolk Natural Living toiletries, plus a map of a circular walk you can take directly from the pub. Don't be put off by the lack of TV; you won't miss it!

Quite rightly featured among the UK's Top 100 Gastropubs for 2023, the food is a real draw. Elliot Ketley (formerly at Soho House) is at the helm in the kitchen, and menus feature locally-sourced ingredients – Norfolk muntjac, King's Lynn shrimps with Cromer crab mayo, Walsingham honey drizzled over granola and yoghurt at breakfast (if you can resist the Full English). To drink, kick lunch or dinner off with a cheeky little Negroni or a pint of Duration ale, brewed half an hour away. There are several dining areas, from the wood-beamed pub filled with nooks and crannies to the two eye-catching rooms beyond, and a larger space, upstairs, while in summer, the garden comes to life with a rotating mix of DJs and live jazz to complement lazy al fresco dining. Take a seat out the front or back – both are equally pretty, and the sound of the river provides a soothing soundtrack.

CONTACT Lynn Rd, Fakenham, Norfolk NR21 9QG • 01328 633 001
HOW MUCH? Double rooms from £110 a night, including breakfast.
ROOMS 7 Guest Rooms.

The White Horse

Great food and comfy rooms in a North Norfolk coastal location that can't really be bettered

It's hard to beat the location of this combined restaurant, pub and hotel, which backs straight onto the marshes, lagoons and creeks of the North Norfolk coast. It's something of a local landmark, a special place to eat and also to stay, with seven airy, attractively decorated, en-suite guest rooms in the main building, and eight dog-friendly Garden Rooms at the back with a sedum-roof to blend with the marshes beyond. These have thoughtfully provided wooden-floored entrance halls for dog beds and muddy boots, and their own terraces for sitting out and enjoying the marsh and sea views. All of the rooms are spacious and contemporary, with a blue-green decor inspired by the seascape beyond. Some have sea views, and the top-notch 'Room at the Top' is split over two levels and has its own viewing telescope to take in the best views of the coastline. Whether you stay in the main building or the garden rooms, all the rooms have large comfy beds, Smart TVs, digital radios and wifi, and Nespresso machines.

The White Horse also have a great selection of guest ales at their bar including some from their very own Brancaster Brewery just up the road, and the restaurant is one of the best on a coast that's not short of good places to eat, with excellent fresh fish and seafood, including local mussels, crab and lobster, served either in the pub itself or the delightful modern conservatory at the back, which makes the most of the property's position overlooking the sea. The location certainly makes The White Horse special, with a short stroll down to pick up the coastal path at the bottom of the garden making it a perfect location for dog owners, walkers, cyclists or indeed anyone who wants to explore this unique stretch of coast. The same family also own the excellent King's Head near Holt, and The Farmhouse at Redcoats in Hertfordshire (p.70).

CONTACT Main Road, Brancaster Staithe, Norfolk PE31 8BY • 01485 210 262

HOW MUCH? Double rooms with breakfast from £150 to £285 a night.

ROOMS 15 Guest Rooms.

Morston Hall

A first-rate North Norfolk boutique country-house hotel with a superb Michelin-starred restaurant

A traditional 17th-century flint house surrounded by lush and verdant gardens, Morston Hall is an idyllic spot in a terrific location – right on the North Norfolk coast, just a few miles from picturesque Blakeney and footsteps from Morston Quay and the Coast Path. Chef-patron Galton Blackiston has been here for over 30 years, nurturing the house and garden to become the destination restaurant and hotel it is today – it has held a Michelin star for a whopping 24 years. You couldn't hope for somewhere more comfortable to stay, and it's easy to understand why Norfolk-born Blackiston was so taken with the place.

First, the guest rooms, which divide between the main house, including one accessible room on the ground floor, and the 'Pavilion' rooms in a purpose-built annexe. The latter are like mini-suites, with easy chairs and a private terrace. They all have Smart TVs, digital radios and coffee- and tea-making facilities (including a Nespresso machine), and come with homemade cookies, fresh milk and still and sparkling water. The en-suite bathrooms are large, with a walk-in shower, robes and Noble Isle toiletries and a separate bathtub (with TV!). The main house rooms are more mixed but just as comfortable and have similar amenities.

Most guests opt for a Dinner, Bed & Breakfast package, but you don't have to, although it would be a shame to skip breakfast, which Galton cooks himself every morning so he can chat to guests about their meal the night before. The seven-course dinner menu changes daily according to what's available – from local fish and seafood suppliers, the Hall's kitchen garden or the hotel's own smokery. The food is seasonal, simple and delicious, served at a single sitting every evening (and lunch on weekends) in the lovely conservatory-style restaurant. They also serve a sumptuous afternoon tea.

CONTACT Hall Lane, Morston, Near Blakeney, Norfolk NR25 7AA • 01263 741 041
HOW MUCH? Double rooms with breakfast and dinner from £260 a night for two people.
ROOMS 13 Guest Rooms.

The Old Rectory

A family-friendly country house B&B in the heart of the Norfolk Broads

Visit the Norfolk Broads and you'll soon come to realize that every winding country lane leads to a little treasure of pastoral paradise. One such place is the sleepy village of Catfield, home to The Old Rectory, a striking ivy-clad 19th-century house straight out of central casting with six gorgeous guest rooms that is one of Norfolk's most comfortable – and family-friendly – places to stay, with a heated pool, tennis court, and gorgeous grounds and gardens.

High ceilings and big windows give the house a bright, airy vibe while the tasteful decor, artworks and homely, bulging bookcases make you feel more like an honoured friend than a paying customer. Two of the bedrooms are en-suite while the others share bathrooms that have roll-top baths and rainfall showers. For those here with little ones, there's a well-equipped playroom, plus an inviting communal sitting room with a Smart TV. Dogs are welcome too. Breakfast is served in the dining room and the owner Penny provides a spread to rival any hotel.

But for our money, the major draw here is the spectacular grounds and gardens – 20 acres of open fields dotted with wildflowers, ornamental gardens abloom with exotic plants and fragrant flowers, a lake abuzz with dragonflies, and pristine lawns for games. There are friendly goats, pigs and bunnies, and across the road a paddock that's home to a couple of horses. A trail here leads you past Penny's impressive veg patch to a full-sized tennis court. It's the most tranquil of settings, with birdsong and the pealing of bells from the church next door providing a blissful soundtrack to your stay.

Finally, The Old Rectory isn't your typical guesthouse or B&B in that the house is available for exclusive use and you are free to self-cater courtesy of the comprehensive kitchen wing. As Penny puts it, 'we offer more of a house party stay where you will be welcomed as friends'.

CONTACT Catfield, Norfolk, NR29 5DA • 07887 584 790
HOW MUCH? Double rooms from £100 a night including breakfast.
ROOMS 6 Guest Rooms.

The Boathouse

A tranquil waterside restaurant and bar with boutique rooms and garden lodges

Mike and Belinda Minors run the excellent Waterside restaurant a few miles up the road, so they know a thing or two about feeding hungry punters in beautiful Broadside locations. Thus it made perfect sense for them to take over the iconic Eel's Foot pub a decade ago, which enjoys a fabulous location right on the banks of Ormesby Broad but which was then badly in need of a shot of TLC. They went much further than this, however, and have transformed this old Broadside pub into a spectacular wedding venue and restaurant with rooms, with some well-appointed lodges in the garden for good measure. The restaurant is very nice indeed, with two large rooms and comfy chairs by the fire if all you want is a drink; but it's the rooms upstairs that we like best of all, because waking up here is the best way to enjoy The Boathouse's perfect position by the Broads.

There are six rooms in all, funkily furnished, cosy and well-priced, and four have views or partial views over the water. There are two suites, one of which is very spacious with a downstairs sitting room and upstairs bedroom and all are decorated to a very high standard, with free wifi throughout, tea- and coffee-making facilities in each room and beautifully decked-out bathrooms. Downstairs the restaurant is large but has a few cosy nooks, while the wedding venue is a self-contained unit off to the side, with its own waterside decking and gazebo and eating area – which is great if you're getting married here, but even better if you're not and don't want to be knee-deep in wedding guests in the bar. Finally, there are the lodges in the grounds, one of which is used for happy brides and grooms while the rest are comfy two-bedroom affairs, equipped with a sitting room and kitchenette and verandahs to watch the sun setting over the water in the evening.

CONTACT Eels Foot Road, Ormesby St Michael, Norfolk NR29 3LP • 01493 730 342
HOW MUCH? Double rooms £85-£100 a night and lodges from £135 - £165 a night. Breakfast is extra.
ROOMS 6 Guest Rooms & 3 Lodges.

The Gin Trap Inn

Great food and accommodation at this beautifully located North Norfolk coast country inn

Just a mile from Hunstanton and the North Norfolk coast, The Gin Trap Inn advertises itself as providing Modern British food in a 17th-century inn – words to quicken the pulse of any pub lover, and we are happy to say that they deliver on both counts. Based in the village of Ringstead, this ancient inn is nowadays all about making the most of Norfolk's bounty to create great seasonal food. Not only that, it also has 13 very comfortable bedrooms for overnight stays, and a couple of two-bedroom cottages for those who prefer to self-cater.

First the food, which is high-end and locally sourced – oysters harvested by a local fisherman, halibut with brown shrimp, local quail, pork and beef. They also offer a simpler and cheaper bar menu in what is about as pubby a pub environment as you'll find. The rooms (and two split-level suites) are cosy and comfy, each one different in size and shape but all furnished with a mixture of antiques and bric-a-brac that give them real character while not dispensing with modern comforts. They all come with wifi, Smart TVs, luxury linen and spacious en-suite bathrooms with robes and toiletries. They also have tea- and coffee-making facilities, still and sparkling mineral water, homemade cake and biscuits and a complimentary gin and tonic. The cottages are similarly well-appointed, with two double bedrooms each and lots of living space, including a contemporary fitted kitchen. And, if you're feeling lazy, you can eat at the pub – breakfast is included in rates! Dogs are welcome in most rooms, and you will want to get out and explore. The pub is well positioned for exploring the nature reserves at Snettisham and Titchwell, Holkham Beach and multiple other coastal attractions. You're also never far from some superb country walks, including a seven-mile loop you can do from the pub.

CONTACT 6 High Street, Ringstead, Norfolk PE36 5JU • 01485 525 264

HOW MUCH? Double rooms from £120 a night and 2-bedroom cottages from £360 a night, including breakfast.

ROOMS 13 Guest Rooms & 2 Cottages.

Cliff Farmhouse B&B Suites

Luxury B&B suites in a prime North Norfolk location – close to the beach in Old Hunstanton

Situated in a prime location in Old Hunstanton, Cliff Farmhouse B&B Suites goes the extra mile for its guests, many of whom return again and again to sample the hospitality offered by owners Graham and Vicky. With guest suites rather than rooms, and with Hunstanton's glorious beach and cliffs just footsteps away, it's no ordinary B&B, and definitely a cut above many of the others along this stretch of the North Norfolk coast. It's also a tremendous base not just for the seaside resort of Hunstanton but for the coast all the way from Snettisham to Wells, not to mention the rural delights that await you just inland.

Cliff Farmhouse has just three individually designed boutique suites, each with their own private sitting room and spacious bedroom with super-king-size beds and good-quality linen. They're beautifully furnished, with spacious en-suite bathrooms with bath and shower and every other amenity you could need, including a fridge, toaster, and coffee and tea facilities (including a Nespresso machine), robes and environmentally kind toiletries, underfloor heating, wifi and USB charging, Roberts radios, and not one but two Smart TVs! One suite also has its own private outdoor patio, and all three have access to the south-facing garden. They also have a charging point for electric vehicles.

But Cliff Farmhouse is not just about the facilities, it's the personal service and attention to detail that Graham and Vicky provide. Nothing is too much trouble, from the delicious breakfasts they serve in your suite to the in-house holistic massages that can be arranged. Graham and Vicky are a mine of information on the attractions of the surrounding area, which are considerable. Hunstanton is on your doorstep, and they even have their own beach hut you can hire. You'll also find a selection of places to eat and drink within a five-minute walk, including a beach café and Neptune, a Michelin-starred restaurant.

CONTACT 62 Old Hunstanton Rd, Old Hunstanton, Norfolk PE36 6HX • 07941 225 777
HOW MUCH? Suites from around £119 a night, including in-room continental breakfast.
ROOMS 3 Guest Suites.

The White House

North Norfolk luxury B&B where no detail has been overlooked

This wonderful Norfolk B&B ticks a lot of boxes. It's in a beautiful location, midway between the North Norfolk coast hot spots of Brancaster Beach and Burnham Market, and it's a lovely flint-and-white Georgian mansion whose owners seem to have thought of every detail to make your stay more comfortable. They have parking with EV charging points, and the rooms are luxurious and well-equipped, with indulgent bathrooms and contemporary yet cosy furnishings; they serve delicious breakfasts in a bright and sunny garden room; and if you have a large party and something special to celebrate, you can have the place all to yourself. The White House's rooms are an almost perfect blend of traditional comfort and modern amenities. Each one is different – some have high, vaulted ceilings, some have views over the gardens, others the countryside, while a couple are large enough for a family – but all come with super-king-size or king-size, ultra-comfy Hypnos beds with silk duvets and goose-down or allergy-free pillows, Sky and Google Chrome TVs and Roberts radios, super-fast wifi, tea- and coffee-making facilities with Nespresso machines, and bathrooms with underfloor heating and 100 Acres toiletries. Most have spacious walk-in showers, a few baths with showers (the suite has a free-standing bath in the room and separate shower). Two of the bedrooms are dog-friendly.

The White House is so alluring you may not want to go far: there's a sitting room to relax in with squashy sofas and an honesty bar, they have their own tennis court and the walled gardens are gorgeous. Their restaurant is open Thursday–Saturday evenings and serves their vineyard's award-winning wine, and it's also worth knowing that they run 'Big Sky Art' painting courses for budding artists. All in all, the perfect spot for a tranquil weekend break on the North Norfolk coast.

CONTACT Sussex Farm Lane, Burnham Market, Norfolk PE31 8JY • 07785 439 727
HOW MUCH? Double rooms from £150 a night.
ROOMS 11 Guest Rooms & 1 Suite.

Cley Windmill

This gorgeous converted windmill makes a spectacular place to stay on the North Norfolk coast

It was a brilliant idea to turn this old windmill into a B&B – and a very successful venture it has proved too. Fabulously restored, the windmill sits among the reedy marshes on the edge of the village of Cley and the interior is simply charming, its best guest rooms set beneath ancient beamed ceilings. The location is sublime too, right on the edge of the NWT reserve of Cley Marshes, and perfectly placed for the delights of the rest of the North Norfolk Coast.

There are nine guest rooms in all – six in the windmill itself and three in various outbuildings. Plus there's the Dovecote, a charming self-catering cottage with two double bedrooms. It's of course a big draw to stay in the mill itself, where the rooms are all different, though each is beautifully furnished in a sympathetic country-chic style, with rugs, kilim cushions and whitewashed walls, and equipped with en-suite bathrooms. It won't suit everyone – there are plenty of stairs to climb! – but the upper rooms in particular have spectacular views over the coast and marshes, the two most vertiginous connected by a step ladder and making for an exciting place for a family of four to sleep.

The outbuildings – the Boat House with a four-poster and the flint-walled Long House – are equally comfortable and well-appointed. The most recent addition is The Old Cart Shed, a spacious suite with its own kitchenette and living area. Breakfast is served in the beamed dining room and all guests have access to the wonderful circular sitting room with open fire on the ground floor.

The mill is also licensed for weddings, and you can book the whole lot if you want, whether for a wedding or just a rather fabulous house party. It's surely one of the most unique places to get married in the UK and is indeed perfect for any occasion – and not just because of the building.

CONTACT The Quay, Cley, Norfolk NR25 7RP • 01263 740 209

HOW MUCH? Double rooms with breakfast from £215 a night.

ROOMS 9 Guest Rooms & 1 Cottage.

The Globe at Wells

Situated right on a pretty Georgian square in the busy North Norfolk resort of Wells-next-the-Sea, this 19th-century inn is many things to many people. It's a good place to drop by for a drink and is home to an excellent restaurant, and it's also a terrific place to stay. All the rooms and suites combine the quirky Georgian charm of the original building with home-from-home comforts, top-quality mattresses and duvets and luxurious bathrooms complete with Duck Island toiletries; they all come with Freeview TVs and tea- and coffee-making facilities and some rooms welcome dogs. It also has three larger rooms with kitchenettes. Wells is a pleasantly unpretentious seaside town, quite unlike this coast's more chi-chi spots, and also benefits from being close to one of the country's best expanses of sandy beach at Holkham Bay, backed by fragrant pines, plus the considerable delights of the Holkham Estate, whose extensive grounds feature a magnificent Palladian pile crammed full of paintings and sculptures.

CONTACT The Buttlands, Wells-next-the-Sea, Norfolk NR23 1EU • 01328 710 206
HOW MUCH? Double rooms with breakfast from around £150 to £270 a night.

Fritton Lake

Tucked away on the edge of Great Yarmouth, Fritton Lake – and the lavish Somerleyton estate it is part of – straddles the Norfolk-Suffolk border and offers boutique rooms and self-catering woodland lodges and cottages. Technically a private member's club, anyone who stays gains access to the estate's extensive facilities, which include tennis courts, an open-air heated pool, a gym and a studio for yoga. You can go wild swimming, boating, kayaking and paddleboarding on the lake and there are regular organized runs, foraging tours and jeep 'wildlife safaris'. As for the accommodation, the cosy Clubhouse at the heart of the estate has eight dog-friendly bedrooms, decorated in a country style with funky, contemporary touches, and a downstairs restaurant that serves a deliberately simple menu, much of it using produce and foraged ingredients from the estate – beef burgers and ragu, shepherd's pie made with estate lamb, seasonal salads and veg.

CONTACT Church Lane, Fritton, Great Yarmouth, Norfolk NR31 9HA • 01493 484 008
HOW MUCH? Double rooms from around £150 a night.

The Hoste Arms

Decades ago The Hoste Arms almost single-handedly turned the postcard-pretty village of Burnham Market into one of the hottest tourist spots in Norfolk. Now its latest owners (City Pub Co) have turned the Hoste back into what it was originally – a great country inn with good food and comfortable rooms. Its rooms come in all shapes and sizes and are spread between the original pub at the front (one of which Nelson is said to have stayed in), a couple of buildings at the back and the Georgian Vine House across the green. 'Divine' rooms are the largest and offer extras like robes and slippers, but all rooms have wifi, Smart TVs, tea and coffee, water, fresh milk, minibars, air-conditioning and en-suite bathrooms, and they often have separate baths and showers. For food, choose between a bar menu and à la carte menu, and enjoy them in the front bar or the conservatory restaurant at the back. Other facilities include a small spa, a basement gym and a 20-seat cinema.

CONTACT The Green, Burnham Market, Norfolk PE31 8HD • 01328 738 777

HOW MUCH? Double rooms £130–180 a night, not including breakfast.

The Cliftonville

Bang on top of the cliffs at Cromer, there's no better place for a seaside break than The Cliftonville. Built in 1897, the hotel is the epitome of Edwardian splendour and has recently been renovated by the City Pub Co, who have turned it into an affordable and thoroughly up-to-date place to eat, drink and stay. Cromer is accessible by train too, so you can leave your car keys at home. It's a great building, with a grand lobby, sweeping staircases, stained-glass windows and wide ocean views. Yet it has been restored with a flair and sensitivity that has put it firmly in the 21st century. The restaurant is contemporary yet stylishly in tune with the period, making the most of the bay windows and views, and every one of the guest rooms has a sea view, nice en-suite bathrooms, wifi, flatscreen TVs and tea- and coffee-making facilities. They're crisp and contemporary but like the rest of the hotel make the most of the Edwardian touches and it's a lovely spot for a weekend by the sea.

CONTACT 29 Runton Road, Cromer, Norfolk NR27 9AS • 01263 512 543

HOW MUCH? Double rooms from around £110 a night.

The Gunton Arms

Situated in the 1000-acre deer park of Gunton Hall in North Norfolk, the Gunton Arms has a reassuring country estate feel. But it's not a typical country pub by any means. Sure, its 16 guest rooms are comfortable and very homely, with the feel of your richest friend's country house, and its food is renowned for miles around. But, as the project of London art dealer Ivor Braka, its walls are plastered with works by Tracy Emin, Gilbert and George and lots of other Brit-Art biggies, and it would be no surprise to trip over a Damian Hirst creation as you stagger off to your room. The food too is rather special, with main courses literally sourced from the fat of the land with loads of venison dishes, beef, lamb, Blythburgh pork and plenty of locally sourced fish, much of it cooked on the vast French open fireplace in the main restaurant. The pub is ideally placed for exploring North Norfolk, just a few miles from the coast at Overstrand and Cromer.

CONTACT Thorpe Market, Norfolk NR11 8TZ • 01263 832 010
HOW MUCH? Double rooms from £160 a night.

The Feathers

Situated in the picturesque and well-heeled North Norfolk town of Holt, this is a classic coaching inn in style, with an old-fashioned cosy bar, welcoming log fires and various snugs and lounges, some of which now house private dining spaces. Drink inside or on the outdoor terrace, and choose from a menu that revels in local produce, from coastal smokehouse salmon and local seafood to lamb and beef from nearby Swannington Farm. The guest rooms divide between the main building and The Lawns annexe, two minutes' walk away, and are all modern and spacious, with decent-sized, recently refurbished bathrooms with toiletries, Freeview TVs, tea- and coffee-making facilities and either a double or a king-size bed. There are a couple of family rooms in the main building (complete with bunk beds), and those in The Lawns are also good for families, while all the rest have walk-in showers and also welcome dogs.

CONTACT 6 Market Place, Holt, Norfolk NR25 6BW • 01263 712 318
HOW MUCH? Double rooms from £130 a night including breakfast.

Elveden Inn

Midway between London and Norwich, the Elveden Inn is a proper country inn, a thoroughly inviting roadside hostelry with comfy rooms and a restaurant with a large garden outside. It's part of the Guinness family's Elveden estate and as such is a complement to their impressive restaurant and shops across the road. Handily situated on the edge of Thetford Forest, it attracts walkers, cyclists and families heading for Go Ape or the nearby Center Parcs – a homely, family-friendly place, with rooms that are contemporary but cosy, decorated in neutral browns, creams and greys. There are large family rooms at each end of the building, with super-king-size beds and sofa beds and bath/shower, and the rest are doubles/twins with king-size beds and showers. Downstairs, they serve a menu that is a moderately priced, undemanding affair based partly on ingredients from the responsibly farmed Elveden estate– just what you need after a full day in the forest!

CONTACT Brandon Rd, Elveden, Suffolk IP24 3TP • 01842 890 876
HOW MUCH? Double rooms £90–£110 a night, family rooms £100–£140, including breakfast.

Magazine Wood

With its wonderful North Norfolk location, Magazine Wood is a charming country B&B but it also offers some of the things we love about a hotel, such as privacy and a high level of service. Its three luxurious suites are completely self-contained and enjoy a private entrance and views to the large manicured garden; each is stylishly decorated in soothing colours, tasteful fabrics and provided with super-comfy beds. There's a fridge stocked with essentials, a sofa and dining table, binoculars for bird watching, Netflix and an in-room concierge service – namely your own iPad to cater for all your needs, from ordering breakfast to planning great days out. For the technophobes among you, just pick up the phone – owners Jonathan and Pip are always on hand. If you want to get out and about, just go north out of the gate and you're on the Peddars Way, which will take you to the beach of Holme-next-Sea.

CONTACT Peddars Way, Sedgeford, Near Hunstanton, Norfolk PE36 5LW • 01485 750 740
HOW MUCH? Double rooms with breakfast from £115 a night.

Lucky Dip

The Alma Inn

25 King's Head Street, Harwich, Essex CO12 3EE

Not only is this salty old Harwich inn a proper local, it serves memorable and unique food, specializing in local lobster, seafood and steaks, and has a handful of boutique rooms in case you want to stay over. No surprise that it won an award for 'Best Pub with Rooms' in East Anglia a couple of years ago.

The Assembly Rooms

Theatre St, Norwich, Norfolk NR2 1RQ

Run by well-known Norfolk chef Richard Hughes, this beautifully renovated Georgian building multi-tasks as a boutique hotel, restaurant, cookery school and wedding venue. The guest rooms are light, spacious and beautifully decorated, and even the smallest rooms are a decent size. The decor is luxurious, contemporary yet classic, with high-quality beds and linen, wifi, flatscreen TVs, Bluetooth speakers and nice bathrooms, and you wake up each morning to one of Richard's superb breakfasts.

The Guinness Arms

The Street, Icklingham, Suffolk IP28 6PS

This revamped estate pub, situated in a lovely, rural part of Suffolk has eight boldly decorated, very attractive guest rooms and serves excellent, family-friendly pub food in its bright and spacious dining room. Each room is styled after a member of the Guinness family– Alec's room is naturally full of actorish memorabilia, while Lulu's was created by the fashion designer herself and has a hand-painted mural and a gorgeous four-poster bed.

The Ingham Swan

Sea Palling Rd, Ingham, Norfolk NR12 9AB

When the wind blows across the marshes here, there's no better place to be than sitting down to a meal at this renowned Norfolk Broads restaurant with rooms. It's a thatched, originally 14th-century pub with big fireplaces, flint walls and wooden beams. It serves good Modern British food – classic in style and inspiration, with big flavours based on high-quality, often local ingredients – and there's a set of affordable, contemporary and comfortable guest rooms to retire to afterwards.

The Seven Hotel

7 Clifton Terrace, Southend-on-Sea, Essex SS1 1DT

You'll feel a little bit transported staying at this properly posh Southend boutique hotel. Situated among the resort's elegant Regency terraces, opposite the Victorian Cliff funicular railway, it does a pretty good job of injecting a bit of glamour into the resort. Around half the rooms have sea views and it's easy to imagine yourself in a cool joint in Barcelona rather than overlooking the Thames in Southend. They serve good food too in its ground-floor restaurant.

The Sibton White Horse

Halesworth Road, Sibton, Suffolk IP17 2JJ

Neil and Gill Mason's charming old Suffolk inn serves of the best food in the area, and that's reason enough for a visit. But it also makes an excellent base for visiting the nearby Suffolk Coast, and has five simple yet very comfortable and cosy rooms next door so you can do just that. Perfect for birders, walking enthusiasts or just exhausted couples keen to escape the pace of city life for a day or two.

The Guinness Arms

Stoke by Nayland Hotel

Keepers Lane, Leavenheath, Suffolk CO6 4PZ

Deep in the Suffolk countryside, this hotel is owned by the Copella juice family, and it's not only very comfy and well set up for golfers and spa-lovers, but also has 10 beautiful self-catering lodges in its extensive grounds, full of light and fitted with high-spec kitchens and furnishings – the perfect place to make the most of the hotel's facilities.

The Assembly Rooms

The Sun Inn

High Street, Dedham, Essex CO7 6DF

In the heart of picturesque Dedham and Constable Country, this country inn has a set of cosy rooms and serves brilliant food, much like its sister business The White Hart Inn in Mersea (p.136). They also have bikes for the use of guests and can arrange boat trips on the river.

Ingham Swan

Wivenhoe House

Wivenhoe Park, Colchester, Essex CO4 3SQ

Home to Britain's only hotel-based hospitality school, and partially staffed by the students, you could do worse than be a guinea pig in the spacious and very comfortable rooms here.

The Midlands

Birmingham • Warwickshire • Staffordshire • Worcestershire • Shropshire • Herefordshire • Northamptonshire • Leicestershire • Rutland • Nottinghamshire • Derbyshire • Lincolnshire

For many, The Midlands means cities, and in particular Birmingham, and we would be the first to say that these are often overlooked. England's second city has undergone a renaissance in recent years; nearby Warwickshire and historic Stratford-upon-Avon draw the tourists, and the counties further west – Worcestershire, Shropshire and Herefordshire – offer some of the most stunning and unspoilt scenery in the country. On the Midlands' opposite flank, the Peak District of Derbyshire is perhaps the region's busiest spot, and quite rightly – its landscape is magnificent and its tourist heritage second to none, meaning that there are countless great places to stay. Consider also the delights of tiny Rutland and the open spaces of Lincolnshire, both of which are full of great hotels, gastropubs and B&Bs.

The Tawny, p.184

Staying Cool at Rotunda

Stylish accommodation in the heart of Birmingham's city centre

The serviced apartments at Staying Cool may just be one of Birmingham city centre's best-kept secrets – as discreet as you like, with no signage indicating a place to stay. And in fact, Staying Very Cool at Rotunda would be a more apt description as the accommodation here is of rock-star quality, housed within the city's most iconic building – a landmark structure from 1965 that is now a Grade-II-listed building. With nearby Selfridges as your 'corner shop', and British designers given free rein in the classy interiors, these are Instagram-ready city breaks in waiting.

Rotunda's apartments vary in size, ranging from studios (Mini), one-beds (Clubman) and two-beds (Maxi) to two-bed penthouses (Roadsters). The building's circular shape lends these idiosyncratic upper-floor apartments a 'cheese wedge' design, while the floor-to-ceiling windows allow for great panoramic views. Bespoke furniture keeps everything refreshingly light and airy, even in the smaller studios, and they all boast proper pocket-sprung king-size beds and high-end fixture and fittings – Poggenpohl kitchens with dishwashers and washer/dryers, Illy espresso makers, ultra-fast wifi and a SkyTV package, plus aromatherapy bathroom products and complimentary breakfast cereals and a tuck shop for snacks.

Rotunda is also a surprisingly sustainable place to stay, and places an emphasis on paying its staff a living wage, using renewable energy sources and working with local suppliers. So not only can you be comfortable, you can feel good about it too! Service is slick and professional, and you couldn't be more central for the many delights of Brum – it's handy for two train stations, the Bull Ring and pretty much everything else you might want to see in central Birmingham.

CONTACT 150 New Street, Birmingham B2 4PA • 0121 285 1290

HOW MUCH? Mini studios from £149 a night, Maxi 2-bedroom apartments from £450.

ROOMS 35 Apartments.

Edgbaston Park Hotel

Cool and comfortable rooms to suit everyone – including your dog – on the leafy side of Birmingham

Situated on the city's leafy southern side only two miles from Birmingham City Centre, Edgbaston Park Hotel brings together contemporary elegance with period charm. It's a purpose-built place so it's no surprise that modern expectations are met and often exceeded. With electric charging points on-site, free car parking, bar and restaurant and access to a 50-metre pool just a 10-minute walk away, you're spoilt for choice. What might surprise those who miss character and history when staying in contemporary accommodation is that Edgbaston Park Hotel can deliver a healthy dose of that too.

Part of the University of Birmingham's Edgbaston campus, there are a total of 185 bedrooms and three apartments spread across a trio of very different buildings and divided between four tiers of room types, in which

space and luxury increase by degrees. Whatever category you choose, you'll find all the things you'd expect from a hotel of this quality: comfy beds, quality towels and linen, tea- and coffee-making facilities, eco-friendly toiletries and a TV. There's good wifi too, of course, and practical things in every room – a hairdryer, iron and safe. There are also three serviced apartments for those who like to self-cater, and their cosy, comfortable ground-floor double bedrooms in the main hotel are pet-friendly so you can bring your canine companion!

The main building has a light, high-ceilinged restaurant, and a no less modern but slightly cosier bar. Both are named 1900 for the year the university was founded, but you'll not find old-fashioned canteen fare here. There are upwards of 60 gins behind the bar and a selection of innovative dishes on the restaurant menu. The hotel's location on the campus means it's handy for anyone who's visiting the university, but it's also well located for lots more – Edgbaston Cricket Ground, Winterbourne House and Gardens and the Birmingham Wildlife Park. It's also only two miles from the city centre and just a tad more to Cadbury World.

CONTACT 53 Edgbaston Park Road, University of Birmingham, Birmingham B15 2RS • 0121 414 8888
HOW MUCH? Double rooms from £129 a night.
ROOMS 185 Guest Rooms & 3 Apartments.

Hampton Manor

A lovely country-chic weekend escape, serving some of the best food in the West Midlands

Situated in the green and pleasant hinterland of the UK's second city, Hampton Manor is a foodie retreat like no other. This historic manor house – the former home of 19th-century British prime minister Robert Peel – has been reinvented as a grand but rather funky destination for food and rooms that's perfectly in tune with the times. Despite the grandeur of the building, with its chinoiserie, stained glass and sweeping main staircase, it's actually a homely sort of place, with a newly Michelin-starred restaurant – Peel's – at its heart, and 24 very comfortable bedrooms to retire to at the end of the evening. The emphasis is on confident, nothing-is-too-much-trouble service, and the food seasonal and organic, partly based on ingredients from the hotel's own kitchen garden, served in an intimate restaurant that seats just 28 diners.

As for the rooms, they are all different, but the common denominator is William Morris and the Arts-and-Crafts movement, with bold patterns and colours, well-stacked bookshelves and a mix of classic and contemporary furniture. All have air-conditioning, wifi, a fridge and tea- and coffee-making facilities and they range from standard Cosy Double rooms through to Feature Rooms and two junior suites and a master suite. Most have big bathrooms with monsoon showers and robes and toiletries, and it's nice that they all have baths, if not in the bathroom then in the room itself so you can luxuriate while admiring the views over the grounds. The large rooms of the ground floor lend themselves well to hotel use, and in addition to the restaurant, there's a private dining room, bar and lounge. On summer evenings you can relax on the outside terrace and make believe you truly are 'to the manor born', or explore the grounds and the surrounding area using the hotel's own guide which details footpaths around the grounds and beyond. All in all, it's a perfect place for jaded city folk to get their feet muddy.

CONTACT Shadowbrook Lane, Hampton-in-Arden, Warwickshire B92 0DQ • 01675 446 080
HOW MUCH? Double rooms from £170 a night.
ROOMS 24 Guest Rooms & Suites.

The George Townhouse

An updated coaching inn with stylish boutique rooms and a busy bar and restaurant

Located bang in the middle of the handsome Warwickshire market town of Shipston-on-Stour, and by far the grandest building on the short high street, The George Townhouse is a historic 18th-century coaching inn that has been the heartbeat of the town for years. Given a major makeover at the beginning of 2016, it's now a medium-sized boutique hotel, fitted out afresh for the 21st century.

They have done a great job, updating it with flair and style while preserving the historic nature of the building. The rooms all come with king-size beds, high-quality mattresses and stylish bathrooms with rainfall showers, plus Temple Spa toiletries, flatscreen TVs, mineral water and Nespresso machines, and blackout curtains for insomniacs. There are 15 rooms in all, ranging from smallish Classic rooms to larger Superior and Deluxe rooms and so-called Deluxe Plus rooms, which have a freestanding bath and separate walk-in showers. There's also a suite right at the top of the building.

The really nice thing about The George, though, is that it's also a well-known venue for food and drink in the town, with non-residents popping in for breakfast, lunch and dinner to enjoy locally sourced food or just a pint or two, either in the main bar or restaurant or out on the popular terrace behind. They serve a shortish, moderately priced menu with half a dozen starters and mains, plus good steaks and a few classics including a great burger and fish & chips – and we challenge anyone to finish what is a generously portioned and delicious Full English breakfast. The atmosphere is good, and the welcome always warm, and there's a pride and enthusiasm for the town and its area that shines through in the service and surroundings. Shipston was named one of the best places to live in the UK not so long ago, and no wonder: you're perfectly placed for visiting the northern Cotswolds, with the pleasant town of Broadway nearby and Stratford-upon Avon not far away in the other direction.

CONTACT 8 High Street, Shipston-on-Stour, Warwickshire CV36 4AJ • 01608 661 453
HOW MUCH? Double rooms from £80 a night.
ROOMS 16 Guest Rooms.

The Tawny

A quirky and very comfortable deconstructed hotel in a lush 70-acre Staffordshire estate

The Tawny may have a reception, a restaurant and room service but it rather stretches the definition of a hotel. That's because, after check-in, guests are dispersed via leafy pathways rather than carpeted corridors; and instead of boxy rooms clustered under one roof, The Tawny is made up of huts, cabins and treehouses tucked away among trees and lakes. All of them have the facilities you'd expect of a regular hotel room, but none of the immediate neighbours, and each delivers a healthy dose of nature thanks to an outdoor spa bath and its unique setting on this lavish and bucolic Staffordshire estate.

At the heart of the hotel is its well-regarded restaurant: The Plumicorn. It's a strikingly modern, glass-fronted affair, and a quick check of the Oxford English will reveal that, yes, its unusual name is a real word – one that describes the elongated eyebrow feathers of an owl! Somehow the idea of this curious embellishment is rather fitting here: nature with a bit of a flourish and perhaps just a touch of magic, mixing botanical prints with plush upholstery under a high ceiling with huge windows, and with a gorgeous setting at the head of the estate's largest lake, just above the hotel's outdoor heated pool.

The landscaped gardens around the restaurant are home to a quirky collection of Victorian follies, while the lodgings have been just as carefully planned and just as beautifully designed as the restaurant. These range from the simple Wildwood Huts that sleep two in whitewashed, timber-clad Scandi style, to the grand Hillside Treehouses with their private verandahs, and the cedar-clad Retreats with sunken baths. Whichever you choose, you'll have a bed that's no less than king-size, en-suite facilities, a Smart TV, wifi, a complimentary minibar, a coffee machine and fluffy bathrobes to get you to that spa bath outside.

There are bikes to borrow, walking routes to follow and there's always that heated outdoor pool. Bookable extras include private yoga sessions, treatments in the spa and mindful stargazing events. With breakfast included and lunch and dinner available in The Plumicorn, there's little reason to leave the estate. Should you want to, though, the vastly different pleasures of the Peak District and Alton Towers are both within a half-hour's drive.

CONTACT Consall Gardens Estate, Consall Lane, Consall, Staffordshire ST9 0AG • 01538 787 664
HOW MUCH? Double rooms from £250 a night.
ROOMS 34 Guest Rooms.

The Duncombe Arms

Great food and rooms at a terrific Staffordshire country inn – if only all village locals were like this!

It was written that Johnny and Laura Greenall would take over this pub: not in the stars but on the pub sign itself, which bore Laura's mother's Duncombe coat of arms. The couple used to drive past the empty and neglected pub every day and dreamt of restoring it, and that's exactly what they did, taking this 1850s village boozer and turning it into a modern country inn renowned for the excellence of its food and the comfort of its rooms.

Just over the border from Derbyshire, the Duncombe Arms enjoys a great location overlooking the Dove Valley, on the edge of the Peak District National Park. It's a five-minute drive from Alton Towers, making it an excellent place to stay when visiting the resort, and not far from the pleasant country town of Ashbourne, renowned for its antiques dealers. The rooms – 10 in total, in a separate building behind the pub – are individually decorated in a contemporary country style that really works; think stylish artisan fabrics and wallpapers, mood lighting and bespoke art. They are large enough for a comfy chair or two and a writing desk, and the bathrooms are modern and well-conceived, some with spacious walk-in showers, others with a shower and bath, and all stocked with fluffy robes and fragrant Bamford toiletries. Each room also has a Roberts radio, a Freeview TV, tea- and Nespresso coffee-making facilities, bottles of mineral water and homemade biscuits. The ground-floor rooms open up onto a private patio area, while the junior suites are equipped with sofa beds and can accommodate a young family. Dogs are also welcome in two rooms, and they also offer self-catering alternatives – the three-bedroom Old Barn next door and another cottage nearby.

The pub itself still has the feel of a village local but one where the emphasis is on good-quality food, with a menu that features both pub classics and more refined fare, all beautifully presented and using game and meat from nearby farms, local cheeses and seasonal produce. The food is delicious and the surroundings ideal – pretty much everything in the kitchen is homemade, and the ambience is suitably pubby, with various different rooms, a roaring fire in winter and an attractive outside terrace. As for drinks, they serve their own Duncombe Ale and the extensive wine list is carefully chosen, as are the 28 different gins on offer. If only every local pub could be like this!

CONTACT Ellastone, Ashbourne, Staffordshire DE6 2GZ • 01335 324 275
HOW MUCH? Double rooms from £195 a night.
ROOMS 10 Guest Rooms & Suites.

Brockencote Hall

This country house hotel is an oasis of comfort in the heart of Worcestershire

Nestled in the picturesque Worcestershire countryside, Brockencote Hall Hotel is a Victorian gem – a hidden oasis situated just outside the market town of Kidderminster that offers the comforts and treats of a luxury country estate. Once a family residence, this enchanting manor house was transformed into a hotel in 1986 and has 70 acres of grounds to explore.

This historic hotel's 21 beautiful and well-appointed bedrooms offer a choice between sweeping countryside vistas and serene lake views. Five are dog-friendly and one is accessible, making it a destination for the whole family, whether you opt for a Classic room in the main house with a cosy double bed or a Deluxe room with a king bed in the west wing. All are spacious and well equipped, with wifi, a Smart TV, a mini-fridge, tea- and coffee-making facilities, complimentary water, fruit and homemade biscuits. For those seeking extra space, Superior and Master rooms come with king-size beds and en-suites with baths and walk-in showers, and even extra beds or cots to make room for little ones. Or, if you want to live like royalty for a couple of nights, stay in the Feature suite: often booked for special occasions or as a bridal suite, it comes with a large seating area and a king-size bed. For a bit more privacy, the hotel is also home to two-storey Brockencote Lodge. This former gatehouse features three double bedrooms, an open kitchen and a private hot tub.

Beyond the plush accommodation, the hotel's crown jewel is the award-winning Chaddesley Restaurant, which has three AA Rosettes and a well-established reputation for fine dining. It serves breakfast, lunch, an excellent afternoon tea, and has multiple menus, including Sunday roasts and a more relaxed bar menu featuring traditional favourites like fish and chips and steaks. You can also enjoy seasonal six- and nine-course tasting menus!

There's a myriad of possible activities in the hotel's grounds, from tennis to croquet, and while Brockencote Hall offers an oasis of seclusion, it also provides easy access to the scenic countryside around: the Malvern Hills, Shropshire and the Welsh Borders are a brief car ride away, and there are quaint historic villages and walking routes to explore on your doorstep. Back at Brockencote, Le Colonial Bar is a relaxed setting for an evening cocktail or two.

CONTACT Brockencote, Kidderminster, Worcestershire DY10 4PY • 01562 777 876
HOW MUCH? Double rooms from £138 a night, including breakfast.
ROOMS 21 Guest Rooms & Suites.

The Castle Hotel

The perfect country bolthole, with comfy rooms, a cosy bar and restaurant – and a wonderful location

Once you get to the top of the main street of the tiny town of Bishop's Castle, which is where you'll find The Castle Hotel, you feel like you've really got away from it all. There are glorious views over the surrounding countryside, which is beckoning and accessible, and the hotel makes for an inspiring bolthole for aspirant walkers and cyclists, and is very family-friendly.

The Castle has been here since the early 18th century – owners Henry and Rebecca claim Clive of India was once the landlord here – and it's just our sort of place: comfy rather than posh, with eight large and cosy rooms with flatscreen TVs, tea- and coffee-making facilities and wifi throughout. There's a good restaurant downstairs serving a lovely menu that includes lots of local produce and a veggie option or two, and a pleasant bar that is well used by locals and makes a point of serving proper brews from the local area, including the town's two micro-breweries The Three Tuns and Six Bells (the hotel has special rates on brewery tours for real enthusiasts). They also have a fantastic, almost Mediterranean-style garden that overlooks the Shropshire Hills from its high perch behind the hotel, and which is perfect for enjoying an early evening glass of wine from its covered arbours.

Finally, the Castle is one of the most dog-friendly hotels we know, which makes us like it even more. They not only encourage you to bring your pet but also provide a 'Dog Welcome Box' in the room that includes a feeding mat, food bowl, towel, lead, treats and even poo bags. In short, we reckon The Castle is as friendly and relaxing a place to stay as you'll find – and situated in what is frankly a glorious location.

CONTACT Bishop's Castle, Shropshire SY9 5BN • 01588 638 403

HOW MUCH? Double rooms with breakfast from £125 to £210 a night.

ROOMS 12 Guest Rooms & 1 Cottage.

Old Downton Lodge

A beautiful hotel in a great location with lovely rooms and award-winning food

Nestled in the rolling green south Shropshire hills, Old Downton Lodge has been here so long that it almost feels part of the landscape. It's a mixture of timbered medieval and Georgian houses and barns and outbuildings that have been ingeniously converted into one of the most comfortable rural boltholes in the region. Atmospherically housed in the lodge's grand Norman hall, its three-AA-Rosette restaurant has been voted one of the best 100 places to eat in the UK, serving tasting menus every night from Tuesday to Saturday.

There are only nine guest rooms (plus a bridal suite in the separate building), grouped around a herb- and flower-filled courtyard which provides an appealing sense of seclusion. There is a comfy sitting room fashioned out of the old stable, with a wood-burner and a bar squeezed into a corner, and a mighty timbered roof that echoes the look and feel of the guest rooms. Fashioned from spaces that were once stables and barns, the guest rooms are as different from each other as you might expect, and as well as the high-timbered ceilings many have stone walls and wonderful flagstoned floors covered with Turkish rugs. They all have comfortable beds, including three four-posters, and well-chosen furniture, as well as wifi, Freeview TVs, tea and coffee-making facilities, homemade biccies and complimentary water. Most of the bathrooms have been recently refurbished: some have en-suite showers, others a bath, and all have Noble Isle toiletries.

As for the location, it couldn't be better, with glorious walks and countryside right outside the door, and the foodie town of Ludlow just 10 minutes' drive away. They have a couple of electric car-charging points too. So, just throw away those keys, charge up your car, and... relax!

CONTACT Downton on the Rock, Ludlow, Shropshire SY8 2HU • 01568 771 826
HOW MUCH? Double rooms £155–£175 a night, including breakfast.
ROOMS 9 Guest Rooms.

The New Inn

This Herefordshire coaching inn has been converted to a fabulous restaurant with rooms

When the new owners bought The New Inn five years ago, it was well in need of some TLC. And, as a pub close to their own hearts, they were more than ready to take on the challenge of giving this 16th-century coaching inn a new lease of life, with a winning combination of old-fashioned beams and plaster, chic rooms and fabulous food. As a result, it's a wonderfully warm and friendly place, with tasteful, stylish rooms and exquisite food, set in breathtaking Herefordshire countryside just outside Ross-on-Wye.

The pub was voted one of the UK's 'Top 100 Gastropubs' in 2024 and it boasts a lovely bar, restaurant and a little snug for private dining. Although it still maintains a traditional look, it's very sophisticated and contemporary, with stripped-back light oak beams. The restaurant serves first-rate food with a strong emphasis on local produce and seasonality. They have three very elegant bedrooms, rated five-star by the AA, which come with cosy throws and robes, ultra-comfy beds, wifi and Smart TVs, tea and coffee facilities, and crisp, modern en-suite bathrooms. The rooms are all spacious but the largest one is almost a suite, with a wow-factor glass-walled bathroom and a free-standing bath – very romantic, and perfect for a weekend away. They also offer beautiful, contemporary self-catering accommodation less than a five-minute drive away at Teal Barn, which sleeps eight people.

The New Inn is above all a pub for those looking for something a little bit special, with over 50 wines by the glass and a great choice of ales, bespoke cocktails and an enormous list of gins – including plenty of local specialities! The food is worth coming for alone – think orchard pork, wild sea bass, blackberry souffle… and as well as the contemporary yet rustic dining room, there's a lovely secret terrace to enjoy eating and drinking al fresco. Recently awarded three AA rosettes, and winner of the AA's 'Best Restaurant with Rooms' award, they offer à la carte, a set lunch option, two fabulous tasting menus, and lighter dishes at the informal bar. The pub also enjoys an excellent location, close to the bustling market town of Ross-on-Wye, with the beautiful Wye Valley and Symonds Yat, and the gorgeous small town of Ledbury not far away.

CONTACT St Owen's Cross, Hereford, Herefordshire HR2 8LQ • 01989 553 387
HOW MUCH? Double rooms from £160 a night including breakfast.
ROOMS 3 Guest Rooms.

The Cavendish Hotel at Baslow

A lavish country house hotel in the Peak District's Chatsworth Estate

For a taste of life on the Chatsworth Estate, book yourself in for a stay at The Cavendish Hotel at Baslow. This country house hotel is firmly rooted in the Duke of Devonshire's vast 35,000-acre estate in the Peak District – and you'll feel that while you're here. Every bedroom offers views across the parkland surrounding Chatsworth House itself and the hotel's two restaurants use fresh produce from its gardens. There's antique furniture and artwork from the Duke's collection on the walls and the Duchess herself had a hand in the decoration of some of its rooms.

The style here is as classic as the destination, and while each of the 28 bedrooms is different, they all share the same aesthetic. Quality carpets, curtains and upholstery soften the crisp white linen on the beds. And whether you book a standard room or a suite, all boast stunning countryside views. The difference comes in the space. The Superior Rooms, for example, have a four-poster or a king-size bed and the top-notch Redesdale Suite is split over two floors with comfy seating arranged around a fireplace. The hotel is also contemporary where it counts. En-suite bathrooms have underfloor heating, heated towel rails and high-quality toiletries. Every room has wifi, a Bluetooth speaker and a flatscreen TV. Downstairs, there's a choice of two restaurants – the fine dining of the three-AA-Rosette Gallery Restaurant or the relaxed warmth of The Garden Room which opens to the outside in warmer weather.

From the terrace around the hotel, you'll probably be tempted into the great outdoors. After all, this is what this place is all about. The Chatsworth Estate offers endless walks through parkland and woodland. The magnificent house at its centre is open for public viewing and has a vast art collection, while outside its landscaped gardens are a further attraction. Beyond that? Well, this is the Peak District, so there's a whole National Park to explore.

CONTACT Church Lane, Baslow, Bakewell, Derbyshire DE45 1SP • 01246 582 311
HOW MUCH? Double rooms from £260 a night.
ROOMS 28 Guest Rooms & Suite.

The Devonshire Arms at Pilsley

A stone's throw from Chatsworth House, this popular pub has 13 stylish bedrooms and terrific food

The Devonshires are very well-connected, and the Duchess of Devonshire has applied her great eye for design to the pub in this tiny estate village, a mere stone's throw from Chatsworth House, and even nearer to a peerless farm shop at the top of the lane. Pilsley is chocolate-box pretty, the soft sandstone buildings glowing in sunlight, and the inn has a stylish, contemporary vibe that makes it a tremendous place to stay and eat right in the heart of the Peaks.

The Dev (as it's known locally) has been here for 300 years. It's a great place to make yourself comfy before striking out for a tour around Chatsworth House. There's a collection of 13 stylish guest rooms in all, individually designed by the Duchess herself and divided between the main building and the next-door farmhouse. The rooms above the pub are slightly more contemporary, divided between Petite, Classic and Deluxe, while the farmhouse rooms are a bit more countrified, with plaid soft furnishings and four-poster beds. All are dog-friendly and come with good wifi, tea- and coffee-making facilities, Freeview TVs, comfy beds with good-quality linens and en-suite bathrooms with toiletries. The Deluxe and Farmhouse rooms are more spacious and the Farmhouse rooms have larger bathrooms and some have walk-in showers as well as baths.

The food is upmarket pub grub, beautifully cooked and presented, and makes the most of the produce from the Chatsworth Estate, with the likes of partridge breast with artichoke, venison with cabbage, local lamb shoulder and hogget loin, Chatsworth-raised beef and oxtail, plus good steaks and fish dishes, including classic fish and chips and crispy whitebait. Try the local faggots or beef and ale pie.

CONTACT Pilsley, Bakewell, Derbyshire DE45 1UL • 01246 565 405
HOW MUCH? Double rooms with breakfast from £190 a night.
ROOMS 13 Guest Rooms.

Sheriff Lodge

A boutique Derbyshire B&B in Matlock on the edge of the Peak District

Comfortable beds and tasty breakfasts are just two of the things that make Sheriff Lodge a fantastic place to stay in the old spa town of Matlock on the edge of the Peak District National Park. But both are merely indicators of what's really special about this adults-only B&B, something that can be summed up in just three words – attention to detail, which owner Ziz has applied to every aspect of this place. The reason the beds are so comfy? The mattresses are a minimum of eight inches deep, seven-foot long and made up with Egyptian cotton bed linen, and beds are all super-kings (some convertible to twins). The reason the breakfast is so tasty is because it's fresh from the farms around you – as much as possible is locally sourced.

There are also fresh flowers, up-to-date magazines and a little box of 'things you may have forgotten' in all of the five guest rooms, and guests are offered tea and cake on arrival. Each room is individually decorated, mostly in tasteful neutrals with a touch of colour here and there, to suit the age and elegance of the place. Originally built in 1740, this stone-walled townhouse was extended in 1908 and in some ways retains the feel of the Edwardian gentleman's residence it once was. The long curtains, upholstered chairs, a drawing room where you can take a nightcap, and someone to serve your breakfast all help with that. But elegant as it is, this place is also homely. There's a garden for guests' use, plenty of parking and even a couple of EV charging points. Ziz also offers foodie extras like sharing platters and packed lunches, plus homemade afternoon teas and truffles.

Each en-suite bedroom has tea- and coffee-making facilities, a Smart TV and even a hot-water bottle. There are games, DVDs and books to borrow downstairs, and one of the rooms – The Warren – has a separate entrance. Each room has its own personality, tied to the British countryside by both the paintings on the walls and the views of the Derwent Valley.

Whichever room you stay in, it doesn't take long for you to be out in the Great Outdoors. You can walk down the hill to the centre of Matlock in 10 minutes and then strike out into the surrounding countryside – maybe on the riverside walk to Chatsworth or the more challenging route up High Tor. Further afield are some of the Peak District's greatest attractions: Haddon Hall and Bakewell, both 15 minutes' drive away, and guests qualify for discounts at many nearby restaurants and attractions.

CONTACT 51 Dimple Road, Matlock, Derbyshire DE4 3JX • 01629 760 760

HOW MUCH? Double rooms with breakfast from £115 a night.

ROOMS 5 Guest Rooms.

Losehill House Hotel & Spa

A boutique treat in the Peak District for both walkers and weekenders

If you're a walker you couldn't dream of a better setting than the one enjoyed by Losehill House Hotel & Spa. Deep in the heart of the Peak District, just outside the village of Hope, it's surrounded by enticing views that beckon you each day to enjoy the pleasures of the gorgeous Derbyshire countryside. No surprise, then, that it was the Sunday Times' 'Country Hotel of the Year' a few years ago, and continues to provide an enticing mix of traditional and modern comforts in the midst of some of the Peaks' most enchanting scenery.

One of the many nice things about Losehill House is that it makes a good car-free weekend break from either Manchester or Sheffield, with regular trains running from both cities to Hope, two miles away. An Arts-and-Crafts property from the turn of the 19th century, it was built as a ramblers' hostel but has been superbly updated by Paul and Kathryn Roden, who have turned it into an extremely comfortable spa hotel with a two-AA-rosette restaurant that attracts plenty of non-residents. It's a tremendously relaxing place to stay, with a country house vibe that is deliberately comfortable rather than full-on posh; wooden floors, squashy sofas and mismatched comfy chairs blend well with the low-key but attentive service and a range of thoroughly up-to-date facilities. The hotel has three treatment rooms, a sauna, steam room and a lovely indoor pool, plus an outdoor hot tub that's ideal for soothing those aching limbs after a hard day's hiking.

There are 22 guest rooms in all, ranging from Doubles to De Luxe Kings and four suites; all are furnished in a simple, contemporary style and come with en-suite bathrooms (De Luxe rooms have separate showers), big comfy beds (king- or super-king-size), Freeview TVs, tea- and coffee-making facilities, robes and slippers for the spa, and decent wifi. There's a lift to the upper floors, which is helpful for less mobile guests, and most of the rooms have wonderful views over Edale. Breakfasts are waiter-service and full of local treats like black pudding and oatcakes – indeed the food here is one of the highlights of any stay. They serve a great-value four-course menu that starts with canapes in the bar, or you can choose from their daily changing à la carte menu, with a focus on duck and game from nearby estates, free-range chicken and pork, local honey, herbs and artisan cheeses. Just what you need after a day visiting the varied attractions of Britain's first ever National Park.

CONTACT Losehill Lane, Edale Road, Hope, Derbyshire S33 6AF • 01433 621 219
HOW MUCH? Double rooms with breakfast from £168 a night.
ROOMS 22 Guest Rooms & Suites.

Dannah Farm

High-end B&B luxury in an informal setting

This beautiful boutique B&B is situated on the edge of the Peak District in the heart of the Derbyshire Dales, looking down onto the Ecclesbourne Valley. The elegant late-18th-century farmhouse lies at the centre of a 154-acre working farm on the Chatsworth Estate at Shottle, and although it's easy to reach, it's a very rural place to stay, with levels of luxury that compare favourably to a top-end hotel but in a gloriously informal setting. We also like it because it's a proper family business, created by Joan and Martin Slack back in the mid-1980s and now – along with its sister self-catering cottages – run by Joan and daughter-in-law Helen.

There are seven large rooms and suites, and all have flatscreen TVs, wifi, tea- and coffee-making facilities and large well-equipped bathrooms, but there the similarities end, because each room is utterly individual, varying from large two-level suites with private sitting rooms and hot tub to spacious doubles with four-poster beds. One has an en-suite bathroom complete with flatscreen TV, another is a two-bedroom suite that is big enough for a small family or group of friends. But throughout there is an emphasis on space, luxury and comfort.

True lotus-eaters can also book the 'Secret Garden' for exclusive use for the duration of their stay: a deliciously enclosed space equipped with a hot tub from which to enjoy the views of the countryside. Breakfasts are the other thing worth leaving your room for – generous affairs featuring homemade bread, free-range eggs and excellent local bacon, sausage and black pudding (veggies are well catered for too). There are some wonderful places to eat out nearby offering a range of fabulous food, or you can order in a take-away to enjoy at your leisure. If there is a more comfortable family-run place to stay in this part of Derbyshire, then we have yet to find it.

CONTACT Bowmans Lane, Shottle, Belper, Derbyshire DE56 2DR • 01773 550 273
HOW MUCH? Double rooms with breakfast from £270 a night.
ROOMS 7 Guest Rooms & Suites.

Ye Olde Bell

A historic Nottinghamshire coaching inn with sumptuous suites, lodges and spa facilities

At first glance, Ye Olde Bell looks like any other traditional inn, but step inside and you'll see that it's comfortably and sumptuously furnished to look more like a country house hotel. What's more, if you slip out the back, you'll find a spa with an impressive array of thermal facilities. Situated just off the A1 in Nottinghamshire, it has been hosting overnight guests for centuries, including some illustrious names (a young Queen Victoria among them). These days, however, thanks to its restaurants and restorative relaxation rooms, it's not just part of the journey but a destination in its own right.

The hotel has 59 rooms, including four suites and two spacious lodges – all rooms have been individually designed to make the most of the historic features of the building. The suites, of course, are the most luxurious, with canopied beds and roll-top baths in the bathrooms, but whichever you choose they are all well-designed with elegant touches. Heavy curtains and antique furniture sit alongside the upscale hotel staples of flatscreen TV, hairdryer and tea- and coffee-making facilities, and there is wifi throughout. The en-suite bathrooms all have power showers and breakfast is included with every stay.

For those interested in a spot of pampering, the hotel has a lavish spa complex with a wide range of facilities, including an Alpine sauna, herbal laconium, outdoor pool and treatment rooms. There are plenty of packages on offer, from 30-minute massages to multi-day experiences. If you're using the place as a stop-over, you might be happy to rest in a classic room and refuel in the relaxed St Leger bistro. If you're heading here to visit the local area, the spaciousness of a lodge might suit you better. If you're here for a treat, book a suite, spend some time in the spa and get yourself a table at the Restaurant Bar 1650.

CONTACT Great North Road, Barnby Moor, Retford, Nottinghamshire DN22 8QS • 01777 705 121
HOW MUCH? Double rooms from £130 a night.
ROOMS 59 Guest Rooms & Suites.

Lucky Dip

The Barnsdale

The Avenue, Near Oakham, Rutland LE15 8AH

A collection of typically honey-stoned buildings around a central courtyard, this is a very comfortable recently updated Rutland hotel, with 45 stylish, country-style guest rooms and a collection of cedar-clad self-catering cabins across the road. It's close to Rutland Water and has a well-established restaurant, split between a traditional dining room and a contemporary conservatory, which serves a menu based around local ingredients. There's also a cosy, dog-friendly bar and a lovely bright garden room with doors opening out onto a central courtyard.

The Devonshire Arms at Beeley

Devonshire Square, Beeley, Derbyshire DE4 2NZ

Another fine member of the Chatsworth stable, Beeley's Devonshire Arms is one of the Duke and Duchess's oldest pubs – and very handsome it is too, its stone facade sitting squarely in the pretty hamlet of Beeley. Above all, this hotel is a perfect place to stay close to Chatsworth House, and it has 18 lovely guest rooms divided between the pub itself and two adjacent buildings.

Fischers Baslow Hall

Calver Road, Baslow, Derbyshire DE45 1RR

Max and Susan Fischer have been in residence at this stunning Grade II-listed manor house since 1988, and their care and attention to detail shines through. Their restaurant is Michelin-star territory, and unsurprisingly the accommodation matches at this wonderful boutique country house hotel, with six traditional bedrooms in the main house and five more contemporary rooms in the adjacent Garden House, from which you can admire Max's veg garden. Oh, and it might be posh, but it's really friendly and no one stands on ceremony.

The Fish Hotel

Farncombe Estate, Broadway, Worcestershire WR12 7LH

Deep in the heart of the Cotswolds, near the charming village of Broadway, the sprawling Farncombe Estate is home to The Fish Hotel. Tucked into the hillside, with wide views of the valley below, it has a set of appealing rooms and suites decorated in a crisp modern style. The grounds also harbour a number of deluxe 'Hideaway Huts' with private hot tubs, en-suite bathrooms and wood-burning stoves, along with several woodland treehouses with the same conveniences.

Flore House

The Avenue, Flore, Northamptonshire NN7 4LZ

Originally a 17th-century hunting lodge, this superb adults-only boutique guesthouse gives you a rare chance to experience a weekend in your very own country house in one of two beautifully updated guest rooms, each with its own entrance and access to 20 acres of grounds. The rooms have been updated with great taste and a flair for design, with contemporary features blending well with the historic character of the building.You receive a breakfast hamper on the first morning that provides everything you need for your stay, including cereals, bread, butter and jam, teabags and coffee, fresh milk, and mineral water, and each room has a fully equipped kitchenette with fridge, boiling water tap and toaster. All very private and perfect if you're after a secluded break.

The Fuzzy Duck

Ilmington Road, Armscote, Warwickshire CV37 8DD

A beautifully revamped north Cotswolds gastropub with boutique rooms, rescued by the brother and sister team behind soap and bath product company Baylis & Harding. It's still very much a traditonal inn at heart, serving superb seasonal food and with four comfy bedrooms upstairs, named after ducks, all with big beds, fine linen and a host of Baylis & Harding toiletries of course!

The Olive Branch

Main Street, Clipsham, Rutland LE15 7SH

With its beams and bare walls, this delectable Rutland gastropub is a great base for exloring England's smallest county, and manages to be folksy and rural without being twee. It serves outstanding food and has six elegant, individually decorated rooms in the attractively restored Beech House, across the road.

The Olive Branch

The Devonshire Arms at Beeley

Flore House

Yorkshire & The Northeast

South Yorkshire • East Yorkshire • West Yorkshire • North Yorkshire • Durham • Northumberland

Is there a region that has as much to offer the visitor as the North East of England? Home to no less than three National Parks – the Yorkshire Dales, North York Moors and Northumberland National Park – its interior is mostly dramatic and unspoilt, and the coastline is a treat, from salty old towns like Whitby to the glorious open skies and sandy beaches of Northumberland further north. It's a region that's very much used to visitors, and as a result has a wide range of hotels and B&Bs, including some superb gastropubs and country inns that are the match of anywhere in the UK. No wonder they call it 'God's Own Country'!

Matfen Hall, p.220

New Holgate

A stylish boutique hotel in York just a 10-minute walk from the station

Just 10 minutes' walk from the train station and 15 minutes from the city's medieval walls, New Holgate is a cool, sophisticated boutique hotel occupying two Grade II-listed Victorian townhouses. Opened in 2023, New Holgate has 12 guest rooms and shared spaces including a brick-walled dining room and a cosy, low-lit whisky lounge. It's all been carefully curated by Yorkshire-based interior designers, and while the style might have a touch of stateside city cool, there's plenty that's local too. There are nods to Holgate's industrial heritage in the use of metal work and there are works by modern local artists on the walls. The food on the breakfast menu and drinks on offer in the evenings are locally sourced and even the toiletries in the bathrooms are made not far from here.

There are no 'bedrooms' in New Holgate – it offers only suites, spread over all four floors of this townhouse hotel. Choose from double, king and luxury, each larger than the last. Even the doubles have a sofa that can convert into a bed, making every room family-sized if you want it to be. That said, none of them feel too large to be enjoyed by a couple, not even the super-sized luxury suite – although unusually this has the capacity to sleep up to six, thanks to a separate living room with an extra sofa bed. Some of the suites – on the ground floor – are dog-friendly and one has access to its own private garden.

All this space extends further outside, where, in the summer, guests can enjoy a contemporary patio. There's also ample parking, with a space for every suite. The location, outside the city walls but a short stroll from York's historic centre, is ideal for anyone who's visiting by car. But the proximity to the station makes it good for car-free visits too. From here, you can walk to see all of central York's sights: its castle, its Minster, its museums, its medieval walls and The Shambles. There are lots of reasons to visit York and this stylish new hotel offers one more.

CONTACT 106 Holgate Rd, Holgate, York YO24 4BB • 01904 217 208
HOW MUCH? Double rooms from £125 a night.
ROOMS 21 Guest Rooms & Suites.

Tickton Grange

One of Yorkshire's finest country house hotels, garnering award after award for its accommodation, food and highly personal service

When the Whymant family came to the Georgian country house of Tickton Grange over 40 years ago, it was dilapidated and unloved in the extreme. Now it's one of Yorkshire's finest country house hotels, renowned for the standard of its accommodation, food and highly personal service. The family story is writ large across the hotel – successful Northamptonshire shoemakers who moved back to the place they used to come on holiday, and who have renovated every inch of the building using local craftsmen and artisans. It's a terrific place to stay by any standard.

There are 21 guest rooms spread across various buildings – apart from the main house, lodgings are also in the renovated stables and pump room, servants' quarters and workers' cottages. Family members grew up in these rooms and played in the gardens, so the sense of pride here is palpable. As you may imagine, no two rooms are the same, but you can expect country-house-chic and plenty of welcoming touches throughout – homemade biscuits, fresh flowers, good Italian coffee and high-quality tea, a thoughtful selection of books, and Bramley toiletries in well-appointed en-suite bathrooms. The larger rooms have king-size beds and all rooms have good wifi and flatscreen TVs. Nothing is too much trouble, and service comes with a broad smile from staff who have been with the family for years. Dogs are welcome at Tickton Grange and they'll provide a dog bed, towel, bowls and treats in the, room in readiness for canine guests.

With Beverley and Bridlington on the doorstep, this is the perfect romantic East Yorkshire weekend getaway. The hotel is embraced by its own 16 acres of grounds and gardens, while beyond lie the wild landscapes of the Yorkshire Wolds that so inspired Bridlington boy David Hockney. You can pay further tribute to our most famous living artist by indulging in an afternoon tea in the eponymous Hockney Room – one of a trio of beautiful dining spaces within Tickton Grange's renowned restaurant, The Bloomsbury Room. With a kitchen headed up by their long-standing chef James Pulford, the food served is delicious, organic and local, and echoes the individuality, style and passion that sums up the rest of the hotel. Breakfast too is always local, fresh and bountiful – this is Yorkshire, after all!

CONTACT Tickton, Beverley, East Yorkshire HU17 9SH • 01964 543 666
HOW MUCH? Double rooms from £149 a night, suites from £220, including breakfast.
ROOMS 21 Guest Rooms & Suites.

The Devonshire Arms

An extraordinarily welcoming North Yorkshire country house hotel and spa

Must be a pub, with a name like that? Perish the thought! In fact The Devonshire is an extraordinarily welcoming country house hotel set among the rolling acres of the Duke of Devonshire's Bolton Abbey Estate, just a few miles outside Skipton, North Yorkshire. It is quite a grand sort of place – of course it is, given that the other Devonshire family seat is Chatsworth. But it isn't stuffy or even particularly formal, and with only 40 individually designed rooms and suites there's a genuinely familiar welcome backed up by some highly polished service. Located in a brilliant North Yorkshire location, with the 'Great Outdoors' right on your doorstep, and dogs welcome too, the whole thing's a treat.

The Devonshire's array of portraits, antiques and mementoes keep the ducal connection very much in mind. This place exudes luxury and comfort, with great facilities, including an excellent restaurant and a spa with gym, state-of-the-art vitality pool and other relaxation inducing facilities. Guest rooms vary in size and aspect, but most have lovely rural views, and those situated in the original 18th-century part of the hotel have ornate four-poster beds. Even the lowest category – Classic, housed in the 'New Wing' – comes with king-size beds, lots of space for seating, mini-fridges, complimentary water and tea- and coffee-making facilities and welcome treats.

The Devonshire's guest rooms all have good wifi, Freeview TVs and en-suite bathrooms with Noble Isle toiletries. Deluxe, Luxury and Superior rooms often have super-king-size beds and a bath as well as a walk-in shower, plus more space and views, while the hotel's suites have large four-posters, separate sitting rooms and predictably glorious countryside vistas. Throughout, there's a keen sense of modern country style and classy little extras: umbrellas at the door, and, at the other end of the scale, the hotel's own helipad out on the lawn.

All guests have complimentary access to the Devonshire's Spa, housed in a separate building, where there are treatment rooms, gym, sauna, and they are building a natural outdoor pool. Eating and drinking are similarly as relaxed or posh as you want. There's a lovely cocktail lounge available for a drink or two, a bright and contemporary brasserie serving lunch and dinner, while the more upscale Burlington restaurant, which looks out onto the hotel's courtyard garden, offers both seasonal tasting menus and à la carte options.

CONTACT Bolton Abbey, Skipton, North Yorkshire BD23 6AJ • 01756 710 441

HOW MUCH? Double rooms with breakfast from around £200 a night.

ROOMS 40 Guest Rooms & Suites.

Low Mill Guest House

A truly special place to stay in a beautifully restored mill building in the heart of the Dales

'Small but special' is what one award citation said about Low Mill, and it's bang on. Just three rooms keep your stay on the intimate side, but what wonderful rooms they are, fashioned from an 18th-century watermill on the gushing riverside in Bainbridge, in the heart of Wensleydale, four miles from Hawes. There's no mistaking the building's heritage – owners Neil and Jane have restored the lot to working order, so the grindstones and cogs form a dramatic backdrop in the eye-popping guest lounge, while the wheel itself lies underneath the dining room (a tour by Neil, who did the work himself, is very much part of the experience).

There's a story to tell in every lavishly appointed room – the old 'Store Room' sits under gorgeous beams, while the 'Kiln Room' retains its vintage ceramic floor tiles where the grain used to be spread to dry. And if you think you're been-there-done-that as far as boutique goes, be prepared to swoon at 'The Workshop', which is an absolutely massive space running the length of the building, complete with winding gear and pulleys, wood-burner and free-standing copper bath. Low Mill is a chic affair all round, from polished wood floors and exposed stone walls to cheeky fabrics and designer bathrooms, and it's wi-fi-ed, flat-screen-TV-ed and fluffy-bath-robed up to its eyeballs. But style aside, there's comfort and fun here too, whether it's the deep, deep bedside rugs or the leopard and tiger standing guard in the lounge. Mornings see serious breakfasts, strong on local produce and outside is a riverside terrace and sitting areas, where you can lie in wait for the visiting herons. Small but special indeed – well said, Yorkshire Life!

CONTACT Bainbridge, Leyburn, North Yorkshire DL8 3EF• 01969 650 553

HOW MUCH? Double rooms from £110 a night.

ROOMS 3 Guest Rooms.

Stow House

An exceptionally comfortable and contemporary Yorkshire Dales B&B run with style and enthusiasm

A boutique bed and breakfast in the heart of the Yorkshire Dales, Stow House occupies an artily (and artfully) renovated Victorian vicarage with magnificent views from every room. The excellent breakfast is freshly cooked to order, with homemade bread and granola alongside sausages and bacon supplied by the local butcher, and they can also make packed lunches or an evening meal for larger groups. There's an honesty bar, should you fancy a drink or a snack, and the powerful cocktails mixed by your hosts, Sarah and Phil, between 6pm and 7pm each evening, also come very highly recommended. Sarah, meanwhile, cannot help enough when you're settling in, or if you need advice on the local area: Aysgarth Falls are just a short stroll away, and there are plenty more challenging local walks as well as country pubs and National Trust sites to visit. Wensleydale cheese is made nearby, and the surrounding countryside will be familiar to fans of 'All Creatures Great and Small'.

The seven exceptionally comfortable and playfully named rooms are all different, but each is light and airy, with unique modern artwork and a well-appointed bathroom, most with large baths. Our own favourites are the two bright modern spaces on the top floor – Shotgun Clare and Cowboy Balance – with wood beams and big Velux windows cut into the eaves. The living room, snug/library and dining room downstairs all have woodburners. Dogs are welcome in most rooms, and on fine days can join the owners' pets in the extensive gardens. Nearby places to eat include the Aygsarth Falls Hotel, which is a short walk away, and the Wensleydale Heifer, on the way to Leyburn, where there are also a number of good pubs and restaurants.

CONTACT Aysgarth, Leyburn, North Yorkshire DL8 3SR • 01969 663 635
HOW MUCH? Double rooms with breakfast from £120 to £180 a night. Family room £200.
ROOMS 7 Guest Rooms.

Falcon Manor

Small and charming boutique country house hotel on the edge of the Yorkshire market town of Settle

Well, this is rather nice – a handsome manor house set in lush grounds on the edge of Settle, one of the most interesting market towns in the Yorkshire Dales. Falcon Manor is a very elegant place, with its leaded windows, baronial staircase and manicured lawns, and a restful weekend or longer stay here would do very well indeed. The classic rooms are done out in an appealing country-chic style, boasting either courtyard or countryside views. A white-painted four-poster here, a raised slipper bath there – there is plenty to like about these rooms, and even the smaller ones have a harmonious feel and all the creature comforts you need, from goose-down duvets to great showers.

If you want to make your better half swoon though, pick one of the suites – Rafters (the honeymoon suite) or Turret, both beguilingly large spaces, beautifully appointed, with massive beds, hanging chandeliers and luxurious bathrooms. The Falcon Suite, meanwhile, would make a good family room, and has a small kitchen attached.

The bar and restaurant has elegance stitched right through it too, with a modern, stripped-wood feel and a menu that can best be described as Yorkshire-Mediterranean – tapas nibbles to Yorkshire ham and eggs. It's at its best – or at least its most attractive – when you take advantage of the gorgeous terrace overlooking the grounds, whether that's a champagne afternoon tea or a G&T sundowner. Settle is a short stroll away, with its market square pubs and local walks up the nearby crags and fells. Malham's not far away either, a wild drive over the tops, or take a day trip on the famous Settle to Carlisle Railway – you can catch the train right in town after a Yorkshire breakfast that will set you right up for the day.

CONTACT Skipton Road, Settle, North Yorkshire BD24 9BD • 01729 823 814

HOW MUCH? Double rooms from £135 a night.

ROOMS 17 Double Rooms & Suites.

La Rosa Hotel

This unique Whitby hotel puts Victorian seaside fun centre stage

Described as 'more boudoir than boutique', La Rosa puts Victorian seaside fun centre stage in eight lovingly furnished rooms in an elegant Georgian townhouse that was once a favourite of Lewis Carroll. Facing the hotel across the picturesque harbour are the ruins of Whitby Abbey, the inspiration for Bram Stoker's Dracula, making this place one cool literary stay – and a romantic one too.

La Rosa is certainly unique, but it's also elegant and comfortable, with guest rooms each individually decorated according to a specific theme. Quirky retro furniture, found objects and fabulously sourced bric-a-brac evoke various dreams and themes, from the Swan-themed La Rosa and French-themed Sacre-Coeur (both with sea views and free-standing baths), to cosy Little Red with its four-poster bed and shower. One room evokes Lewis Carroll's study, another – Stoker – looks across to the ruins of Whitby Abbey, while the top-floor Crow's Nest apartment can comfortably accommodate six people in three bedrooms.

Four of the rooms have sea views but even those that don't are adorned with luxury features, from the huge bed in 'Arabesque' to the massive bath in 'Saloon'. What's more, half the rooms and also the apartment are dog-friendly. There are no TVs – the hotel provides quite enough entertainment without that! – but there is good wifi and a great selection of books and vinyl in the hotel's cosy Cocktail Library, which is the perfect complement to the hotel's Victorian Tearoom, where homemade cakes and other goodies are available throughout the day. Breakfast is delivered to your room each morning in a picnic hamper and is a delicious mix of eggs, yoghurt, fruit and pastries.

Finally, La Rosa is handy for just about everywhere you might want to see in Whitby, from the Abbey to the beach to the town's legendary Magpie chippy, and also a terrific base for the rest of the North Yorkshire coast.

CONTACT 5 East Terrace, Whitby, North Yorkshire YO21 3HB • 01947 606 981
HOW MUCH? Double rooms from £105 to £165 a night, including breakfast. Apartment £285 a night.
ROOMS 8 Guest Rooms.

Devonshire Fell Hotel

A dozen chic rooms in an intimate hotel high above Burnsall in the Yorkshire Dales

Situated in an idyllic Yorkshire Dales location on a hillside above the small village of Burnsall, not far from Grassington, the boutique little sister to the nearby Devonshire Arms offers a more intimate setting than the larger hotel, with just 16 boutique-style guest rooms. It's a small, originally Edwardian hotel, and we love the feel here since it's so unexpected, switching from traditional exterior to contemporary interior in the blink of an eye.

First the rooms, which are a thoroughly modern experience all round – 'city chic in the countryside' they say – with bold colours, vibrant designs and stylish furnishings contrasting with the timeless rural views. Little extras make you feel special, from herbal teas to hot-water bottles in each room, and all rooms – from the entry-level Classic to Superior and Luxury – all come with flatscreen Freeview TVs, Bluetooth speakers, king-size beds, contemporary bathrooms with posh toiletries, tea- and coffee-making facilities and complimentary biscuits. More expensive rooms are on the whole more spacious with slightly better views and maybe a walk-in shower as well as a bath, while the open-plan Fell Suites are large enough for a family of four, with a spacious seating area, sofa bed and two bathrooms. All rooms are dog-friendly, which is just as well, given the countryside – and country walks – on offer from your doorstep. Downstairs there's a bar and a conservatory where you can enjoy afternoon tea, while the two AA-rosette Fell restaurant serves a terrific, well-priced menu based around the estate's local produce. Bear in mind too that if you drive down to Bolton Abbey you can use the Devonshire's health club and spa facilities there – very welcome indeed if you've made the most of the walks on offer there, or to Grassington, or the Craven Arms pub in Appletreewick.

CONTACT Burnsall, Grassington, North Yorkshire BD23 6BT • 01756 718 111

HOW MUCH? Double rooms £129–£259 a night.

ROOMS 12 Guest Rooms.

Lord Crewe Arms

A cosy country hotel in a glorious location, with history to spare

This much-loved inn on the Durham-Northumberland border is an extraordinary building with an extraordinary history – a 12th-century former abbot's lodgings that dominates the impeccably preserved village of Blanchland, tucked under the local moors. Inside the main building, it's all stone corridors, soaring ceilings, heraldic shields, hidden nooks and majestic fireplaces, including one that hides a secret Priest's Hole, where Jacobite rebels once sheltered.

There are guest rooms in the old abbot's residence and the restored miners' cottages that flank the adjacent cobbled square, and while no two are the same, you can count on a certain updated country-chic style. They're classed as Cosy (the smallest), Canny or Champion (the best), though all feature king-size beds, robes, aromatherapy toiletries and carefully selected art and furniture. The Champion rooms and the two suites also boast Nespresso machines, and the suites are particularly lovely, especially Blackdene, a charming cottage duplex with an open log fire and a winding staircase to an upstairs bedroom. Colours throughout are earthy and muted, as restful as the peaceful surroundings, where the loudest sound you'll hear in the morning is birdsong. Breakfast is a sophisticated start to the day, with homebaked bread, locally smoked salmon, eggs benedict or the full fry-up. Drinking in the medieval Crypt bar and eating in the Bishop's Dining Room is as atmospheric at it sounds, while grassy gardens back onto the old priory church.

The hotel is a perfect place from which to explore either County Durham or Northumberland – it's a short trip over the lonely moors either way, to Stanhope in Weardale or Hexham and Hadrian's Wall. They're a bit of a venue for country sports and outdoor activities, too, or for just enjoying the local walks and bike rides. It's also a pretty sensational wedding venue.

CONTACT The Square, Blanchland, Durham DH8 9SP • 01434 675 469

HOW MUCH? Double rooms from £139 a night.

ROOMS 24 Guest Rooms & Suites.

40 Winks Guesthouse

An opulent Durham guesthouse with luxury rooms and views of the cathedral

They didn't hold back when decorating 40 Winks, a fancy Durham guesthouse that is a place of plush fabrics, patterned wallpaper and chandeliers. It's a little bit of opulence in a peaceful part of the city and a lovely place to stay if you want to explore historic Durham and its surroundings. Situated on a cobbled street above the river Wear, you can see the cathedral tower from four of the guest bedrooms – and you can walk to it in under 10 minutes.

This Grade II-listed Victorian townhouse offers nine guest bedrooms spread across its first and second floors. All have themes that tend towards opulent decor, whether that's floral, Gothic or regal. They range from the garden-view Woodland Rooms to the Cathedral Rooms at the front, including the master Gala Room, which has both a roll-top bath and a super-king-size bed, plus tremendous views of the cathedral. For all its modern conveniences (Smart TVs and wifi included), 40 Winks retains the character of its era, all set off with elegant upholstery and damask wallpaper. It's a similar story in the other named rooms. The Woodland Rooms are cosier and share a modern aesthetic, which means more pared-back styling but no less comfort. Whichever you choose, you'll have a king-sized bed, an en-suite with Molton Brown toiletries provided, and the usual inclusions of tea, coffee and a TV (the Cathedral Rooms even have decanters of whisky for a cheeky nightcap).

The grand staircase that leads from the reception to your bedroom is a striking introduction, with a bold bird-print on the walls and tiered chandeliers. The Snug room is a guest lounge with playful prints on the cushions and walls and an honesty bar with an impressive selection of wine and the hotel's own branded spirits. The breakfast room is no less flamboyant – all reds and golds – and makes a luxurious backdrop for a highly-rated breakfast that's the perfect start to a day in the city.

CONTACT 40 South Street, Durham DH1 4QP
• 01913 803 000
HOW MUCH? Double rooms with breakfast from £199 to £240 a night.
ROOMS 9 Guest Rooms.

Headlam Hall

Elegant rooms in a Durham country house hotel with a spa and golf course on site

Headlam Hall has all the elements for a relaxing stay in the Durham Dales. It's a country house hotel between Barnard Castle and Darlington, with comfortable bedrooms, a cosy bar, a great restaurant and well-tended gardens — not to mention its golf course and spa. The list of facilities is one that you might expect from a large hotel in the hands of a corporate giant, but this place is family-run and has just 38 rooms. Stay here and when you're walking in the walled garden, eating dinner in The Orangery, or just swimming a few lengths of the pool, you experience a sense of fortunate exclusivity that befits the surroundings of this elegant 17th-century mansion house.

Bedrooms range from the spacious Lord Gainford suite in the main house, with its four-poster bed and garden views, to the light and airy modern rooms above the spa. There are dog-friendly options, too, in The Mews which offers direct access to the outside, or the hotel's self-catering Hideaway. Whichever room you opt for, you'll find a flatscreen TV and wifi and tea- and coffee-making facilities, and Molton Brown toiletries to top it off. For breakfast, lunch and dinner, head downstairs in the main house for Modern British food served in The Orangery or, in warm weather, out on the patio. The Library Bar offers a cosy place for a drink and a less formal place to dine that's dog-friendly too.

Spa and golf breaks are available, or you can pay a small additional charge to access the spa facilities, which include a 15-metre pool, a sauna, steam room and gym as well as treatment rooms and café. With all this on site, there's little reason to go off exploring, and the hotel is basically a good place to do nothing at all. But you're well placed should you want to do so. There are lovely walks in Teesdale, and Barnard Castle, with the fascinating Bowes Museum, is only a few miles away. The Yorkshire Dales are half an hour's drive, as is the coast.

CONTACT Near Gainford, Darlington, Durham DL2 3HA • 01325 730 238
HOW MUCH? Double rooms from £145 a night.
ROOMS 38 Guest Rooms & Suites.

Matfen Hall

An elegant country house hotel in Northumberland with a golf course and spa

On arrival at Matfen Hall the valet will park your car, the concierge will whisk your luggage to your room and you will be offered a welcome drink in The Great Hall as you check in. All this sets the tone for your stay at this five-star hotel, which occupies a Gothic mansion in the Northumberland countryside, not far from Hadrian's Wall. Set in 300 acres of stunning parkland, there's a championship golf course, a spa and a choice of places to eat. It is the quintessential country house hotel, with all the comfort and luxury that implies, and yet it is so much more – with grandeur, opulence and an attention to detail that sets it apart.

There are 65 rooms and suites – book any and you can expect classic but contemporary decor in tune with the elegance of the place. Of course, your room has a minibar, and yes, good coffee is available, courtesy of a Nespresso machine. Toiletries are from Penhaligon's of London, and all beds are fitted with the finest 300 TC Egyptian cotton sheets. These may be minor details for some (not us), but it's this sort of attention to them that is evidence of the service and style you can expect at Matfen Hall. And there's more besides. Book a suite for the extra space and marble bathroom, and get a seasonal flower arrangement too. For guests staying in the luxury suites and rooms, who arrive by plane or train into Newcastle, a chauffeur service is included in the rate.

Everyone who stays here has access to the spa's swimming pool, sauna and treatment rooms – and all guests are welcome to explore the beautifully-manicured grounds. Booking in for a round of golf or an afternoon tea in The Orangery are two pleasant ways to while away the day. Then, when evening arrives, dress for dinner and head to the Emerald Restaurant for fine dining after a cocktail in the cosy 1832 bar. There's a timeless appeal to all this that many will love, but if it's too formal for you, there's steak and seafood to enjoy at the more contemporary Cloisters Restaurant, ingeniously designed in a former courtyard .

Matfen Hall works equally well as a place to rest and relax as it does to celebrate a special occasion, but it's also well located as a base to explore the Northeast region. It's midway between Newcastle and the best-preserved bits of Hadrian's Wall, with Northumberland National Park stretching away to the north. Whether you get to see any of this will depend on whether you can tear yourself away from the hotel and its manifold comforts.

CONTACT Matfen Hall, Matfen, Northumberland NE20 0RH • 01661 886 500
HOW MUCH? Double rooms and suites with breakfast from £299 to £749 a night.
ROOMS 65 Guest Rooms & Suites.

Chillingham Manor

An elegant and very welcoming luxury B&B in a gorgeous Northumberland location

It would be hard to imagine anywhere more peaceful than this gorgeous three-bedroom B&B, tucked away in the tiny village of Chillingham in north Northumberland, very close to Alnwick, and handy for Bamburgh and its sandy beaches, the Cheviot Hills and the long-distance St Cuthberts Way. Set amid glorious countryside, it's a tempting stop-off for walkers looking for a bit of comfort, but really anyone would appreciate its to-the-manor-born elegance and the warm attentions of owners Ed and Mhairi Seymour, who are keen to make every guest's stay as special as possible.

The rooms on the first floor of this handsome late-18th-century property are extremely spacious and beautifully furnished, with a homeliness and attention to detail that would be impressive in a five-star hotel. All are light and welcoming, with views over the garden and castle grounds, and come with Smart TVs, Roberts radios, good wifi and tea- and coffee-making facilities. Two have super-king-size beds which can be configured as twins (the third has a regular king-size), with colourful and stylish headboards, while two of the bathrooms have separate showers as well as lovely deep baths; the other has a deep bath with a hand-held shower. All come with robes and White Company toiletries.

Among the public spaces, there's a cosy Morning Room with a wood-burning stove, full of books for lazy days, a large drawing room with a wood-burner, and a sociable dining room where they serve breakfast on demand between 8.30am and 10.30am (especially late risers can opt for brunch instead, which is served until midday). Breakfasts are delicious and encompass everything from a sumptuous 'Full Northumbrian' to pancakes, smashed avocados on sourdough and much more. Mhairi (a cook by trade) will provide dinner too, if you book the entire property.

Ed and Mhairi are huge advocates of the local area and are happy to help you seek out the best places nearby. They have dogs, so unfortunately you can't bring your own but you're welcome to take one of theirs for a walk, and there are lots of routes to choose from. The village itself is home to its own castle and the Visitor Centre for the world-famous Wild Cattle of Chillingham is a two-minute stroll away. All in all, if you're looking for somewhere comfortable and elegant to stay in a beautiful part of Northumberland, it would be hard to find a better or more welcoming place.

CONTACT Chillingham, Northumberland, NE66 5NP • 01668 215 614

HOW MUCH? Double rooms with breakfast from £155 a night.

ROOMS 3 Guest Rooms.

The Cookie Jar

A stylish and very comfortable boutique hotel in Alnwick's Castle Quarter

This ultra-stylish boutique hotel occupies a prime position between Alnwick Castle and the town's Bailiffgate Museum. Stay here and you're in capable hands. The Cookie Jar's quirky name is a nod to the experienced hotelier behind the business, Debbie Cook, who has put together a hotel that lives up to the family reputation for great places to stay (her husband was formerly chief exec at Hotel Malmaison/Hotel du Vin), and the property shares a sense of design-led luxury, but offers something altogether more personal. You'll feel it as soon as you step inside to be greeted by warm smiles and the hotel's signature treat – a jar of homemade cookies.

There are just 11 guest rooms in this converted former convent, a Grade-II listed building that's been thoroughly softened from its more austere previous incarnation while retaining a lot of character. Nowhere is that more apparent than in the flagship room – The Chapel – a spacious suite complete with stained glass windows, beneath which you can bathe in a free-standing copper bath. Other guest rooms vary in size and price but each is individually designed and decorated. What ties them together is the quality of furniture and amenities – Hypnos beds, en-suites with drench showers, Penhaligon's toiletries and locally-roasted coffee. You may notice that there's a common colour throughout: blue is extensively used, but it's so cleverly done that it's never too much. It's calming and warming thanks to different textures and shades, with complementary wood, leather and lights. You'll notice it everywhere, from the walls in your bedroom to the upholstered chairs in the 30-seater bistro downstairs. This, with its seasonal menu and 'aficionado' wine list (alongside a regular one), is a destination in its own right for dinners and afternoon teas. Breakfasts are served here too, and there's also a terrace overlooking the garden if you want to simply sit with a drink, and a lovely book-lined lounge at the front of the building.

Alnwick Castle, seat of the Duke of Northumberland and the backdrop for Harry Potter's Hogwarts, is just outside, so you don't need to travel to sightsee. For more inspiration, just look at the names of the guest rooms: all Cook family favourites in the Northeast area that make up a tick-list of places to visit. There's Harehope for shooting, Goswick for golf, the Holy Island of Lindisfarne and the castles of Bamburgh and Dunstanburgh. Thoroughly recommended!

CONTACT 12 Bailiffgate, Alnwick, Northumberland NE66 1LX • 01665 510 465
HOW MUCH? Double rooms from £180 a night including breakfast.
ROOMS 11 Guest Rooms.

Beadnell Towers

Boutique seaside hotel, restaurant and bar on the gorgeous Northumberland coast

A boutique hotel, restaurant and bar on the Northumberland coast, Beadnell Towers is one of those places that just feels right the minute you walk in. From the classy rooms to the welcoming bar and restaurant, we're going to be absolutely fine here, is the general vibe. 'Don't worry, be happy', in fact – and there's plenty to be happy about.

This 18th-century building in the small seaside village of Beadnell was given a complete makeover a couple of years ago, and the rooms now display a modern, country-house feel. You can expect original beams and fireplaces, plump cushions and thick, draped curtains, but also individually designed feature walls, bespoke furniture and sharp, stylish bathrooms. All have king-size or super-king-size beds. Some rooms have free-standing copper baths (the 'Muckle House' heritage room has two!), while the top-floor 'Craa's Nest' room has windows on three sides and sea and hillside views. One room is fully accessible with an en-suite wet-room, while several others on the ground floor are dog-friendly. Your pooch is all right in the bar too, and there's a dog-wash to the side of the hotel – handy, as you're close to lots of sandy beach walks.

The bar and restaurant change the tone and style slightly – less country, more seaside, and very cosy and hospitable. The menu's great, strong on fish and locally sourced produce, and the kitchen's open from breakfast until dinner via afternoon tea. It's a really handsome space, whether you're settling down for some oysters, a posh fish pie or a decent steak, and the locals use the bar as a place to drink so it has a buzzy feel a lot of the time, especially in summer.

Drag yourself away from the comforts of the Towers and you'll find yourself in one of the most dramatic parts of England, on perhaps the finest coastline in the country. The white sand beaches nearby are outstanding, and you can walk north to Seahouses (where owners David and Anna also have the Beach House Hotel) or south towards Dunstanburgh – the former has boat trips out to the puffin-filled Farne Islands, the latter is the site of a hugely atmospheric, ruined clifftop castle. Hop in the car and it's a five-mile drive to Bamburgh – site of another extraordinary castle and golden beach – or further to the causeway crossing to Lindisfarne, known as Holy Island. You really are spoilt for choice, but don't worry – all you have to do when you get back is choose another dish from the tempting menu and sink into your plump bed at brilliant Beadnell Towers.

CONTACT The Wynding, Beadnell, Northumberland NE67 5AY • 01665 721 211

HOW MUCH? Double rooms with breakfast from £119 to £179 a night.

ROOMS 18 Guest Rooms & Suites.

The Whittling House

Country-seaside chic at a restaurant with rooms on the spectacular Northumberland coast

It's not hard to put together a great seaside break – a walk along the beach, a terrific meal and a comfortable night in stylish surroundings. Even better if you can do it all in the same place and under the same roof. Step forward The Whittling House in Alnmouth, a restaurant with rooms in an under-the-radar location on the spectacular Northumberland coast, just yards from the most alluring of golden beaches.

The pretty village is something of a timewarp, with its painted houses and quiet streets, set back from a wide, sandy beach that's perfect for pottering, beachcombing and long coastal walks. While The Whittling House fits right into the overall vibe, however, there's nothing old-fashioned about it at all. Ten gorgeous, characterful bedrooms offer a comfortable night's sleep in king-size or super-king-size beds, each with a smart en-suite bathroom. Colours and furnishings echo the overall seaside-country theme, and amenities have been carefully thought through, from bathrobes and ironing boards to coffee machines. Some of the rooms are dog-friendly too – and your pooch even gets their own bed.

Meanwhile, the restaurant is their secret weapon – a handsome wood-panelled, fire-warmed space where a hearty cooked breakfast is included in the rate. Enjoy an Alnmouth G&T here while they serve up a mostly Northumberland-inspired menu that is big on the local seafood, from Lindisfarne oysters to locally-caught lobster from around the Northumberland shores – the same owners run the renowned Potted Lobster in nearby Bamburgh. The restaurant is a modish British delight throughout, whether it's rib-eyes and fillets from the grill, rare-breed pork, or classic fish and chips (with lager-and-lemon batter, pea puree and triple-cooked chips).

Suitably fortified, it's time for you to discover what the locals already know – that the Northumberland coast really is one of the UK's hidden gems. The sands and dunes stretch from Alnmouth up to historic Bamburgh and Lindisfarne (Holy Island) and beyond, to the border town of Berwick-upon-Tweed and its extraordinary stone ramparts. There are amazing, ruined castles at places like Dunstanburgh and Warkworth; or you can spend the day just five miles up the road at mighty Alnwick Castle and Garden, film location for the 'Harry Potter' series. That's just for starters on a great seaside break staying – we couldn't help ourselves! – at the magic Whittling House.

CONTACT 24-25 Northumberland Street, Alnmouth, Northumberland NE66 2RA • 01665 463 001
HOW MUCH? Double rooms with breakfast from £150 a night.
ROOMS 10 Guest Rooms.

THE POPPY
SAFETY MATCHES
MADE IN INDIA
WIMCO

Lucky Dip

Bar Convent

17 Blossom Street York YO24 1AQ

Dating from 1686, this B&B occupies England's oldest living convent – pretty cool and very York, given the history all around you in this city. There are smart twins and doubles with either en-suite or shared facilities, some good-value singles and a couple of larger family rooms, plus use of a sitting room, kitchen and top-floor recreation room with rooftop views – so it's a good self-catering base for couples and families. Breakfast is served in an extremely handsome ground-floor courtyard café and a tranquil hideaway garden out back.

Beach House Hotel

12A St Aidans, Seahouses, Northumberland NE68 7SR

Seahouses is the closest you get to a seaside resort in this part of Northumberland, and this small seafront hotel offers terrific sea views and has 30 family and dog-friendly contemporary guest rooms, making it an ideal base for this glorious stretch of coast. Very handy for the Farne Islands and with a restaurant and bar open all day every day.

The Black Swan at Oldstead

Oldstead, North Yokshire YO61 4BL

Oldstead's 16th-century country inn has the ambience, ales and rolling rural views that are de rigueur in these parts, but let's be honest, you're probably here to worship at the table of local boy Tommy Banks, and why not? He has turned his family's Black Swan pub into a Michelin-starred destination of some renown, with a field-to-fork ethos that starts in the vast kitchen gardens and plunders neighbouring farms for the very best produce. Luckily, its guest bedrooms are all gorgeous, and each comes with a table reservation.

The Blue Lion

Main Road, East Witton, Leyburn, North Yorkshire DL8 4SN

Current owners Paul and Helen Klein have built an impressive reputation for this beautifully located Yorkshire Dales inn, which has 15 simply decorated and contemporary bedrooms and great food and drink on offer too. Things to do nearby? Well, that's the Yorkshire Dales right out there, and the team have walking maps available at reception.

Jesmond Dene House

Jesmond Dene Road, Newcastle-upon-Tyne, Tyne & Wear NE2 2EY

This beautifully converted Arts-and-Crafts mansion enjoys a leafy location in the heart of Newcastle. Twice winner of 'Best Small Hotel' in the region, it has 40 distinctive and individually decorated bedrooms and a pretty wonderful restaurant, serving both informal all-day food and haute cuisine in the evening (plus a famous cream tea). You may find yourself not going into the centre of Newcastle at all. Which would be a pity, but quite understandable.

Jet Black Jewel

10 Skinner Street, Whitby, North Yorkshire YO21 3AH

Situated in the unique Yorkshire seaside town of Whitby, this boutique accommodation wears its idiosyncratic heart on its sleeve, with eight rooms individually decorated to represent a historical tale about Whitby, from exiled Maharajahs to Robin Hood. The ground-floor café-bar is open from breakfast onwards, and it has a similarly inspired decor as well as a wide-ranging menu that does more to sell the offbeat charms of the town to you.

Pipe and Glass Inn

West End, South Dalton, Beverley,
East Yorkshire HU17 7PN

This picture-perfect East Yorkshire country inn has nine boutique guest rooms, its own kitchen garden and fabulous Michelin-starred food. Romance-seeking couples will find all they need for a sumptuous weekend.

Yorebridge House

24 Northumberland St, Alnmouth, Northumberland
NE66 2RA

Made out of a former Victorian school and some associated farm buildings, this is a truly stylish boutique hotel that just happens to be set amongst some of the most compelling scenery the Yorkshire Dales has to offer.

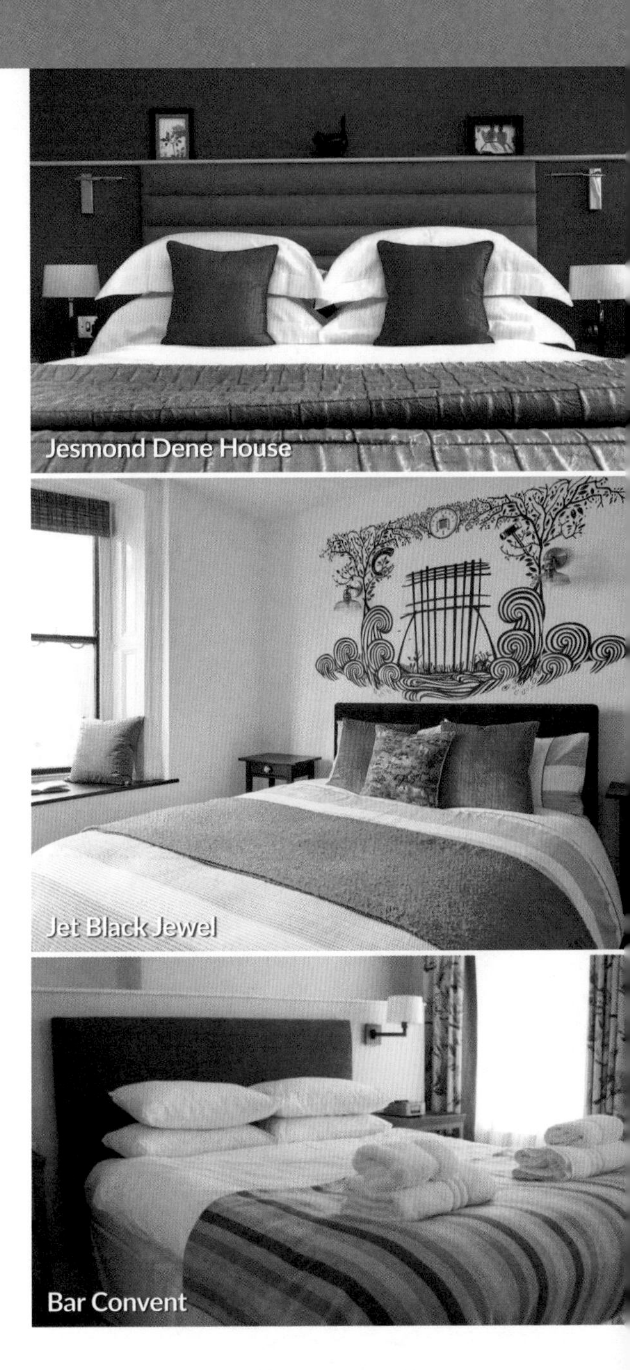

Jesmond Dene House

Jet Black Jewel

Bar Convent

The Northwest

Cheshire • Lancashire • Cumbria

We reckon that the Northwest is England's most diverse region by some way. It's contains the largest metropolitan areas in the country after London, with Manchester and Liverpool and the large towns in between more or less one large conurbation, and these give way to the gentle countryside of rural Lancashire to the north – an often overlooked county that is home to some magnificent countryside in the Ribble Valley and Forest of Bowland along with some terrific places to stay. Beyond are the high peaks and fells of Cumbria and the Lakes and the western fringes of the Yorkshire Dales. Needless to say, there are some very cool places to stay in Manchester and Liverpool, both of which make perfect destinations for a short or weekend break. As for Cumbria, it has been catering to tourists for a century or more and has hotels and B&Bs for all tastes and budgets in every scenic corner.

Another Place, The Lake, p.244

The Spinning Block

Gorgeous boutique rooms in a fabulous designer conversion of an historic mill building in the Ribble Valley

It's hard to think of a more triumphant re-imagining of an old industrial space than the 1823 Spinning Block Hotel. It forms part of the Holmes Mill complex in Clitheroe, a small town at the heart of Lancashire's gorgeous Ribble Valley that two centuries ago was a thriving textile centre, spinning and weaving cloth that was sent around the world. The old mill buildings – long disused – have been lovingly restored as a food, drink and entertainment venue, capped now by this fine addition of a boutique hotel in the former spinning sheds.

The Victorians built industrial complexes like they built cathedrals, so the scale and space is magnificent. Thirty-nine individually designed rooms and suites occupy carved-out quarters in a soaring building that retains much of its original structure, from the original brickwork and solid beams to the cast-iron pillars. These handsome, grown-up rooms in earthy, on-trend colours hit all the right notes, from sharp bathrooms with walk-in, monsoon rain showers to chunky wooden furniture and classy fabrics. Two family rooms and two suites provide more space, while in the tower penthouse suite you get loft-style living on the edge of beautiful Lancashire countryside.

The hotel is only the half of it though, because the entire mill complex is at your service – and it's stunning. You can have breakfast in the bistro, bar and grill, a sensational space fashioned from the old spinning block, with a sinuous bar, clubby leather sofas and chairs, and a dramatic warehouse-style feel that's straight out of New York. The old boiler house contains the popular Beer Hall and Brewery, there's a farm shop-cum-deli and juice bar called the Food Hall, as well as an indie cinema, in the former weaving shed, and plenty of outdoor space for summer drinks and lazy lunches. You want to grab an artisan ice cream or some air-dried ham? This is the place.

If it sounds like the ideal urban-country getaway, that's because it is, and if you don't already know the area, you're in for a treat. Although its heyday as a centre of textile production is long gone, this is no old industrial wasteland. Clitheroe is a charming market town with the smallest Norman castle in England, and you're on the doorstep of the Forest of Bowland AONB. The Ribble Valley sculpture trail is one of the gems of the town, with 20 works of art set in peaceful Brungerley Park. However you spin it, the Spinning Block is a winning choice for a modern take on a country weekend away.

CONTACT Holmes Mill, Greenacre Street, Clitheroe, Lancashire BB7 1EB • 01200 407 120
HOW MUCH? Double rooms from £80 a night.
ROOMS 39 Guest Rooms.

HY Hotel

Great family-friendly accommodation in a serviced apart-hotel in genteel Lytham St Annes, close to miles of sandy beach

Looking for a traditional seaside family break in the northwest of England, with a long promenade, Victorian pier and golden sands? No, not Blackpool – we're talking the altogether more refined setting of Lytham St Annes, just three miles south of the big resort, which offers a far more gentle experience all round. And there's accommodation to match, too, in the shape of the welcoming self-catering apartments at HY Hotel, just a block back from the promenade and a short walk from the vintage pier.

These are terrific, open-plan home-from-home apartments, handy for seeing the local Fylde coast or zipping up the road to Blackpool by bus and tram. They come in one, two and three-bedroom versions, sleeping two to eight people, and are handsomely decorated and furnished in a thoroughly modern style. There's plenty of space for families to spread out – a fully equipped kitchen in each, and a washer-dryer, while each bathroom has a walk-in rain shower. But where HY Hotel scores over a regular apartment complex is in its hotel-standard facilities. That means 24-hour reception and daily housekeeping, but also real bonuses like an on-site gym, a pool and a spa, with all sorts of treatments, a Jacuzzi, a sauna and a steam room. And with the wide sands and the promenade close by, you've really got the best of both worlds, whatever the weather. The apartments are dog-friendly, too, and with the open coastline and nearby woods and gardens, Lytham St Annes is a great place for a break for all members of the family. Top tip – take your bikes and explore the seafront – if you're feeling adventurous you could even make it all the way to Fleetwood for a plate of fish and chips before heading back.

Grab-and-go Starbucks coffee and croissants are available for breakfast, and there are supermarkets close by for self-caterers (delivery can be arranged). There are plenty of nice places to eat in St Anne's in any case – either in the seaside area or in the nearby town of Lytham, a 10-minute drive away. Our favourite lunch spot, and completely in keeping with the genteel vibe of St Anne's, is the pavilion café in the town gardens just over the road from the hotel.

It's not full-on, kiss-me-quick Blackpool, not by a long chalk, but it is a different side of the traditional British seaside break, and this luxury apartment option makes a comfortable base for seeing the sights.

CONTACT 318–328 Clifton Drive North, Lytham St Annes, Lancashire FY8 2PB • 01253 720 072
HOW MUCH? Apartments from £110 a night.
ROOMS 35 Guest Apartments each sleeping 2–8.

The Freemasons at Wiswell

A slice of country refinement in the heart of Lancashire's Ribble Valley

Tucked down a lane in the middle of Wiswell village, this pub sits among the moors and hills of Lancashire's Ribble Valley – not only a locally renowned place to eat but also a comfortable base for what is a very underrated spot. Hundreds of years ago, The Freemasons was actually three cottages, one of which was a masonic lodge. Nowadays, it's the food that is the star of the show here. Local fresh produce is always part of the menu so expect the freshest veg, Lancashire beef, Manx lobsters and scallops, plus unusual signature starters like truffle cheese hot dogs and lamb fat and rosemary brioche. You can even book a table in the kitchen if you want to be close to the action!

We're glad to say that breakfast is included in their rates, and it's almost worth coming here for this alone (duck fat fried bread, anyone?), although the rooms themselves are pretty special too. Named Mr Fox, Mr Hare, Partridge and Grouse, and located in the building next door, each is uniquely styled and elegant, with a contemporary country look and feel, comfortable super-king-size beds and high-quality linen, underfloor heating, all singing-all-dancing lighting, plus tea- and coffee-making facilities (including Nespresso machines) and bottled water. Reinforcing the no-expense-spared feel, they also all have 50-inch Smart TVs, Sonos sound systems and fast wifi. Bathrooms are gorgeous and spacious: two rooms have mezzanines with roll-top bathtubs and they all have enormous showers, toiletries and robes.

There's no question that it's a terrific place to stay, not only for the food and the overall sense of being thoroughly pampered, but also because it's such a great base for the countryside around. There are fabulous walks into the nearby Wiswell Moors, and you're also close to the glorious landscapes of the Forest of Bowland.

CONTACT Wiswell, Clitheroe, Lancashire BB7 9DF • 01254 822 218
HOW MUCH? Double rooms £280–£330 a night.
ROOMS 4 Guest Rooms.

Shireburn Arms

This 17th-century pub with rooms makes a great base for exploring the Ribble Valley and the Tolkein Trail

The rural scenery around Hurst Green in the Ribble Valley brings walkers from far and wide to enjoy the tranquillity of this relatively undiscovered area, and we're pleased to report that this 17th-century hostelry offers excellent and reasonably priced food and a handful of rooms to those who want to stay overnight. Most of the pub's rooms have been refurbished in a contemporary country style with antique furnishings, comfy beds with goosedown pillows, en-suite bathrooms with toiletries, flatscreen TVs, ample storage, bottled water and tea-making facilities. The bedrooms nearest the reception desk are probably the best, while at the other end of the hotel, room three has an enormous four-poster bed.

Breakfast is included with the room price, and head chef Nathan Riddehough and his band of merry men create consistently good dishes at lunch and dinner, with roast dinners, beef brisket, steak pies, delicious risotto and scrumptious desserts. The service can't be faulted, and, with its roaring fire and plenty of seating, the pub is also a good place to stop by for just a drink. During summer, an outside patio space is utilized for outdoor dining.

There are views out to Pendle Hill and two significant rivers, the Ribble and the Hodder, the latter spanned by a 16th-century packhorse bridge that Cromwell and his troops used to cross the river when advancing on Preston during the Civil War. Not far from here, there are more historic sights, notably Stoneyhurst College – a collection of mainly 16th-century sandstone buildings famous for being the place where JRR Tolkien wrote 'The Hobbit' and 'Lord of the Rings' when he stayed here during World War II. You can even follow a Tolkien Trail, which begins near the Shireburn Arms and circles back via the river to the pub – a walk of around five miles that gives you a good taste of the Ribble Valley.

CONTACT Whalley Rd, Hurst Green, Clitheroe, Lancashire BB7 9QJ • 01254 826 678
HOW MUCH? Double Rooms with breakfast from £77 a night, Suites & Family Rooms from £125.
ROOMS 21 Guest Rooms & Suites.

Number One St Luke's

An award-winning B&B in a quiet part of Blackpool that prides itself on a personal service and attention to detail

Definitely not your average Blackpool B&B – when Mark and Claire Smith first opened Number One St Luke's in a regular house in a residential street in a quiet part of South Shore, the boutique stylings and all-round gorgeousness stuck out like a sore thumb. Roll on a few years, and Blackpool has upped its game in all respects, insofar as there are now a fair few contemporary accommodation choices around. But Number One still manages to keep its nose in front – it was Visit Britain's 'B&B of the Year' a few years back, and there's a personal service here that's very appealing if you're tired of bland, identikit places to stay.

The house style is glam-boutique rather than understated – this is Blackpool, after all! – and you've got the lot in each of three individually styled rooms, from whirlpool baths to a hot tub outside in the garden. For an intimate Blackpool romantic retreat, we reckon you could hardly do better.

There are also more rooms (and sea views) at their bigger seaside hotel, Number One South Beach, which is not far away and offers a choice of 14 rooms with names like 'Passion' and 'Decadence', many with balconies and sea and promenade views, king-size beds and whirlpool baths, while two of the front rooms ('Indulge' and 'Spirit') have contemporary four-posters and spacious balconies. The in-house bar here is always open for guests while a bookings-only restaurant takes care of lazy nights when all you want to do is chill, South Beach style!

From either hotel, it's just a short walk to the Pleasure Beach or to the seafront for the tram into town. So you can leave the car at home. Or, like Claire, if you have an electric car, you can charge it overnight at their very own, universal electric car charging socket, making both hotels a perfect car-free option.

CONTACT 1 St Luke's Road Blackpool FY4 2EL • 01253 343 901

HOW MUCH? Double rooms from £130 a night, including breakfast.

ROOMS 3 + 14 Guest Rooms.

The Cartford Inn

This Lancashire inn is a shining beacon of good cooking and warm hospitality

If ever there was an advertisement for the benefits of the entente-cordiale, then The Cartford Inn is surely it – a contemporary inn situated in a perfect position on the river Wyre in deepest rural Lancashire. It's the creation of Anglo-French couple Julie and Patrick Beaume, who founded this foodie inn almost 20 years ago, and is a shining beacon of good cooking and warm hospitality in a beautiful rural location. Originally confined to just the front of the building, Julie and Patrick added an extension and more bedrooms in 2011, and since then have converted the outbuildings to a deli and gallery and private dining space. They have also added a couple of modernist cabins that serve as high-end suites. The guest rooms are all different, and reflect Julie's tastes in contemporary art, with bright and vibrant colours and all sorts of eclectic features. They vary from cosy Deluxe doubles to the fabulous cabin suites across the car park, which not only have record decks and a supply of vinyl but also heated balconies so you can enjoy your rather special view all year round – just one detail among many that sets The Cartford Inn apart from more run-of-the-mill places. Seven rooms have baths as well as spacious walk-in showers, and all the rooms come with comfy beds, good wifi, Smart TVs, tea, coffee and water; some also have Sonos sound systems and digital radios.

The bar and restaurant is a relaxed space that matches the playful style of the rest of the inn, with up-cycled timber and intriguing art. The menu includes a few French crowd-pleasers – snails, French onion soup, fruits de mer – along with more recognizably local dishes, such as cockles and suet pudding, and seasonal ingredients like locally foraged mushrooms and hearty Lancashire staples like black pudding, oxtail and lamb's hearts. Stop off at the deli to get something to take home, and say a big fat 'merci' to Julie and Patrick for meeting up all those years ago and creating something unique – vive la difference!

CONTACT Cartford Lane, Little Eccleston, Near Preston, Lancashire PR3 0YP • 01995 670 166
HOW MUCH? Double rooms £190–£280 a night, including breakfast.
ROOMS 15 Guest Rooms & Suites.

Randy Pike

A one-of-a-kind boutique bolthole featuring stunning suites with huge bathrooms

There are boutique B&Bs – and then there's the glorious, one-of-a-kind Randy Pike, the designer bolthole that's also the home of local restaurateurs Andy and Chrissy Hill. Three suites have been carved out of this Victorian gentleman's residence, and they are simply stunning ensembles featuring hand-carved beds, designer fabrics, rococo touches and absolutely massive, luxurious bathrooms (variously described as nearly the size of Belgium, Luxembourg 'or another small European principality' – you get the idea, these are big bathrooms).

Individual they most certainly are, but the suites do have some common features, with wonderful wooden floors and great views looking out over the woods around the building. Andy makes his fab music collection available on the in-room sound systems, and there are drinks on arrival and private gardens to stroll in, which come complete with their own Dr Who Tardis. There is a further place to stay in the amazing Juniper House, which is basically another spacious suite with a vast bedroom and views over the lake, equipped with an Alexa speaker, big squashy sofas, a minibar and Nespresso machine. The owners bring breakfast to your door so you don't even have to move, and transfers are offered to their excellent Grasmere restaurant, the Jumble Room, which serves up hearty seasonal food in a relaxed and bohemian environment.

As for the location, not only are you within reach of plenty of attractions, including the local National Trust properties, but Randy Pike is also within easy reach of the magnificent lakeland fells, which offer some of the best walking routes in the UK. There are plenty of B&Bs to be found around nearby Ambleside, but for a different kind of stay in glorious surroundings, Randy Pike really does stand out from the crowd.

CONTACT Low Wray, Cumbria LA22 0JP • 01539 436 088
HOW MUCH? Double rooms with breakfast from £200 a night.
ROOMS 3 Guest Suites.

Brimstone Hotel

Boutique luxury combined with sublime landscapes and the best walking the Lake District has to offer

The Lake District has something for everyone, not just thrill seekers, and nowhere proves that point better than The Brimstone Hotel. The region prides itself on its fine dining with 11 restaurants sharing 13 Michelin stars between them, so where better to base yourself than in the heart of the National Park where the sumptuous surroundings of the Brimstone will make soggy sandwiches in a howling gale feel like they are creations from another universe. This is one of the Lakes' finest boutique hotels, and is housed in a slate-clad building perfectly in keeping with its surroundings. Situated in one of the Lake District's most beautiful valleys, and with some of the region's best walking on its doorstep, it has everything that people come to the Lake District for, but the approach is as contemporary as it gets, with an emphasis on comfort, good food and creating a welcoming home-from-home.

There are 16 rooms in all, which are large and clad in cool and contemporary colours and brimming with gadgets, notably groovy dimmer switches and pushbutton curtains, though ironically only the best rooms also boast a suitably retro open fire. However, although the Brimstone may be a metropolitan sort of place, it's firmly anchored in the Lakes and the breathtaking landscape that surrounds them, and they make it easy to get out and about.

Breakfasts are as hearty as you need for a spot of fell-walking, and anyone who doesn't have their own kit can rent waterproof clothing and rucksacks with OS maps. And when you come back, cold and hungry, they can have scones and tea or sizzling steak sandwiches waiting for you in the cosy lounge and reading room. There's also an indoor-outdoor pool, sauna and steam room where you can soak away hiking induced aches and pains, or just relax and drift away.

CONTACT Ambleside, Cumbria LA22 9JD • 01539 438 062
HOW MUCH? Double rooms £490–£620 a night.
ROOMS 16 Guest Rooms & Suites.

Another Place, The Lake

A contemporary lakeside hotel on the shores of Ullswater that does everything just right

If you're going to go to the trouble of updating a country house hotel in the Lake District – where there's lots of competition – you need to do it right, so kudos to Another Place, The Lake. Handsomely sited on the shores of Ullswater, it's stylish yet unstuffy, and properly family- and dog-friendly – the sort of place that offers wild swimming, stand-up paddleboarding and kayaking from their own jetty and has muddy wellies by the door. But there are also romantic lake views, convivial public spaces and three restaurants, all of which makes it a fabulous grown-up retreat too, handy for exploring the less-visited northern Lakes.

Rooms are split between the original Georgian country house and a new contemporary wing, shepherds huts and a treehouse in the grounds. They range from standard doubles up to family suites, with lake views a premium (and dog-friendly options available). If you want a four-poster bed, high ceilings and an original feature or two, then the main house is for you, though even here the rooms have been given a light, modern touch. Other rooms and suites feel more contemporary, so you might get a lake-view Juliette balcony, a designer sofa with a sheepskin throw, and a slipper bath. Bluetooth radio, fridge and drinks flask are standard throughout, and we love the thought that has gone into the overall guest-friendly concept – for example a stargazing beanbag under a bathroom skylight. Beyond the main building, you'll find Willow Cottage, a large family suite, while the latest additions are a contemporary treehouse and six lakeshore shepherds huts, sleeping two to four people.

Public areas flow seamlessly through both sections of the hotel in a kind of 'open-house' manner – you feel that you can plonk yourself down in any one of a number of cosy corners. The Living Space is a Scandi-style café-bar with a family-friendly bistro menu of burgers, salads, pasta and the like, and it spills out onto a lake-view terrace. The indoor pool is a beauty – 20 metres long with its own lake view – and there are also spa facilities for adults, with a sauna, treatment rooms and outdoor hot tub too. Outdoor activities loom large – there is wild swimming, stargazing swims, kayaying and stand-up paddle boarding, or you can drop the kids off at the impressive supervised Kids' Zone. The Rampsbeck Restaurant channels contemporary British cooking at its best, including produce from the vegetable patch in the grounds. Seasonal and fresh, every dish comes with signature flair and individuality.

CONTACT Watermillock, Ullswater, Cumbria CA11 0LP • 01768 486 442
HOW MUCH? Double rooms from £210 a night, family suites from £295, breakfast included.
ROOMS 47 Guest Rooms & Suites.

Storrs Hall Hotel

A beautiful Grade II-listed country house hotel right on the shores of Lake Windermere

With a position to die for right on the shores of Lake Windermere, Storrs Hall is like no other hotel in the area – a family-owned and -run country house that combines low-key intimacy with every contemporary comfort you could wish for. Situated in a beautiful Grade II-listed Georgian mansion, it has 36 rather special rooms, some of which are dog-friendly, a cosy bar and excellent restaurant and 17 partially wooded acres of lakeside grounds. It's also just a five-minute drive from the tourist honeypot of Bowness-on-Windermere. Little wonder that it was featured as one of The Times' 'Top 80 British Hotels' a few years back.

The 28 rooms in the hotel's main house range from cosy Classic rooms through to Superior and larger Deluxe rooms that come with or without lake views. Individually designed with a contemporary country feel, they're furnished with king-size beds, tea- and coffee-making facilities, good wifi and recently fitted bathrooms. The main difference between the different categories – and rates – is in the size of the rooms and bathrooms and whether they have a view of the lake. In addition there are six very contemporary (adults-only) glass-walled lakeside suites and a unique converted Boathouse for two, complete with lake-facing terrace, fire pit and hot tub. The Lakeside suites are inspired by the classic Georgian style of the main house and the natural environment they nestle in, and they have incredible views of the lake. They're somewhat Japanese in feel, open-plan and spacious, with super-king-size beds, chaise-longues, free-standing baths, separate walk-in showers, Smart TVs and a private terrace with a cedar hot tub. You can laze on the terrace with a book, utilize the space for some forest bathing therapy crossed with yoga, or enjoy a hot coffee after a dip in the lake. There's nothing else quite like them and like the rest of the hotel they work a rather special and welcoming magic.

Service throughout is terrific, and the hotel has a properly enticing bar, The Tower, so named for its ornate wooden bar which came from Blackpool Tower. They serve a menu of staples and classics between noon and 9pm, while a more formal restaurant with gorgeous lake views serves a refined and locally sourced menu each evening and for Sunday lunch. They'll also sort you out a packed lunch or picnic if you're taking off for the day on a hike; for the less energetic, afternoon tea is served every afternoon until 4.30pm.

CONTACT Bowness-on-Windermere, Cumbria LA23 3LG • 01539 447 111
HOW MUCH? Double rooms from £210 a night with breakfast; lakeside suites form £550 a night.
ROOMS 35 Guest Rooms & Suites + Boathouse.

The Yan

Boutique rooms and first-rate food in a gorgeous Lakeland location

It means 'number one' in local dialect, and there's a good chance that The Yan will be number one on your agenda after spending a night or two here or eating in the downstairs bistro. Part of the successful The Yan at Broadrayne business, which also includes glamping and a set of comfy holiday cottages, this bistro with rooms is their latest venture. A short hop north of Grasmere, it occupies a lovely old country property that enjoys panoramic views over the surrounding landscape and is decorated in a rustic contemporary style that will make anyone feel at home.

The seven upstairs rooms are each individually decorated and come in various shapes and sizes, as you would expect in a historic building like this. There are three cosy standard rooms and four deluxe rooms (with a full-sized double sofa bed) that will easily accommodate a family of four; and two rooms are dog-friendly – a nice thought in a region that is the perfect getaway for dogs as well as humans. Of the Yan's five self-catering options (three cottages, two apartments), the cottages are also dog-friendly. All of the rooms come equipped with Smart TVs, tea- and coffee-making facilities, great wifi and super-king-size beds with good-quality linen, and the beds can be changed into twins, if you prefer. Bathrooms are crisp and modern and come with rainfall showers and backlit heated mirrors.

Downstairs, there's a comfy open-plan lounge decorated in a similarly contemporary yet cosy country style, as well as the bistro, which is open to the public and serves hearty British comfort food from 3pm till 9pm – from huge helpings of homemade shepherds pie to gut-busting local burgers with all the trimmings: just the sort of food you need after walking on the fells. There's also a choice of sumptuous sharing platters as well as a range of delicious breakfast dishes. And if sustainability is important to you then The Yan ticks that box too, with eggs from their own chickens, honey from their bees, and electricity from a hydro-generator in nearby Tongue Gill.

Owners Dave and Sally are usually around, as is their daughter Jess, who's the operations director of the farm, while her husband and executive chef Will oversees the kitchen. All in all, then, a family affair, offering beautiful, very well-priced boutique rooms and great food in a gorgeous location. A winning formula, if ever there was one!

CONTACT Broadrayne Farm, Grasmere, Cumbria, LA22 9RU • 01539 435 055
HOW MUCH? Double rooms from £160 to £220 a night, including breakfast.
ROOMS 7 Guest Rooms.

Victorian House

A stylish and characterful B&B in Grasmere, one of the Lake District's most charming and historic villages

As one of the most popular spots in the Lake District, the charming village of Grasmere sees a lot of comings and goings during the day, with visitors hot on the Wordsworth trail or heading out onto the fells. But there's something magical about staying the night, as the sun sets on the hills and lake, and even better if it's somewhere with the style and character ofVictorian House. It's been a guest house since it opened in 1872 and retains its original quirks and proportions, but it has also been updated with real flair and style, designer furnishings, and a highly personal touch.

The rooms are right on the button – stylish, comfortable, and with locally-sourced hot drinks and coffee machines on request. They're beautifully turned out, with lots of natural light and garden views. 'Stargazer' rooms at the top of the house look straight out through large feature glass windows onto the fells, with telescopes provided to make the most of the superb dark skies. Some rooms are spacious enough to accommodate extra beds or travel cots for families, or you could book interconnecting rooms for a real family-friendly stay. 'Cosy' rooms do have a double bed but are more suited for solo guests, and there are dog-friendly rooms with hard flooring throughout. Other options include a two-room suite in an adjacent cottage – the feel and style is the same as in the main house – and even a gorgeous, light-flooded, riverside shepherds hut with full mod-cons: underfloor heating, rolltop bath and a private fire pit.

Meanwhile, Grasmere itself is a beauty, with its historic churchyard and Wordsworth graves, old-time gingerbread shop, and short stroll to the famous Wordsworth houses of Dove Cottage and Allan Bank. There are walks right from the doorstep to some of the Lake District's most alluring beauty spots or jump on the 599 for an open-top bus ride down to Ambleside and Windermere for boat cruises and more. The celebrated 555 bus also stops in the middle of the village and a ride on the top deck up to Keswick is not to be missed. And when the sun goes down, and the crowds go home, you have the quiet lanes and lakeside strolls to yourself, not forgetting the sanctity of Victorian House and its genteel comforts and home-from-home feel.

CONTACT Broadgate, Grasmere, Cumbria LA22 9TA • 01539 435 217
HOW MUCH? Double rooms £120–£150 a night, including breakfast.
ROOMS 20 Guest Rooms.

The Belsfield Hotel

An elegant hotel on the banks of Lake Windermere

Picture the kind of hotel you dream of staying at in the Lake District and you might well come up with somewhere that looks like The Belsfield. It's a quintessential English Lakes getaway, situated on the banks of Windermere with views of the water from its tranquil gardens, restaurant and best bedrooms. This place has been welcoming guests for well over a hundred years and retains a timeless appeal thanks to its classic architecture, refined decor, friendly staff and tempting afternoon teas. It's also just a short walk across the lawn to the Bowness-on-Windermere jetty, from where you can hop aboard a cruise around England's largest lake.

The Belsfield's bedrooms are set in six acres of grounds. All are en-suite and have the usual inclusions, but to really make the most of the location, we advocate a lake-view room or suite. There's simply nothing like waking up to views across Windermere and the Cumbrian peaks beyond. The style here is classic but contemporary – up-to-date but fitting the age of the place, with a soft colour palette, elegant fabrics and occasional period furniture, whether you choose the four-poster suite or a compact double. That style continues downstairs, where you can enjoy glorious vistas at breakfast time in the hotel's brasserie and restaurant, where huge sash windows frame panoramas across Windermere. High ceilings and white tablecloths make this a sophisticated setting for dining, but if the weather is favourable, the Garden Terrace is hard to beat for al fresco eating. Lunch includes sharing platters, salads and small plates. Enjoy a lazy afternoon's Aperol Spritz while admiring the beauty of Bowness Bay.

There's also an airy and welcoming lounge bar that comes into its own in the evenings when the marblesque bar gives off a cosy amber glow. It's the perfect place for an aperitif or a nightcap, with a varied menu of classic cocktails on offer. The hotel's location also means there are plenty of nearby options if you decide to venture out: it's a short stroll into the heart of Bowness while the charming village of Windermere makes for a pleasant afternoon excursion. For daytime adventures, World of Beatrix Potter is less than half-a-mile away and Windermere Lake Cruises depart beside the hotel. Beyond that, the rest of the Lake District National Park spreads in every direction – or you can relax and enjoy the views of the distant fells from your room.

CONTACT Kendal Rd, Bowness-on-Windermere, Cumbria LA23 3EL • 01539 442 448
HOW MUCH? Double rooms from £150 a night including breakfast.
ROOMS 62 Guest Rooms & Suites.

The Royal Oak

Contemporary comfort at a charming hotel in the Lake District's Borrowdale Valley

Stay at The Royal Oak and the windows of your room will offer a framed scene of the charming stone buildings of Rosthwaite village or of babbling Stonethwaite beck. Either way, the backdrop beyond will be the high fells of the northern Lake District. It's an area best described by walker, writer and champion of the area, Alfred Wainwright, who claimed: 'The Lake District is the loveliest part of England, and Borrowdale is the fairest of its valleys.' We're not going to argue with that.

Situated in the heart of this fair and lovely valley, The Royal Oak offers 24 double and triple rooms, along with a self-catering apartment that sleeps four people and a pair of 'bunk barns' out back that house four to six people. The hotel has been hosting visitors for at least 200 years but you might be surprised by the contemporary comfort of its guest rooms, which were fully refurbished in 2022. Crucially, for a village of stone cottages in the nation's most-loved National Park, it's been done with taste and style. Indeed, The Royal Oak was runner-up for the 2023 Cumbria Tourism 'Best Small Hotel Award'.

There's a modern feel throughout and bathrooms are particularly slick, with heated towel rails, metro tiles and backlit mirrors. The bedrooms are warmed by earthy, natural tones to complement both the original features and what you'll see outside. Crisp white bed linen, fluffy towels, toiletries and tea- and coffee-making facilities are among the standard room inclusions. All this will delight anyone who stays, but it's downstairs that identifies this as a place where walkers and dogs are as welcome as guests who simply want to relax. There's a bar, lounge and snug with patterned upholstery and feature walls, and spaces to read, play games or simply chat about the day's adventures. They serve a seasonal menu of farmhouse-style dinners and hearty breakfasts, and packed lunches are available to take away on your walks, and it's no surprise that the hotel recently won the Cumbria Life Magazine 'Casual Dining Experience' award.

It's the walking that most people come for, and there's something to suit most tastes, from gentle strolls along the beck to the serious hike up Scafell Pike. Keswick and Grasmere are easy enough to drive to, and Derwentwater and Buttermere are nearby. As Wainwright himself noted: 'Long experience of the needs of walkers has made Borrowdale folk adept at catering for outsize appetites and tired bodies.' The Royal Oak certainly does that – and in modern style.

CONTACT Stonethwaite, Cumbria CA12 5XB • 01768 777 214

HOW MUCH? Double rooms with breakfast from £100–£165 a night, Bunk Barns £180–£220, Apartment £220.

ROOMS 24 Guest Rooms.

Applegarth Villa

A glam five-star Lake District retreat up in Windermere village, this boutique hotel has 15 individually fashioned rooms with bold colours, designer furniture, sumptuous fabric and super-smart bathrooms with underfloor heating and mood lighting. They start at Deluxe and go up to Ultimate Luxury – which, in the case of the top two suites, means lavish apartment-sized spaces with the choice of either an enormous spa bath and private sun terrace or an eight-foot-wide circular bed in front of two panoramic windows. Most rooms have sweeping mountain views. Breakfast is a joy on a sunny day, with everything from crepes to eggs florentine on the menu, and there's no need to go elsewhere for dinner either, which is good value and artfully presented, with plenty of local produce (plus gluten-free dishes and catering for special diets). There's also a handsome oak-panelled bar with open fire for cosier Lake District nights.

CONTACT College Road, Windermere, Cumbria LA23 1BU • 01539 443 206

HOW MUCH? Double rooms £160–£385 and hot tub suites from £485 a night.

The Cavendish Arms

A perfect Lakeland hideaway and also an ideal base for exploring the Southern Lakes, this 450-year-old coaching inn oozes history from every exposed beam. It has a range of rooms to suit most budgets, and each room is modern, fresh and stylish, from the quirky Cavendish Loft to its spacious Superior doubles and more affordable Classic and Small doubles. In the restaurant, they pride themselves on offering a contemporary selection of seasonal English dishes and also serve sandwiches at lunchtime and a choice of roasts on Sunday. Finally, do explore the village while you're here: it's pretty hard to beat, with tiny, winding streets, an ancient village centre and priory, arguably Cumbria's most beautiful medieval church, and great indy shops and delis. A couple of long-distance footpaths pass nearby – the 33-mile Cistercian Way and the longer Furness Way – and of course you're just a short drive from Windermere and the honeypot sights of the Lake District to the north.

CONTACT Cavendish Street, Cartmel, Cumbria LA11 6QA • 01539 536 240

HOW MUCH? Double rooms with breakfast from £135 a night.

Lindeth Fell

Set back from the shores of Lake Windermere, overlooking the Coniston Fells, Lindeth Fell is a luxury B&B where food is very much part of the offering. The house is the work of renowned local Arts and Crafts architects, and the terraced gardens in which it stands are by a celebrated landscape artist. Together they offer a private, secluded and pretty place to retreat to, while inside there's a garden-facing dining room where breakfast and afternoon tea are served, although when the weather is good you won't be able to resist sitting out on the terrace. There's a menu of simple but well-executed fare available throughout the day and into the evening. The bedrooms are set across three storeys and all are rooted in the Arts and Crafts aesthetic, with panelling, fabric and furnishing to match. All this is paired with inclusions you'd traditionally expect from a hotel rather than a B&B: a Nespresso machine, a Roberts radio, a Smart TV, bathrobes and toiletries.

CONTACT Lyth Valley Road, Windermere, Cumbria, LA23 3JP • 01539 443 286

HOW MUCH? Double rooms with breakfast from £125 to £315 a night.

Pentonbridge Inn

Less than a mile from Liddle Water, whose meandering course marks the England-Scotland border, the Pentonbridge Inn has a reputation for serving well-presented, flavourful British food that warrants an overnight stay. The inn's nine elegant bedrooms divide between the main building and a converted barn connected to the hotel, and the decor throughout makes use of tweed, wood and slate to reinforce the Cumbrian countryside location. Cushioned seats on window ledges in some of the rooms offer views of the surrounding landscape, and Egyptian cotton bedding and modern bathroom fittings bring a hint of luxury. It's nice to know also that dogs are welcome in the three barn rooms. Food is served in a chic and airy bar and dining room, and locally sourced meat and fish feature (shorthorn beef tartare, local Herwick lamb) on an impressive menu. They also offer a 'signature' 10-course tasting menu if you really want to go to town.

CONTACT Penton, Cumbria CA6 5QB • 01228 586 636

HOW MUCH? Double rooms from £175 a night, including breakfast.

Lucky Dip

The Inn at Whitewell

Whitewell, Near Clitheroe, Lancashire BB7 3AT

Deep in the heart of the Forest of Bowland, this is the ultimate country escape, surrounded by miles of stark, stunning, moorlands and offering a set of unique bedrooms, each with their own style and decor ranging from cosy and historic to sleek and modern. Dog-friendly too, and serving wholesome, hearty meals.

King Street Townhouse

10 Booth Street, Manchester M24AW

A luxury hotel with a boutique feel, this place is tucked away on a quiet street but otherwise perfectly placed for Manchester city centre. Its rooms are beautifully decked out, and it has the relaxing feel of a proper, small-scale boutique hotel. Downstairs, the King Street Tavern serves drinks and good food, while there's also a gym, steam room, sauna and a spa offering treatments and an indoor infinity pool on the roof.

The Midland Hotel

Marine Road, West Morecambe, Lancashire LA4 4BU

An icon of Art Deco design, Morecambe's Midland Hotel is beautifully positioned, with superb views across the famous bay to the Lake District fells. Built in the 1930s when Morecambe was in its seaside heyday, it was sympathetically restored almost a decade ago. Having recently changed hands, it still represents a unique place to stay, and you can also enjoy the views from its restaurant and Rotunda bar.

Mitton Hall

Mitton Road, Mitton, Whalley, Lancashire BB7 9PQ

A contemporary country house hotel in the charming Ribble Valley whose rooms come with a touch of romance – river views and rich baronial tones. Also, whether you're after a lazy lunch, afternoon tea, cocktails on the terrace or a special dinner, it offers the kind of all-day dining and drinking that you'd expect from a city brasserie but with the bonus of lovely rustic surroundings.

The Resident

29 Seel Street, Liverpool L1 4AU

Situated in one of the city centre's most popular districts, The Resident is perhaps Liverpool's most affordable yet stylish place to stay. Occupying an old printworks, its strikingly modern rooms are cosy and well-equipped, and instead of a bar or restaurant each has its own kitchenette with fridge and microwave for making a cuppa or heating up some food. A great location, too, with everything just a few minutes' walk away.

The Vicarage

Holmes Chapel, Knutsford, Cheshire, CW4 8EF

Based in a Grade II-listed 17th-century Georgian house, this stylish Cheshire inn near fashionable Knutsford is handy for Tatton Park and other Cheshire landmarks. It's extremely family- and dog-friendly too – part of the local Flatcap group, whose signature is good food and drink and comfortable rooms at decent prices.

Waddington Arms

Waddington, Clitheroe, Lancashire BB7 3HP

Six, smallish en-suite rooms provide a light, contemporary cottage backdrop for a relaxed night's sleep at this charming country pub with rooms in the heart of Lancashire walking country. The current incarnation is a handsome renovation that's heavy on country comfort – think a modern huntin', fishin', shootin' vibe inside and a sunny terrace and beer garden that's more lounge-bar than pub trestles.

Wild Boar Inn

Crook, Windermere, Cumbria LA23 3NF

A short distance from Lake Windermere, The Wild Boar springs a surprise to those expecting a traditional Lakeland inn. Yes, there are stone floors, oak beams, a log fire, and a bar serving real ale courtesy of the on-site microbrewery, but a keen sense of style brings things up-to-date in the guest rooms, which sport bespoke wallpaper, canopy beds, cast-iron wood burners and Bluetooth speakers along with free-standing copper baths and the like. Work up an appetite in their 70-acre woodland, complete with 'green gym' exercise trail and private tarn, before browsing a menu that takes in everything from melt-in-your-mouth beef brisket to local mallard and burgers and steaks from the on-site smokehouse.

Waddington Arms

The Inn at Whitewell

The Vicarage

Wales

Glamorgan • Powys • Monmouthshire • Pembrokeshire • Carmarthernshire • Ceredigion • Snowdonia • Anglesey

Very much part of Britain, yet exotic and dripping with mystery and legend, Wales is one of the most beautiful playgrounds the country has to offer. Catch it on a good day, when the sun is beaming and the clouds are sparse, and you might forget that you're in the UK at all. It has a phenomenal 870 miles of coastline, studded with coves and caves, cliff drops and cliff edges, sandy beaches, dunes and roaring waves, while inland the Brecon Beacons, Cambrian Mountains and the rolling uplands of The Borders are ripe for exploration. There's a definite divide between north and south. Up north, the landscape is rugged and sparsely populated, overlooked by the mighty mountains of Snowdonia, and the vibe more foreign and remote. In contrast, South Wales is a diverse mix of blissful coastal villages and thriving cities – softer and more accessible, yet still scenically spectacular. Both regions are home to some of Britain's most idyllically located hotels, inns and restaurants with rooms, and a selection of high-grade B&Bs – often in breathtaking locations.

Penrhiw Farm, p.268

The Oyster House

Boutique rooms above a Mumbles seafront restaurant and bar

Downstairs is a stylish restaurant and bar, upstairs are boutique rooms with a soft seaside feel – and, if you choose wisely, sea views to add to the mix. This is The Oyster House, in the seaside village of Mumbles on Swansea Bay, five miles south of the city at the gateway to the Gower Peninsula. A stay here offers a comfortable base from which to explore it all and rooms include accessible and dog-friendly options.

Each bedroom is decorated in muted pastels with bright splashes of colour and a nod to the seaside here and there. If you can, opt for one of six sea view rooms, which really make the most of the location. Whichever you choose, you'll find a flatscreen TV, wifi, hairdryer and tea- and coffee-making facilities, plus really nice en-suite bathrooms with Bramley toiletries.

The hotel is owned by The City Pub Company, whose properties are typically well styled and have a contemporary feel, and that's certainly the case here, with a glass-fronted restaurant and bar and a roof terrace and patio to make the most of the views. A wall of framed prints reference seaside themes, as do the colourful painted ceilings which are a central feature. Most important of all is the menu – oysters, seafood and fish feature alongside modern gastropub favourites, with produce from named local butchers and fishmongers.

You are close enough to Swansea to make this a handy base if you have business there. But it's also an escape from the city. Book a weekend in one of its rooms and you can spend time eating seafood, walking the seafront mile to the Mumbles Pier, exploring Oystermouth Castle and basking on beautiful Langland Bay Beach. Stay for longer and the Gower Peninsula beckons, with clifftop walks and beautiful beaches stretching west.

CONTACT Oyster Wharf, Tivoli Walk, Mumbles Rd, Swansea SA3 4DN • 01792 823 159
HOW MUCH? Double rooms from £129 to £149 a night, not including breakfast.
ROOMS 16 Guest Rooms.

The Heathcock

A relaxed and informal Cardiff dining pub with terrific food and lovely guest rooms

From the same stable as the renowned Hare & Hounds pub in the Vale of Glamorgan comes a Cardiff neighbourhood stalwart, The Heathcock, re-imagined as a destination dining place, with two lovely guest rooms upstairs (and another three on the way). The bar is still a terrific local hangout – just a couple of miles from the city centre, near the river in Llandaff – but an increasing number of visitors are making their way here to sample some of the best in contemporary regional Welsh cooking. Expertly executed and presented sharing dishes are popular here, with a tasty rotation of pies, Pembrokeshire oysters, succulent slow-cooked lamb shoulder, and whole baked Welsh seabass.

It's not at all pretentious, with plenty of tables inside so that drinkers can just turn up. Maintaining a neighbourhood pub feel is a priority here, and there are plenty of events to get involved in, from lively board game evenings to a popular quiz night. There's regular live music, and on weekends the late-night upstairs bar opens, serving a selection of charcuterie, cheese, old-world wines, champagne and a seasonal and carefully crafted Welsh-influenced cocktail menu.

Make a real night of it by staying in one of two charming en-suite guest rooms on the top floor. Room one has a contemporary country house feel, with bold colour splashes, plush fabrics and flashes of exposed brick, plus a luxurious super-king bed, rain shower, roll-top bath and Nespresso machine. Room two is larger and features scenic views over the green hills to Castle Coch. You'll also find an additional seating area and an extra large bath – ideal for a post-dinner soak. Breakfast, of course, is a high point, with the terrific produce from the bakery at their sister pub just outside town, The Hare & Hounds, setting you right up for a day's sightseeing.

CONTACT 58-60 Bridge St, Cardiff CF5 2EN • 029 2115 2290

HOW MUCH? Double rooms £100–£140 a night.

ROOMS 2–5 Guest Rooms.

The Felin Fach Griffin

No better place for a Welsh weekend away doing nothing much amid glorious surroundings

'The simple things in life done well' is the motto of this rather special inn – and we reckon it's perfectly suited to this gastropub with rooms, situated on the edge of the Brecon Beacons National Park. It lives up to its billing in every way possible. There are seven very comfortable rooms above a restaurant that is one of the best in the region. It's also a proper pub, with all that implies, serving well-priced, well-kept local ales – a bit of a haven for local drinkers and a welcoming place for everyone else, with a roaring fire in winter. And dogs and children are very definitely welcomed.

The rooms are all different in size and style, but they all have big beds, Roberts radios, homemade biscuits, fresh flowers and posh toiletries. There are no TVs, and they make a thing of this, so embrace the good old days and read a book. Breakfasts are delicious (scrambled eggs and smoked salmon, local apple juice, homemade soda bread), and a good indicator of the quality of the dinner you'll enjoy – namely, seasonally influenced dishes and ingredients from the Welsh borders, whether it's beef or lamb, local cheese, or herbs and veg picked from their own kitchen garden. There's no shortage of things to do during the day either, to work up that appetite, from a hard day's walking to book-browsing in Hay or just pottering around nearby Brecon, Abergavenny or Crickhowell.

There's no better place, then, for a Welsh country weekend away – and if you like the style, it's good to know that the owners use the same motto for the other hotels they run in Cornwall: The Gurnard's Head near Zennor (p.129) and Old Coastguard in Mousehole (p.122).

CONTACT Felin Fach, Brecon, Powys LD3 0UB • 01874 620 111
HOW MUCH? Double rooms with breakfast from £175 a night.
ROOMS 8 Guest Rooms.

The Neuadd B&B Suites

A boutique B&B with luxury suites in the heart of the Brecon Beacons

Situated in the heart of the Brecon Beacons National Park, and with spectacular panoramic mountain views, The Neuadd is a pretty special B&B. From this splendid location, guests need only venture through the flower meadow to access a wealth of wonderful walks. There are paths leading into the Black Mountains or along the Usk River; you can also follow the Monmouthshire and Brecon Canal or stroll into Crickhowell, a charming town recently selected as the 'Best Place to Live in Wales' by The Sunday Times. For aspiring stargazers, The Neuadd is also a perfect base, with some of the highest quality dark skies in the UK.

The Neuadd operates a concept it calls 'Freedom B&B' – a pleasingly flexible arrangement where there's no need to arrange an arrival time – you just let yourself in after 4pm with a unique key code. Best of all, your luxurious continental breakfast can be enjoyed at any time, giving you the chance for some deliciously long lie-ins. There are three large suites to choose from, each varying in size and character, though there is a broad uniformity to decor and feel. Each has a bedroom, living area, and dining area and all come with a king-size bed and plenty of space for outdoor gear. All have tea- and coffee-making facilities and a fridge, wifi and Freeview TVs, plus access to a laundry and drying room. The Courtyard Suite is on the ground floor and has a walk-in shower; the Loft and Vinetree Suites are accessed via a short stairway and have individual bathrooms with showers over the bath. If you'd prefer to self-cater, note that The Neuadd also has several cottages and apartments.

Your helpful hosts Julia and Peter are invaluable sources of local information. They even supply you with a detailed 'holiday planner' before you arrive for inspiration on things to do. Be sure to take them up on their suggested scenic route to get here, which takes in spectacular views via a truly epic mountain road.

CONTACT The Neuadd, Llangattock, Crickhowell, Powys NP8 1LE • 07854 773 419
HOW MUCH? Suites from £132 a night mid-week, £146 a night at weekends, including breakfast.
ROOMS 3 Guest Suites.

The Angel at Abergavenny

Contemporary boutique hotel based in the historic, foodie market town of Abergavenny

Abergavenny, the so-called 'Gateway to Wales' – is making a real name for itself as a foodie town and activity base, with its annual food festival and a backdrop of the Brecon Beacons. The Angel Hotel is a long-established former coaching inn, dating from 1829, and in its current incarnation as a contemporary, boutique inn it makes for a terrific place to stay in this historic and very lively market town.

A sleek makeover has retained the Georgian facade and vintage ambience but added 31 beautifully designed rooms that offer a chic twist on the coaching-inn style. The decor is cool and soothing, and all rooms feature designer fabrics, silky soft linens, and calming neutral colours. The rooms come in various sizes – Executive, Superior and Deluxe – and with a range of beds (doubles, twins and kings), and the outlook varies depending on where you are in the old building. The best room is the super-spacious suite on the second floor, which has a huge bed, a sitting area and a bay window overlooking town, and there are also two Mews rooms set apart from the hotel in the old stables buildings. Breakfast is a real high point, from French toast to smoked haddock, and the bread and pastries are from their own excellent Angel Bakery.

The food, in fact, might have brought you here in the first place, given Abergavenny's rising reputation – the sister property to the hotel is Shaun Hill's renowned Michelin-starred Walnut Tree, which gives you an idea of The Angel's pedigree (for some rooms the hotel offers complimentary taxis out to The Walnut Tree). Locals come to drink in the hotel's Foxhunter Bar, while the Oak Room restaurant is the place for up-to-the-minute Welsh dining using locally sourced ingredients from farm and coast. There's a famous seafood platter, or you can order anything from a whole lemon sole to a Welsh beef ribeye.

You get the picture – you're going to be extremely well looked after from breakfast through to dinner, and thoroughly rested for another day in one of Wales' more exciting destinations. There's canal boating, kayaking, cycling and walking close by, and with Cardiff only 45 minutes away by car or train, The Angel makes a superb weekend away or a good base for city day-trips. And if you prefer to self-cater, its worth knowing that the hotel has some delightful holiday cottages too, both in town and out near The Walnut Tree Inn.

CONTACT 15 Cross Street, Abergavenny, Monmouthshire NP7 5EN • 01873 857 121

HOW MUCH? Double rooms from £145 a night, not including breakfast.

ROOMS 31 Guest Rooms.

Penrhiw Farm

Cosy and colourful B&B rooms on an organic dairy farm close to the Pembrokeshire Coast Path

In the quieter northern reaches of Pembrokeshire, a Georgian farmhouse has been lovingly renovated into a boutique B&B with four cosy and colourful rooms. It's less than half a mile from the Pembrokeshire Coast Path and a similar distance from ferries on the Fishguard-to-Rosslare route. Both of these make it a handy stop for weary travellers but it's also much more than that. It's a place of both style and substance, with views of the Preseli Hills in one direction and farmland that rolls down to the coast in the other.

Penrhiw Farm is a 200-acre dairy farm with its farmhouse B&B in the middle of it all. And while it's an authentic, organic, still-working farm with a herd of Jersey cows, the accommodation has less of a 'country cottage' feel than you might expect. Instead, the four rooms here have all been brought up-to-date with a modern en-suite bath or shower room in each, a flatscreen TV and a comfy double bed. Each room has individual charm thanks to a mixture of vintage furniture and finishing touches to suit modern tastes. We're talking exposed bulb lighting and reclaimed-wood walls for the bathrooms. Even though the style is on-trend not much comes without provenance or sustainability here. The reclaimed wood is the farm's original flooring re-purposed, and the colourful blankets on the bed are from a mill just down the road. The farmhouse is partly powered by sun and wind and kept warm by wool carpets, new insulation and an air-source heat pump.

If you've walked here on the Pembrokeshire Coast Path, you'll be grateful to know that you don't have to go a step further for dinner. Alan, your host, is an experienced chef who can provide dinner as well as breakfasts, served in the elegant dining room downstairs. You might also want to head the half a mile or so to the seaside village of Goodwick (pronounced with a silent W, if you want to sound like a local) or to neighbouring Fishguard where there's a good pub or two. Walking and cycling are great ways to explore this quieter, unspoilt side of Pembrokeshire, and Penrhiw Farm is a great place to base yourself while you do it.

CONTACT Penrhiw Farm, Llanwnda, Goodwick, Pembrokeshire SA64 0HS • 07875 219 746
HOW MUCH? Double rooms from £89 to £139 a night, including breakfast.
ROOMS 4 Guest Rooms.

Manor Town House

Home comforts with super style – this is the perfect contemporary seaside B&B

If you're looking for a B&B room with a view over the beautiful Pembrokeshire coast, then look no further. The lovely Manor Town House, overlooking the sea in Fishguard, provides a warm welcome and fabulous views in what is one of the best places to stay in the area.

The affable owners, Helen and Chris, have a distinguished fan club – Bill Bryson declared their B&B 'lovely' and Nick Crane reckoned it to have the UK's 'best breakfast view', not to mention the 'best breakfast'. And Bill and Nick are not far wrong. Along with the inspiring views, Manor Town House has six lovely guest rooms, four of which have sea views – and two of these have beds perfectly positioned for watching both sunrise and sunset over the sea! All rooms are en-suite – one with a bath and five with showers. Each is individually decorated with flair and style, with well-chosen antique furniture and super-comfy beds (Chris, or maybe it's Helen, have even counted the number of springs to ensure you have a good night's sleep!). You can also expect all the other comforts you get in five-star establishments, such as TV & DVD, dressing gowns, high-end toiletries, bottled water, Nespresso machines and more.

Downstairs there's a room stuffed full of DVDs and books, an honesty bar, and a couple of cosy rooms with log fires that are regularly adorned with work by local painters and photographers. There's good free wifi, and the breakfasts here have won awards for the best use of local produce, so you'll be well fed too. Helen and Chris are extremely welcoming and you will be greeted with tea and homemade warm Welsh cakes served on the terrace on arrival. In short, no stone has been left unturned at Manor Town House, which is as close to the perfect contemporary seaside B&B as it's possible to get. We think you'll love it!

CONTACT 11 Main St, Fishguard, Pembrokeshire SA65 9HG • 01348 873 260
HOW MUCH? Double rooms from £140 a night, including breakfast.
ROOMS 6 Guest Rooms.

Hen Ffermdy

Gorgeous, luxury farmhouse B&B with millpond, woods and walks, near the Pembrokeshire coast

The thing that no one tells you about 'living the dream' is that it's hard work. Take beautiful Hen Ffermdy, a gorgeous country B&B on the edge of the Preseli Hills, close to the stunning north Pembrokeshire coastline and path: the name means 'Old Farmhouse', and, where others saw an abandoned stone building (parts of which date back to the 16th century) that had lain derelict for 50 years, Adrian and Sue saw their dream home and set about lovingly renovating the house, millpond, woods and gardens. Now there are three luxurious guest rooms available, with almost all the work done by the owners, from stonework to upholstery. They've planted a thousand trees to turn the former agricultural land into a wild wood, while the serene millpond – with its encroaching trees and rushes – forms a stunning foreground scene for wide-eyed visitors.

It really is a delight, and Adrian and Sue love sharing their dream with guests. They're well travelled, and know the local area intimately too, so they can point you towards the best walks and activities – anything from cliff-jumping to mushroom foraging. There are two great beaches a couple of miles away reached via a National Trust woodland walk (beautiful in spring, rich in bluebells and wild garlic), while cosy pubs, fish and chips, and fine dining are all on their radar too.

None of that, of course, would be half as good if the accommodation wasn't up to scratch, but you need have no worries on that score. 'Barney' is a standard-sized room – the king-size bed can also be made up as twins on request – with a private bathroom across the hall; 'Brinley' and the larger 'Mabel' are king-sized and en-suite, both with stunning views over the millpond. 'Mabel' also has a seating area, window seating and a separate bath in the en-suite. Decor is harmonious country-chic, with attractive furniture; bathrooms are lovely and light. There's superfast wifi, Smart TVs, and underfloor heating, plus games, books and DVDs in the comfortable guest lounge.

CONTACT Llangloffan, Castlemorris, Haverfordwest, Pembrokeshire SA62 5ET • 07967 818 824
HOW MUCH? Double rooms £100–£140 a night.
ROOMS 3 Guest Rooms.

Twr y Felin Hotel

A contemporary Welsh hotel par excellence, a brief stroll from St Davids

Just a short walk from the centre of the little city of St Davids, Twr y Felin is ideally situated for exploring one of the loveliest counties in Wales. The scenery in this part of the world can be breathtaking, and the hotel is only 10 minutes away from the 186-mile-long coast path, so is ideally placed for all kinds of hiking trips. The Oriel y Parc Visitor Centre and Gallery is actually opposite the hotel and hosts the changing exhibitions of the National Museum Wales collections.

A former windmill set in its own grounds, and dating back to 1806, it's anything but rustic, with public spaces that are seriously – and very deliberately – chic, with minimalist grey and black furnishings, subdued lighting and a wealth of contemporary art, most of it commissioned specially for the hotel and inspired by the St Davids peninsula. The 39 guest rooms are similarly contemporary, and have robes, slippers, aromatherapy toiletries and Nespresso coffee makers, as well as a mini-fridge. The best room in the house is the Windmill Tower suite – spread over three stories, it has a spacious bedroom and lounge and a spiral staircase that takes you to the original observatory, located on the highest floor of the hotel, giving you spectacular 360-degree views of the whole peninsula, including the nearby coastline at Caerfai Bay. You couldn't be anywhere else in the world, and indeed Twr y Felin revels in its 'Welshness': the menu of its three-AA-rosette restaurant – Blas (literally, 'taste' in Welsh) – features specialities such as local lamb, crab and delicious Welsh cheeses.

All in all, Twr y Felin is a quite rare thing – a place where you can immerse yourself in Wales, in the most contemporary of surroundings. There's also a sister hotel nearby called Roch Castle – see p.277.

CONTACT St Davids, Pembrokeshire SA62 6QT • 01437 725 555

HOW MUCH? Double rooms with breakfast from £200 a night.

ROOMS 39 Guest Rooms & Suites.

The West Arms

A super-inviting pub with comfy rooms and terrific food in majestically rugged surroundings

In such majestically rugged surroundings as those around Llanarmon Dyffryn Ceiriog, this gentle, whitewashed old inn comes as a welcome surprise. It dates back to the 16th century, and Nicky and Mark Williamson took it over a few years ago and have devoted bundles of attention since then to bringing it bang up-to-date. The result? A fabulous pub with rooms that you won't want to leave!

The beamed interior is super-inviting, with a snug lounge with a wood-burning stove and a more formal slate-floored dining room with an inglenook fireplace. At the back, the wide, grassy beer garden is almost the only level ground around beneath the Berwyn Mountains' undulating uplands. Of the 15 bedrooms, there are Character rooms, with big old beams, king-size beds and views over the village; newly refurbished and slightly more contemporary King Valley rooms, with super-king-size beds offering wonderful views over the mountains; and Classic rooms either in the main pub or in the converted stables; they also have rooms with one double and a single for small families, and a couple of suites. The Bunny Warren Suite is spread over three levels and has a chunky timber brace encasing the sleeping area, while the beamed Howard Room is centred around its amazing four-poster bed. All the rooms come with en-suite bathrooms, wifi, tea and coffee, telephone, hair dryer, flat-screen TVs and some have robes too. All of them also welcome dogs.

Above all the inn has a reputation for sensational cuisine, and it's nice that the menu mentions by name the people supplying many of the ingredients. As for things to do, just get outside: hiking in the Berwyn Mountains includes walks to the breathtaking Pistyll Rhaeadr waterfall, one of Wales's highest and perhaps familiar from the Timotei shampoo advert!

CONTACT Llanarmon Dyffryn Ceiriog, Wrexham LL20 7LD •01691 600 665

HOW MUCH? Double rooms from £165 a night including breakfast.

ROOMS 16 Guest Rooms & Suites.

Plas Weunydd

Boutique hotel, bar and restaurant in the heart of Snowdonia's adventure tourism zone

It's all very well boasting that you've got a pool and a hot tub, but name us another boutique hotel that comes complete with Europe's longest zip wires, adventure caverns, underground trampolines and world-class mountain-biking right on the doorstep. There really isn't another place quite like Plas Weunydd, a 19th-century former slate-mine owner's home in North Wales that's part of the UK's newest World Heritage Site. You might come for the adventures at Zip World Lechwedd, but the wonderfully atmospheric hotel is a destination base in its own right – perfect for exploring this wild part of Snowdonia, amd with brooding mountain views on all sides.

There are 24 spacious rooms ranged across the sympathetically restored building, whose elegant decor and stylings give a nod to the surrounding slate quarries and mountains. You can opt for double, king-size or super-king beds, depending on the room, and some of the bathrooms feature a bath as well as a shower – essential if you've spent the day making every bone in your body ache. Meanwhile, public spaces throughout are geared towards an outdoorsy clientele – meaning you don't have to worry if you arrive at the hotel looking like you've been dragged through a mine backwards. If you do want a more thoroughly back-to-nature experience, it's good to know that they also have glamping tents and shepherds huts on-site.

Guests are treated to a hearty Welsh breakfast, while the bar and restaurant are great for all-day brunches, sharing platters and pizzas. An outdoor terrace gives views over the activity zone and the mountains beyond, while other exciting days out might include the Ffestiniog heritage mountain railway, the castle and beach at nearby Harlech, or trips to Portmeirion or Caernarfon. And, of course, looming large (literally) over Blaenau Ffestiniog are the mighty peaks of Eryri or Snowdonia. for which the hotel is the perfect base.

CONTACT Llechwedd, Blaenau Ffestiniog, Gwynedd LL41 3NB • 01766 610 006
HOW MUCH? Double rooms from £75 a night including breakfast.
ROOMS 24 Guest Rooms & Suites.

Driftwood Boutique Guest House

A truly idyllic seaside place to stay on the west coast of Anglesey

For us, there's something about the name Driftwood Boutique Guest House that conjures up summer trips to the seaside, basking on the beach and enjoying endless sunny days without a care in the world. If you feel the same, you won't be disappointed by this gorgeous boutique B&B, recently refurbished and offering six beautiful guest rooms and a self-catering lodge in a glorious beachside location.

Situated on the popular northwest coast of Anglesey, Driftwood's rooms either enjoy wonderful views of the sea or of the mountains. Of the six double rooms, three have king-size or super-king-size beds, one is a regular double, and there are two larger rooms that can be used as twins or family rooms. They are bright and contemporary, with a seasidey, almost New England look and feel, and they all come with high-quality, comfortable beds and bed linen, good wifi and Smart TVs, tea- and coffee-making facilities, large wardrobes and dressing tables, and en-suite bath or shower rooms equipped with towels, robes, slippers and posh toiletries. Some rooms also accept dogs, plus, for those who prefer to self-cater, there is a one-bedroom lodge in the grounds that comes with all the same facilities but has its own entrance. Its bedroom has a king-size bed, and there's an en-suite bathroom, a fully-fitted kitchen, a sofa bed so you can accommodate extra guests, and a dining table and chairs – plus you can still order breakfast in the main house if you're feeling lazy!

Finally, the location is truly idyllic, right in the heart of the seaside village of Rhosneigr and just footsteps from not one but two huge sandy beaches – both of which are among the best on the island. There are lots of opportunities for watersports, and Rhosneigr itself is home to a couple of great pubs and some decent restaurants and cafés.

CONTACT Station Road, Rhosneigr, Anglesey LL64 5QP • 01407 521 125
HOW MUCH? Double rooms from £110 to £180 a night.
ROOMS 6 Guest Rooms & 1 Lodge.

Lucky Dip

The Bell at Skenfrith

Skenfrith, Monmouthshire NP7 8UH

With views of either the pea-green hills behind or the murmuring river out front, 11 delightful rooms await at this whitewashed 17th-century drovers' inn, which is also something of a foodie destination in its own right.

Billycan

Lower Frog Street, Tenby, Pembrokeshire SA70 7HS

Situated in the heart of Tenby's old town, this former British Legion is now a successful and contemporary bar-restaurant with five minimalist rooms and a two-bedroom/two-bathroom penthouse apartment complete with Jacuzzi. Billycan's owners also run fish and chip shops in the Rhondda Valley so it comes as no surprise that this British favourite is one of the star dishes on the menu, sitting alongside the likes of burgers and various tempting veggie options.

The Bull at Beaumaris

Castle Street, Beaumaris, Anglesey LL58 8AP

Overlooking the Menai Strait, with its ever-changing light and views of Snowdonia's brooding mountains, this coaching inn has propelled itself into the 21st century, with inventive food and chic rooms, without jettisoning its 400-year-old history. Rooms interweave period features with intricate wallpaper, bursts of colour, Hypnos mattresses, Nespresso coffee machines and Welsh Cole & Co toiletries, while the restaurant pleasingly mixes the old and new, with lots of attention-grabbing art and photography on the walls, a flower-adorned courtyard for outdoor dining and a menu that sings of the season and region.

Druidstone Hotel

Druidstone, Broad Haven, Pembrokeshire SA62 3NE

The Dru is a national treasure: a family-run Pembrokeshire coast hotel, with 10 guest rooms and five cottages. It's extremely dog-friendly too, and serves fabulous breakfasts, good bar meals and proper kids' teas. It also has a bar that stays open as late as the last customer, and fabulous views out to sea.

The Falcondale

Falcondale Drive, Lampeter, Ceredigion, Mid Wales SA48 7RX

This Ceredigion country house hotel just outside Lampeter is very comfortable and ultra-welcoming to both humans and their hounds. Great for walking and nearby beaches.

The Grove of Narberth

Molleston, Narberth, Pembrokeshire SA67 8BX

This small Pembrokeshire hotel provides understated luxury and fine dining in beautiful surroundings. It has 25 rooms and suites – 14 in the hotel itself and 11 in the grounds – all of them large, elegant and comfortable. Just the place for strolling out into the Preseli Hills, knowing that The Grove's cosy rooms and superb food await you at the end of the day.

The Kinmel Arms

The Village, St George, Abergele, Conwy LL22 9BP

Not far from the sea, and only half an hour from Snowdonia, this contemporary village pub makes for the perfect North Wales luxury escape. The food is superb: locally sourced and seasonal but also riddled with other influences, and they have four enormous guest rooms – suites, really – each with a large en-suite bathroom.

Roch Castle

Roch, Pembrokeshire SA62 6AQ

Once voted Wales' Best Bed & Breakfast, there are few places to stay in Britain as gobsmackingly awesome as Roch Castle. It's a 12th-century Welsh castle – and looks like one, perched high above the Pembrokeshire landscape with panoramic views over St Brides Bay and the Preseli Hills.

The Rocks at Plas Curig

Capel Curig, Betws Y Coed, Conwy LL24 0EL

A chic and comfortable mountain hostel with stunning views in the heart of Snowdonia National Park.

Stackpole Inn

Jasons Corner, Stackpole, Pembrokeshire SA71 5DF

Tucked away just a pebble's-throw from one of Wales' loveliest beaches, the ivy-swathed Stackpole Inn is one of the most welcoming places to stay for miles around, and it offers really good, locally sourced food, too.

The Bell at Skenfrith

The Grove of Narberth

Roch Castle

Scotland

Edinburgh • Glasgow • Dumfries & Galloway • Scottish Borders • Fife • Perthshire • Stirlingshire • Scottish Isles • Scottish Highlands

Accommodation in Scotland can rank with the best, with a range of comfortable and welcoming country house and resort hotels, boutique hotels and B&Bs that make the most of Scottish hospitality and produce. Scotland is also much more than just rugged castles, brooding mountains and swishing kilts. It has more than 10 per cent of Europe's coastline and more than 800 islands. It's also home to seven thrilling cities – Glasgow and Edinburgh can hold their own with any in Europe when it comes to sights, architecture and nightlife – and also boasts some of the most remote and wild landscapes on the continent. And that is just the point: Scotland is diverse, deep, and very hard to pin down – as much 'Trainspotting' as 'Braveheart,' with as many fine-dining restaurants as there are chippies and curry houses!

The Art Bank, p.288

House of Gods

A blingy and luxurious adults-only hotel in the heart of Edinburgh

Prepare to be seduced by the vintage glamour at this decadent address in Edinburgh's Old Town. Tucked off the Cowgate, this flirtatious adults-only hotel has 22 rooms, each with butler service across three different categories. It's a unique place to stay, deliberately blingy and for some people it will be completely over-the-top. But the prices are keen and there's an emphasis on luxury, discretion and privacy that are the hallmarks of a great hotel.

The hotel's subtly lit corridors lead to three types of guest room - Cabin rooms, Classic rooms and a sumptuous Suite. There are 11 wood-panelled Cabin'rooms in all, each of which consciously channels the furnishings and atmosphere of the Orient Express, with a snug, berth-like feel, luggage racks for storage, cosy beds and wet-room-style showers; the 10 Classic rooms are larger, with four-poster beds and sofas, while the highly-in-demand Suite has all of the traits of the Classic but with more space and a free-standing bathtub. Privacy is everything at House of Gods. Breakfast hampers are delivered to the rooms, which also feature call buttons for a glass of fizz or just milk and cookies after hours. Given the nature of the building, the rooms have been designed with glass panels for light but no windows, thus ensuring complete seclusion.

This place eschews the traditional, so you'll be checked in with a glass of bubbly in the Resident's Bar, where the walls are adorned with flamboyant heron-print wallpaper beneath a dazzling paint-dripped disco ball. You can also pimp your stay with various packages to elevate your experience – above all, don't miss the drag show and karaoke at adjoining Donatella's. Should you want to venture out, it's worth remembering that you are bang in the middle of Edinburgh, in an extremely handy position for seeing the sights.

CONTACT 233 Cowgate, Edinburgh EH6 1JQ
• 0131 230 0445

HOW MUCH? Double rooms from £120 a night.

ROOMS 22 Guest Rooms & 1 Suite.

The Witchery

The most theatrical, dramatic and indulgent place to stay in Edinburgh

It's one of the most stellar, storied addresses in Edinburgh, a supremely glamorous dining destination by the castle that also offers fantastically theatrical accommodation. Created with couples in mind, The Witchery offers opulent accommodation across two historic properties situated on either side of the Royal Mile, with nine of the most dramatic, theatrical, indulgent suites imaginable.

These adults-only boudoirs, accessed via winding stone staircases, ooze decadence with their velvet drapes, Gothic beds, oak panelling, tapestries, ornamental fireplaces, turrets, secret bookcases, mosaic shower rooms and free-standing bathtubs. The buildings may date from the 16th century but the suites artfully conceal all mod-cons including Smart TVs and Bluetooth speakers, Nespresso machines and Dyson hairdryers. Book direct and you'll enjoy a bottle of champagne on arrival, while the choice is yours when it comes to breakfast: opt for a continental-style hamper delivered to your suite or a cooked breakfast by candlelight in one of the two intimate dining rooms.

As for the location, leave the close and you're at the gates of Edinburgh Castle. It's the most romantic location in the most romantic city. It's a busy place to stay in terms of the tourist numbers right outside your door, but it's very handy for the sights of the city centre, and it's very easy to forget the crowds outside once you're safely within the cosy confines of The Witchery. It's certainly the place to book if you're after a one-of-a-kind experience in the Scottish capital.

CONTACT Castlehill, Edinburgh EH1 2NF
• 0131 225 5613
HOW MUCH? Suites from £595 a night with breakfast.
ROOMS 9 Guest Suites.

Bonnie Badger

Tom Kitchin's label is a sign of meticulous cooking and sophistication, all reflected in the Bonnie Badger

Situated in the highly desirable town of Gullane, some 20 miles east of Edinburgh, the Bonnie Badger is an award-winning pub and restaurant with rooms in deepest East Lothian. The creation of acclaimed Scottish chef Tom Kitchin and his wife Michaela, it's the only property in their portfolio of four fine-dining destinations with accommodation. It's a foodie getaway that's well worth leaving the city for, and even more rewarding for a cosy weekend. Situated in one of the country's sunniest regions – and one of its most seriously underrated outside the country – Gullane is an ideal setting, with big skies, excellent local produce and an escape-the-city vibe. There is golf, walks on the John Muir Way and a slew of coastal villages to explore too.

The Badger has 12 luxurious rooms divided between the main house, and two garden cottages, Hazel and Honeysuckle. Double rooms are in the house, while larger Deluxe rooms are spread between the cottages. Each includes king-size or super-king-size beds, Egyptian cotton sheets, bathrobes, slippers, tea- and coffee-making facilities, bespoke Scottish toiletries, Smart TVs and en-suite showers. There's one Superior room in Honeysuckle, while two Deluxe Loft rooms with fantastic views, and the swish Ridge Suite, which features a chic four-poster, free-standing bathtub and separate lounge space, are located in the main house.

Tom Kitchin is one of Scotland's best-known Michelin chefs, so it's no great surprise that the dishes served in the restaurant here are highly creative and based on local Scottish produce, with everything curated around their trademark 'From Nature to Plate' ethos. What's more, there are various ways to dine: choose from the more formal Stables Dining Room, with its exposed brickwork and huge, light-giving windows; The Broc Bar, a welcoming bolthole for a whisky cocktail; the relaxed Garden Room where breakfast, brunch and afternoon tea are served; or the Garden – as inviting under a blanket in winter as it is on warm summer days.

CONTACT Main St, Gullane, Edinburgh EH31 2AB • 01620 621 111

HOW MUCH? Double rooms with breakfast from £195 a night.

ROOMS 12 Guest Rooms.

The Bridge Inn

A canalside pub not far from Edinburgh with waterfront views, good food and comfortable rooms

If, like us, you tend to associate canalside inns with England, prepare to be surprised by this central Scotland hideaway. Just seven miles from Edinburgh, and even closer to its airport, sits a heritage inn in the conservation village of Ratho, overlooking a stone bridge. This multi-award-winning inn sits on the south bank of the Union Canal, which runs from the remarkable Falkirk Wheel to Edinburgh city centre. From here, you can take boat trips out towards Linlithgow, cycle along the canal into Edinburgh or even hike east to pick up the John Muir Way long-distance trail.

The good news is that you don't have to fight for a waterfront view as each of the inn's four individually designed guest rooms overlooks the canal. Named after famous, characters with links to Ratho, the double rooms feature flatscreen TVs, hairdryers, free wifi and tea- and coffee-making facilities, while each of them remains distinctive. One, Bonnington, has an opulent four-poster; you'll find a brass bedstead in Bryce, while there is simple, predominantly white decor in Burke. The largest room, Baird, has a free-standing bath. Breakfasts are superb, with a generous Full Scottish featuring black pudding and potato scones, although American pancakes make a tasty alternative.

Downstairs there's a proper local pub feel, with a terrace overlooking the canal for dreamy summer evenings and cosy fires inside for the depths of winter. The menu is well above that of standard pub grub, dishing up seasonal favourites made with locally sourced ingredients, all beautifully presented with excellent, friendly service. There is a top selection of Scottish ales on tap, as well as cider and bitter, and kids will enjoy the wooden playboat in the sizeable canalside beer garden, which also has a covered area for dining.

CONTACT 27 Baird Rd, Ratho, Newbridge EH28 8RA • 0131 333 1320
HOW MUCH? Double rooms from £105 a night, including breakfast.
ROOMS 4 Guest Rooms.

Trigony House Hotel

An ultra-relaxed country house hotel with a great restaurant and spa that's also dog-friendly!

Deep in the green, rolling countryside of southwest Scotland, this extremely comfortable 18th-century house is as tranquil a place as you could imagine. Owner and chef Adam Moore and his wife really get that people's needs are much more straightforward than hoteliers sometimes think: a comfortable room with a decent bed, great locally sourced food and the ability to quickly relax and feel at home. Indeed, dogs are welcomed like old friends at an oasis that has been named 'Best Dog Friendly Hotel in the UK'!

Trigony House has the facilities of a luxury hotel (including a spa) but an atmosphere that's more redolent of your best Scottish friends' country house – if, that is, your friends are superb cooks and extremely keen gardeners. Throughout, the emphasis is on quality rather than quantity, with just nine guest rooms, all spacious and unostentatiously furnished in a classic style, with the primary focus on comfort: beds have hand-sprung mattresses and Egyptian cotton bed linen; all rooms come with a butler's tray brimming with homemade shortbread, coffee, tea and hot chocolate; and they all have good wifi, Freeview TVs and DVD players. The bathrooms are decent sizes and very well-appointed, with either a mixed bath/shower or a separate shower and Scottish Ishga toiletries. The larger rooms have a small sitting area, and the largest, the Garden Suite, has a separate bath and shower plus its own conservatory and garden. Most either have views over the gardens and Lowther Hills to the east or over the Kier Hills to the west, while one has views over the woodland behind the hotel and the ruins of a Roman fort.

Service throughout is gracious and as unobtrusive as you want it to be – both in the hotel and restaurant and in the garden spa, which is small but perfectly formed, with a lovely wood-fired hot tub and Finnish sauna. They also offer Japanese reiki treatments, not just for you but for your dog too – something that perhaps expresses what is great about this hotel better than words can!

Finally, the restaurant serves food that is not only delicious but highly local, with ingredients from their kitchen garden, milk from a nearby organic dairy, fish and seafood from the Solway Firth, and Galloway beef and lamb from an award-winning local butcher. Breakfast includes Ayrshire bacon and sausages and amazing local black pudding too.

CONTACT Closeburn, Dumfries and Galloway DG3 5EZ • 01848 331 211
HOW MUCH? Double rooms with breakfast £125–£145 a night; Garden Suite £170 a night.
ROOMS 8 Guest Rooms & 1 Suite.

Murrayshall Country Estate

A luxury boutique hotel that's a perfect place to relax, play golf or explore the glories of Perthshire

Situated amid the rolling green hills of Perthshire, fans of boutique luxury will love this sumptuous, 400-year-old Scottish Manor House. The former home of Lord Lynedoch, the hotel is at the centre of a 365-acre estate and is both easy to reach and hard to leave – just three miles outside Perth and an hour from the Central Belt. It's the perfect place for a spot of Scottish Highland hospitality, and is home to no fewer than two golf courses, a good restaurant and all manner of other activities. The current owners have also spent £3m on refurbishment since they acquired the property in late 2016 so there's really no better time to visit.

The red sandstone castle may date from 1664, but the interiors have a warm, modern feel. There are 40 rooms – all individually designed in a contemporary style with high-quality beds and bed linen and refurbished bathrooms with Scottish toiletries. Whether you choose the Snug rooms, the picture-window-lined Estate rooms or the spacious Deluxe rooms, you'll have a king-size bed, flatscreen TV, tea- and coffee-making facilities, complimentary mineral water – and, the star of the show, Tunnock's caramel wafers as an extra treat!

There's fine dining in the hotel's two AA-rosette Eòlas restaurant (pronounced Olass), where breakfast is served in the morning before being transformed into a super-chic award-winning modern Scottish dining experience in the evening for both residents and non-residents. Laid-back lunchtimes can be enjoyed in the Cairns bar (think burgers, fish and chips, real ales) while afternoon tea is served between noon and 4pm daily in Barossa, the hotel's cosy bar, where the fireplace ensures you're likely to call by for a cocktail at sundown too.

For those travelling with clubs, the estate has two golf courses to choose from, and other activities include hiring bikes, booking a guided walk up nearby Kinnoull Hill, whisky-tasting or simply heading off into the estate for a hike with a pre-prepared picnic. Meanwhile, those after some indulgent R&R can book into the treatment room at the newly refurbished gatehouse, where Scottish seaweed-based Ishga products are used for facials and massages. The hotel also has plans to expand, with a new spa and lodges, glamping pods and an additional 50 hotel bedrooms. Watch this space!

CONTACT 75 Scone, Perth, Perthshire PH2 7PH • 01738 551 171

HOW MUCH? Double rooms from £140 a night including breakfast.

ROOMS 40 Guest Rooms & Suites.

The Art Bank

A creative and welcoming southern Scotland B&B offering dog-friendly rooms and artistic retreats

You'll find this unique bed and breakfast behind the high-street facade of a former bank in Dalbeattie in southwest Scotland. Rescued and renovated after years of neglect, it's a colourful and creative place to stay, with an artistic and innovative host to match. That's Mandy, the welcoming owner of The Art Bank. For most of the year she offers bed and breakfast in the three guest rooms, but on selected dates she also offers 'retreats' – fully-catered events for anyone who wants to explore their creative side and benefit from her experience as both artist and life coach.

As a B&B, Art Bank is certainly different. No fusty old florals here and no modern neutrals either. Each of the three guest rooms has been decorated with bold colours and prints to honour a well-known artist. Choose from the Picasso Room (a family room with access to a shared bathroom), the Monet Room (a double with a shared bathroom) and the Van Gogh Room (a double with an en-suite). Each is a creative cocoon that's as comfortable as it is inspiring. All are dog-friendly, and in addition to the flair in their design, they're also practical and well-equipped, with comfy beds, a TV, a desk and tea- and coffee-making facilities.

Views from the windows are out across Dalbeattie's rooftops, and from some aspects beyond to the surrounding hills and mountains. This is a good place to base yourself if you want to discover this part of Dumfries and Galloway. It's in the centre of town and also close to regional highlights like the Dalbeattie Forest Town Wood, which offers tracks and trails for walking and mountain biking through the trees to Plantain Loch. It's only a couple of miles beyond here to the shoreline of the 'Scottish Riviera' or Solway Coast, while inland Threave Garden is a haven for wildlife on the outskirts of the foodie town of Castle Douglas.

CONTACT 75 High St, Dalbeattie, Dumfries & Galloway DG5 4HA • 07831 125 288
HOW MUCH? Double rooms with breakfast from £120 a night; Retreats from £1300 for 4 nights' full board.
ROOMS 3 Guest Rooms.

The Cross Keys Inn

A cosy pub with rooms and good food in the Scottish Borders village of Ettrickbridge

The Scottish Borders region is a peaceful spot. Admittedly, it wasn't always so but nowadays there aren't many places quite as quiet – perhaps nowhere more so than the lovely Ettrick Valley, which runs west from the historic town of Selkirk. Situated in the village of Ettrickbridge, the recently renovated Cross Keys Inn is a perfect base from which to explore the area, and it offers a good place to return to each night. From the outside, this 17th-century tavern is full of character and inside that's been honoured as well. Old photographs line the walls, and an open fireplace and wooden floors and tables give it old-world charm. Wheelback chairs do that too – but they've been softened with upholstered seats that match the pub's comfy bench seating.

Upstairs, this softness is amplified in seven light and airy guest bedrooms. Floors are carpeted, headboards upholstered, pillows are plump and curtains are floor-length. The windows frame countryside and village views and the walls have paintings by local artists. There's a bedroom here to suit most visitors, whether you're looking for dog-friendly or dog-free, family-sized, a double or a twin. Each is individually designed to fit into this old building but all have the same inclusions – an en-suite bathroom, flatscreen TV, wifi, hairdryer and kettle. A proper Scottish breakfast is included and a Scottish dinner is on the cards too, with a tempting menu featuring seasonal local produce. This place has been brought back to life by Rory and Vicki Steel, son and daughter-in-law of the former MP for the area, Lord Steel. They champion the region in everything from the toiletries to what's on tap. By providing a place to stay in the Ettrick Valley, they are encouraging you to get out and explore. Whether you do that on foot or with a fishing rod in hand, on two wheels or four, is up to you!

CONTACT Main Street, Ettrickbridge, Selkirk, Scottish Borders TD7 5JN • 01750 52224
HOW MUCH? Double rooms from £99 a night including breakfast.
ROOMS 7 Guest Rooms.

Riva Boutique Hotel

A Helensburgh hotel with sea views, good food and easy access to Loch Lomond

If the folk at the Riva Hotel had paid for their location on the Helensburgh seafront, they couldn't have chosen a better one – located on the shores of Gare Loch and the Clyde, with some of the best sea views in the region. The hotel occupies a uniquely accessible spot, at the western end of the Central Belt but also within easy reach of some of the finest highland scenery you'll find. The Loch Lomond and the Trossachs National Park is on your doorstep, and Helensburgh is an attractive seaside destination in its own right, plus Glasgow is just a 40-minute journey away.

Fashioned out of a series of converted townhouses, it's a self-consciously cool sort of place, with a slick bar and a late-night vibe that encourages you to chill out with a nightcap or to order room service from one of their 14 very comfortable guest rooms. Ranging from cosy Standard doubles to spacious king-size rooms, these are crisp and up-to-date, with a palette of blues and greys, Smart TVs with Sky, good wifi, tea- and coffee-making facilities and complimentary water and chocolates, walk-in rainfall showers with Highland Shop toiletries, and – in the more expensive rooms – fabulous sea views and Nespresso machines. Most rooms also have record decks with a selection of classic vinyl. They also have a family room, equipped with a sofa bed and baby cot on request, and most rooms welcome dogs.

Downstairs, the bar serves up cocktails and is open till 4am, and the restaurant offers on-the-money Italian food and bar meals, including pizzas. There's also the rest of Helensburgh to explore, with plenty of cafés, restaurants and shops in what is an undeniably handsome Georgian town. Charles Rennie Mackintosh was born in Helensburgh and you can visit one of his greatest creations, Hill House. The classic Glasgow paddle-steamer, The Waverley, stops here, and you can pick up all manner of hiking trails into the Trossachs, with Loch Lomond just 15 minutes away by car.

CONTACT 12–14 West Clyde St, Helensburgh, Argyll & Bute G84 8SQ • 01436 677 796
HOW MUCH? Double rooms £100–£175 a night.
ROOMS 14 Guest Rooms.

Cromlix

A properly luxurious country retreat owned by Andy and Kim Murray

It's rare to find an award-winning five-star hotel that welcomes dogs. Even rarer to find one with the legendary Murray tennis dynasty behind it. Well, that is exactly what you get at this seriously luxurious hideaway on the outskirts of stately Dunblane, within striking distance of the historic city of Stirling. Proper thought, and money, has gone into making this feel every bit the Scottish country house idyll, but also one that has all the mod cons and comforts that today's discerning guests demand.

The accommodation is spread across 10 bedrooms, five suites and a one-bedroom gate lodge, which are all decorated in their own individual style. They share in common views of the sprawling grounds and the tennis courts (but, of course). Peter Reed 400-thread count Egyptian cotton bed linen and Penhaligon's Quercus toiletries are welcome constants too. A neat touch is that Andy Murray himself has named the hand-painted free-standing baths in the suites after illustrious Scots. So we have Robert Burns and King Robert the Bruce, rubbing shoulders with sports legends Sir Alex Ferguson and Sir Chris Hoy. Impressively, dogs are welcome in any room or suite, though they are not allowed in the public areas. The star attraction is the Chez Roux Restaurant, which had the seal of approval and input of the late French chef Albert Roux. You can watch head chef Darin Campbell work culinary wonders with local produce in the open kitchen. The expansive grounds make up for the restrictions on where dogs can go with plenty of room for them to enjoy themselves while you take in lungfuls of glorious fresh air. Bowls, towels and beds can be arranged for our canine friends too.

CONTACT Kinbuck, Near Dunblane, Perthshire FK15 9JT • 01786 822 125
HOW MUCH? Double rooms from around £300 a night, suites from around £600.
ROOMS 15 Guest Rooms & Suites.

The Ship Inn at Elie

A gem of a beachside property on the coast of Fife, and winner of 'Seaside Inn of the Year'

The East Neuk of Fife remains slightly off the beaten track, which is great for those who already know about it but means that many are missing a trick. The necklace of historic white-washed fishing villages, sandy beaches and links courses sit sandwiched between the Firth of Forth to the south and fertile farmland to the north in this part of east Fife. The Ship Inn at Elie has played its part in putting both the village and East Neuk on the map thanks to its award-winning food, welcoming staff, beachside location and the inn's seasonal cricket schedule, which set it apart as the place to eat, drink and stay around here.

There are six swish, New England-style, nautically-named rooms to choose from as well as some lovingly-fashioned drinking and dining spaces. Four of its six double/twin rooms have sea views; go for the Admiral on the top floor, with its roll-top bath and walk-in shower, whose big windows offer big views over Elie Beach. Meanwhile, the trio of Captain rooms also face the sea and the two Sea Dog rooms are dog-friendly. All feature king-size beds, Egyptian cotton bed linen, Nespresso machines, flatscreen TVs and wifi. It's a family-friendly sort of place, too, with bedrooms that can accommodate additional beds for little ones and a kids' menu in the restaurant.

Speaking of which, the menu stays local, dishing up 100 per cent Scottish fish and meat, including hand-dived scallops as well as East Neuk lobster, which star alongside the inn's renowned fish and chips. You can enjoy all of this in the main bar of the pub, which is bright and light in summer and impressively cosy in winter with a log fire and wood-burning stove; there's also a popular beachside beer garden with a beach bar and a BBQ that fires up seven days a week during summer. Then there's the Ship's Cabin, a private-function space with floor-to-ceiling windows looking over the beach, which, on match days, acts as the pavilion for The Ship's cricket team.

Finally, there's the delightful village of Elie with its golden sandy beach, bracing strolls and year-round chance to watch seabirds. This stretch of the Fife coast is dotted with desirable shoreline villages, while the university town and 'Home of Golf', St Andrews, is only a short drive away. We strongly encourage you to discover this distinctive part of eastern Scotland: just please don't tell anyone else!

CONTACT The Toft, Elie, Fife KY9 1DT
• 01333 330 246
HOW MUCH? Double rooms from £250 a night, including breakfast.
ROOMS 6 Guest Rooms.

The Crusoe

This beautifully located seaside pub with rooms recently won 'Romantic Hotel of the Year'

The East Neuk of Fife, with its fishing villages, golfing heritage and spectacular coastline, is one of Scotland's lesser-known gems, and one of the many picturesque seaside villages here is Lower Largo, a relatively undiscovered spot on the Firth of Forth. It's a pretty place, known to have been the home of one Alexander Selkirk, a castaway and pirate who was the original model for Robinson Crusoe – a fact that is best commemorated in the excellent Crusoe inn, which is perfectly placed on the water's edge. This seaside pub won 'Romantic Hotel of the Year' for the Fife region at Scotland's 2023 National Hotel awards, and no wonder – it's a terrific place to stay, with bright, contemporary rooms all with sea views and really good food.

The pub backs onto Lower Largo Beach and has two types of accommodation across seven airy rooms. There are six Largo Bay rooms, which can be set up as double or twin, some with the option to add an extra bed for children. Each has south-facing sea views as well as super-king-size beds with Egyptian cotton sheets, Bose Bluetooth speakers, USB charging points and Nespresso coffee machines. All Largo Bay rooms are dog-friendly, while four of them have interconnecting doors and en-suite bathrooms with spacious showers (some also have roll-top baths), fluffy towels and Laura Thomas bathroom products. For something extra special, book the exclusive Largo Pier Suite with its claw-foot bath and balcony. Meanwhile, The Crusoe's restaurant dishes up seasonal, fully-provenanced food, from Shetland mussels and Aberdeenshire lamb to cheese and bread from nearby Anstruther. The Seaside Bar, where dogs are welcome, also serves pub favourites as well as plenty of local ales – the perfect end to a good walk along the coastal path or visits to Fife's many other attractions, from St Andrews to the seaside resort of Elie, where you'll find The Crusoe's sister pub, The Ship.

CONTACT 2 Main St, Lower Largo, Leven, Fife KY8 6BT • 01333 406 775

HOW MUCH? Double rooms with breakfast from £110 a night.

ROOMS 7 Guest Rooms.

The Viewmount

Five-star boutique B&B in the Cairngorms National Park with dramatic mountain views

If you've come to the Scottish Highlands for the mountains and the views, then The Viewmount is very definitely for you – a luxurious boutique B&B that's a passion project for its South African host, Esther, who is very much living the dream in her beautiful Victorian home. Luckily, she decided to share it with the rest of us too.

The Viewmount is in the small Highlands town of Kingussie, surrounded by dramatic landscapes and right in the Cairngorms National Park. Careful restoration has retained much of the Victorian feel, and the four en-suite rooms have decorative fireplaces, furniture in keeping with the period and a real sense of genteel comfort. There's a 'no children', 'no pets' policy, which helps maintain the peace and quiet, and the views are simply stunning, especially from 'The Bell' and 'The Leslie' rooms, where panoramic, triple-sash windows look out onto the Grampian Mountains. 'The Reid' is hardly less enticing, with mountain and garden views, while 'The Sharon' is a ground-floor, wheelchair-accessible room that looks out over the landscaped garden. All rooms have king-size beds with the Sharon offering the option of a twin configuration.

The en-suite bathrooms are magnificent spaces with underfloor heating, walk-in showers and slipper baths – and there are lovely touches throughout, from monogrammed bathrobes to hospitality trays with Dalwhinnie whisky. There's nothing vintage about the facilities, though, and you'll find USB ports next to the beds and 55-inch Smart TVs in the rooms, plus free wifi throughout. Breakfast is fabulous, served in the Grampian View library at a time to suit and encompassing freshly-brewed coffee, homemade bread and an impressive pick-and-mix selection of specialities like venison sausages and devilled kidney beans. There's also an honesty bar, with lots to choose from including an extensive choice of wine.

CONTACT East Terrace, Kingussie, Inverness-shire PH21 1JS • 07890 518 836
HOW MUCH? Double rooms from £265 a night, including breakfast.
ROOMS 4 Guest Rooms.

Ravenscraig Guesthouse

Beautiful B&B close to the heart of Aviemore, with mega breakfasts and great hosts

Not surprisingly perhaps, there's a wide choice of accommodation in the Cairngorms resort of Aviemore, but our favourite is this fabulous B&B, located right in the heart of the town and run with verve and enthusiasm by affable owner Scott Burns-Smith. It's a thoroughly welcoming place that revels in its proximity to the outdoor activities that Aviemore has to offer, catering to skiers and snowboarders in winter, walkers in spring and summer and mountain-bikers all year round. And even if outdoor activities aren't your bag, it's as cosy and comfortable a place to stay as you'll find.

The B&B has 12 rooms, made up of four doubles, two singles, a twin and five very popular family rooms situated in a spick-and-span chalet in the garden. They are all beautifully decorated in a contemporary style; each room is individually styled and has a different colour palette, but they all come with good wifi, flatscreen TVs, tea- and coffee-making facilities and en-suite bathrooms with re-fillable toiletries from the Isle of Arran. Some of the double rooms have king-size beds, while the family rooms have a double and two single beds, and an outside seating area with decking.

Breakfast is served in a light, bright room, with porridge, Scotch pancakes and a superb Full Scottish cooked to order among a choice of items designed to set you up for an active day. Scott is big on making things as convenient as possible for his thrill-seeking customers, with a laundry hut and a drying room, and bike storage and a bike wash area for mountain bikers. Scott is also full of good advice on the best slopes, trails and activities in the surrounding area, including adrenaline-fuelled adventures with their partners G2 Adventures. But it's not all about the outdoors: Aviemore is full of family attractions and things to see and do, not to mention places to eat and drink. Best of all, you have your cosy room at Ravenscraig to look forward to at the end of each day.

CONTACT 141 Grampian Road, Aviemore PH22 1RP • 01479 810 278

HOW MUCH? Double rooms from around £100 a night, including breakfast. Family rooms from £130.

ROOMS 12 Guest Rooms.

West Highland Hot Tub Studios

Studios with hot tubs and views of Skye and the Small Isles

You reach the West Highland Hotel from Fort William on one of Scotland's most scenic drives or train rides – and the views from the rooms there will rival anything you've seen on the way. Situated in the fishing village of Mallaig, the hotel looks out across the water towards Skye and the Small Isles. The best rooms in the hotel are orientated to make the most of this stunning scene, and there's no better spot to enjoy it than in a private hot tub. Happily, these can be found on the balconies and terraces of the hotel's brand-new studio apartments. Book one and you'll have a spacious place to stay with a kitchenette and sitting space as well as your terrace and hot tub. They are perfect for those who like the freedom of self-catering with a few luxuries thrown in. You can cook simple meals for yourself and keep to your own schedule – but if you're feeling lazy, there's always the restaurant and bar downstairs, not to mention Mallaig's seafood hot spots.

The studios are a recent addition to this 36-bedroom hotel – cleverly-designed, stylish spaces, with muted tones, warm lighting and sleek bathrooms. Guest rooms, meanwhile, are spacious, comfortable, and very well-equipped, with newly refurbished bathrooms, robes and toiletries, Freeview TVs and tea- and coffee-making facilities. What you can see out of the floor-to-ceiling patio doors of the studios (and guest rooms) is a good indication of what you can do while you're here. The ferry port is a short walk away, from where you can catch one of the regular crossings to Skye or island-hop to the small isles of Eigg, Muck, Rum or Canna. There's also the crossing to Knoydart, a remote peninsula where a visit to The Old Forge, dubbed Britain's most remote pub, is almost obligatory. There are beautiful sandy beaches at Morar and Camusdarach, both less than five miles away. After a day of all this, what could be better than a soothing soak in a hot tub looking out to sea?

CONTACT Davies Brae, Mallaig, Inverness-shire PH41 4QZ • 01697 462 210
HOW MUCH? Studios from £316 for 2 nights (min. stay, off peak). Double rooms from £180 a night.
ROOMS 4 Studios & 36 Rooms.

The Manor House

A small but elegant hotel overlooking Oban Bay and the islands of the Inner Hebrides

In a town that's known as 'the gateway to the islands' and 'the seafood capital of Scotland', it would be hard to find a better place to stay than The Manor House – an elegant hotel in a Georgian building on the south side of Oban Bay, with views across to the Isle of Mull. It has steps down to the shore and a small but excellent restaurant with local produce from land and sea as a highlight of its menu. The ferries to those alluring islands are just a walk away, but island-hopping isn't the only thing to do. In fact, everything you've come to Scotland for is most likely in reach of here – castles, lochs, beaches all included – and there's a whisky distillery in town, too.

You can also opt for your own tasting in the hotel bar, which serves a good selection, and there's an inviting drawing room with an open fire, terrace and garden. The communal spaces give the place a sociable feel where tales of the day's adventures are often shared. What's on offer here is something akin to the experience of a grand country house hotel, but on a smaller and friendlier scale. Built in 1780 by the fifth Duke of Argyll, the building certainly has the heritage to match, its period furniture enhanced with wallpapers, paintings and fabrics that suit the building's age. That's continued in the cosy bedrooms, each of which is individually styled and has en-suite facilities and everything else you'd expect of a modern hotel room, including a Smart TV in most rooms and good wifi throughout.

When local folk have occasion to celebrate, they'll book a table for dinner in The Manor House restaurant, preceded by drinks in the bar or on the terrace. With that in mind, there seems little point in guests wandering further to eat (breakfast is included, while dinner needs to be booked). When you eventually decide to venture forth, a wealth of staggeringly beautiful sights await. The isles of Kerrera, Lismore and Mull are all worthy day trips, as are visits to Loch Etive, Ganavan Sands and the ruins of Dunollie Castle.

CONTACT Gallanach Road, Oban PA34 4LS • 01631 566 429
HOW MUCH? Double rooms from £170 a night.
ROOMS 11 Guest Rooms.

Carradales Luxury Guest House

A very fancy guesthouse on the Kintyre Peninsula on Scotland's West Coast

If you're planning a trip to the Kintyre Peninsula, Carradales Luxury Guest House makes for a great place to stay. And if you're not, Carradales gives you a reason to go. This guesthouse offers hospitality that's worth travelling for. In fact, it's Visit Scotland's only five-star-rated guesthouse on the 30-mile finger of land that Paul McCartney made famous in 'that song.' Stay here, and after days visiting Mull, the mountains and misty seas that he sang about, you'll be grateful for the award-winning hospitality on offer. Carradales isn't just somewhere to stay, but a place to truly relax – in a scenic spot between the forested hinterland and the coastal village of Carradale.

In addition to comfortable bedrooms, there's a lounge where you can have fireside drinks, and an elegant dining room where dinners are served. Indeed, your hosts have got this just right:

it's a lovely place to dine, and co-owner Steve is a talented professional chef, whose finely-tuned menus feature seasonal, local Scottish produce. Championing the region is a theme that's continued elsewhere – bedrooms are named after local castles, Kintyre whiskies are on the drinks list and toiletries are made on the nearby Isle of Arran. There are just four rooms, each with an en-suite bathroom featuring a walk-in shower, and two have a double-ended roll-top bath as well. They vary in size and shape, thanks to the vagaries of what was formerly a Victorian manse, but all boast a king- or super-king-size bed made up with quality Egyptian cotton sheets. Other standard features include a Smart TV and good wifi, and decor includes a tasteful feature wall with designer wallpaper, inspired by the natural world.

Carradales is set on the forested edge of the harbour village of Carradale. You can walk into the trees or down into the village via the Kintyre Way, which passes close by: you can tour this on foot, by bike or by car on a 66-mile scenic drive. Golf, game shooting, fishing and distillery tours provide other things to do. Day trips to Arran are also possible.

CONTACT Carradale, Campbeltown, Argyll & Bute PA28 6QG • 07968 477 563

HOW MUCH? Double rooms with breakfast from £340 for 2 nights.

ROOMS 4 Guest Rooms.

Lucky Dip

The Bonham

35 Drumsheugh Gardens, Edinburgh EH3 7RN

Contemporary style, individuality and understated chic with a few accents of bling, all without the mass-produced feel of a national chain, The Bonham was one of Edinburgh's first boutique hotels and is still a stylishly enjoyable place to stay.

Cathedral House

28-32 Cathedral Square, Glasgow G4 0XA

This stunning baronial brownstone is a fabulous small boutique hotel. Each room has been individually designed and decorated to make the most of the quirky building, like the cosy top-floor loft with its sloping ceiling, built-in bed and rooftop views. There's also an excellent Italian restaurant and unrivalled views over Glasgow Cathedral.

The Courie Inn

Main Street, Killin, Perthshire FK21 8UT

A couple of hours north of Glasgow, this rustic pub offers crisp and comfortable rooms in a beautiful location at the western end of Loch Tay. Its restaurant is a cosy spot with the sort of Scottish portions that will see you right for a day's walking in the nearby Munros.

Eden Locke

127 George St, Edinburgh EH2 4JN

Up in Edinburgh's New Town, Eden Locke offers comfortable stays behind a grand Georgian facade, with each of its 72 suites and apartments furnished in soft, pastel tones and suitable for anything from a weekend away to a month or more on business. They are more spacious than a hotel room, and come with space to work, a fully equipped kitchen, and things like superfast wifi and Smart TVs. There are various configurations, from one-bedroom suites to split-level studios, while there's also a light and airy ground-floor café and working space. It's in a decent location too, and should you not want to venture far at night, you're close to some great places to eat and drink.

The Horseshoe Inn

Eddleston, Peebles, Scottish Borders EH45 8QP

This award-winning and unique country pub with rooms occupies a restored Victorian schoolhouse in the heart of Sir Walter Scott country just a half-hour's drive from Edinburgh. Kids and dogs are welcome; just don't overdo the Tunnock's teacakes in your room or you'll ruin your dinner!

Loch Melfort Hotel

Arduaine by Oban, Argyll PA34 4XG

The unspoilt nature and bountiful littoral of Scotland's west coast boasts many hotels and spectacular views, but the romantic Loch Melfort Hotel is one of those that is in with a shout of having the best of everything. It's a cosy family-run four-star with an excellent restaurant with an outdoor terrace.

The Storehouse

Bridge Street Wynd, Kirkwall, Orkney KW15 1JD

Housed in a converted herring store in Orkney's main town, this boutique hotel is the project of local knitwear designer Judith Glue and her husband David. It has just eight en-suite rooms and a ground floor occupied by a contemporary restaurant that celebrates local cuisine and ingredients. Judith designed each of the rooms herself, with high-end retro furnishings and of course beautiful cushions, throws and other knitwear, and all boasting local Orkney scenes, painted by Judith's sister Jane, a local watercolourist.

The Torridon – Hotel and Stables

Annat, By Achnasheen, Wester Ross IV22 2EY

One of Scotland's grandest lochside hotels, The Torridon is a turreted baronial castle that is a thoroughly indulgent place to stay, with 18 individually designed contemporary guest rooms, two restaurants and its own farm and kitchen garden. Not only that, it's also home to The Stables, a two-minute walk away, which provides a more relaxed alternative that's more suited to walkers and the muddy boot brigade. It's more affordable too – and the location is about as good as it gets if you're keen to get outdoors.

Loch Melfort Hotel

The Storehouse

The Torridon

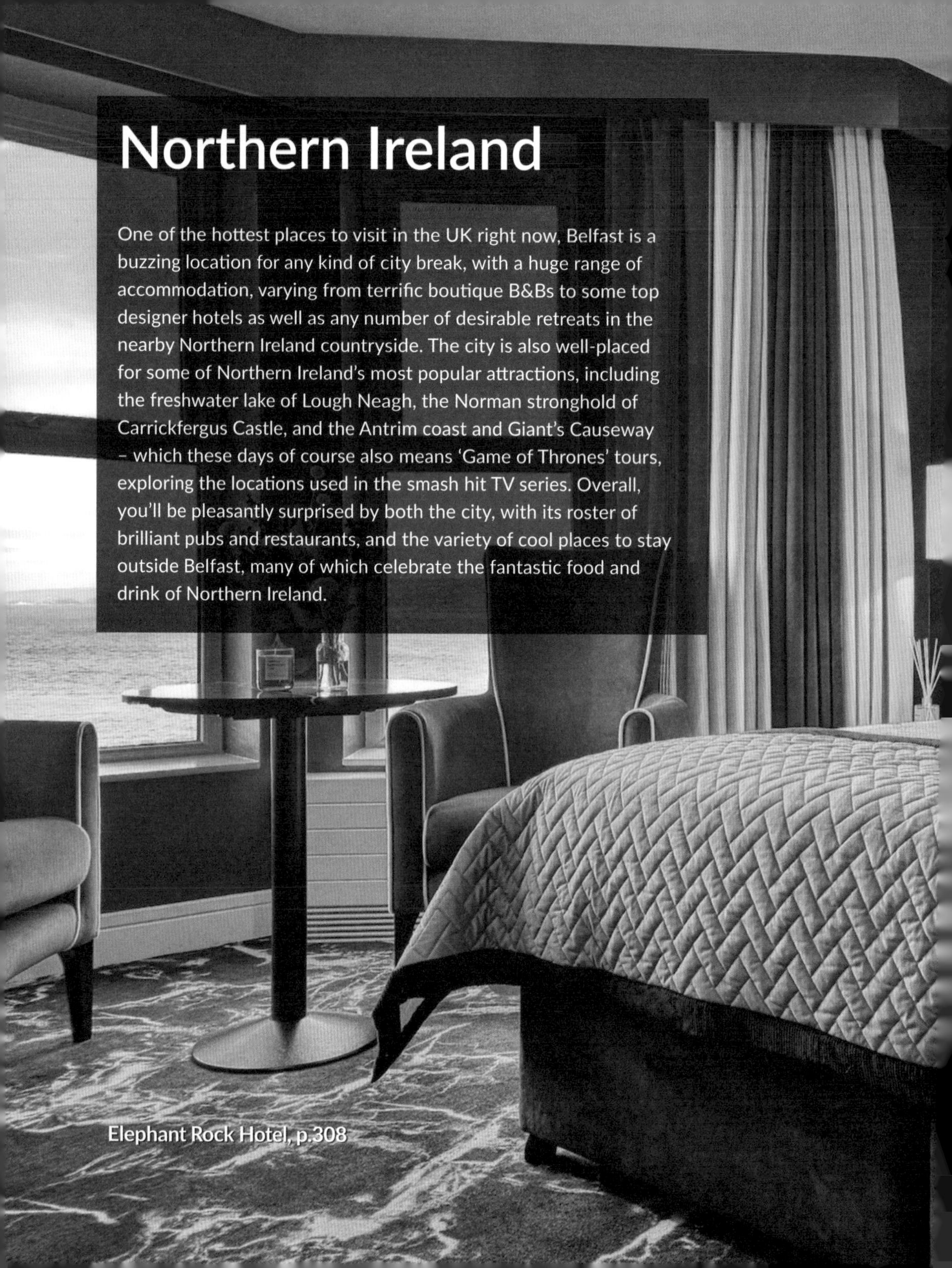

Northern Ireland

One of the hottest places to visit in the UK right now, Belfast is a buzzing location for any kind of city break, with a huge range of accommodation, varying from terrific boutique B&Bs to some top designer hotels as well as any number of desirable retreats in the nearby Northern Ireland countryside. The city is also well-placed for some of Northern Ireland's most popular attractions, including the freshwater lake of Lough Neagh, the Norman stronghold of Carrickfergus Castle, and the Antrim coast and Giant's Causeway – which these days of course also means 'Game of Thrones' tours, exploring the locations used in the smash hit TV series. Overall, you'll be pleasantly surprised by both the city, with its roster of brilliant pubs and restaurants, and the variety of cool places to stay outside Belfast, many of which celebrate the fantastic food and drink of Northern Ireland.

Elephant Rock Hotel, p.308

The Harrison Chambers of Distinction

Joyfully eccentric rooms in a Belfast boutique guesthouse

It's tempting to describe the rooms at this boutique guesthouse in Belfast's Queen's Quarter as quirky. But 'quirky' doesn't quite do this place justice. Indeed, each room in this grand Victorian townhouse is unique, named after a famous creative with a link to Belfast and elegantly decorated to match. It's interesting and intelligently put together, with zeitgeisty work by local artists on the walls, and it hits that sweet spot of being both comfortable and cool. It's also handily located for visiting some of Belfast's major attractions.

Stay in one of the suites and you'll have a Victorian-style free-standing bath in the room and a four-poster, emperor or sleigh bed to sleep in. There'll be plenty of space to spread out and a bay window overlooking the leafy avenue leading to the heart of the city. The decadence continues with a breakfast tray delivered in the morning, so you can savour your first meal of the day in bed. The other rooms are characterised as Gallivanters or Bohemians and are no less charming. Choose the former for a king-size bed, the latter for a cosy double. Either way, you'll find that the owner Melanie has used the same flair and care to put them together. Each room has an en-suite bathroom with a rainfall shower. Standard inclusions are quality linen, locally-made eco-toiletries, tea- and coffee-making facilities and wifi. But those are the only things you could call standard. These are the very antithesis of the 'standard' rooms' of big-chain hotels, all deep tones, colourful wallpapers and velvet curtains – and, unusually, no TVs. Instead, the room's features have been carefully chosen to complement the varied folk they're named after. There's a mini library and a typewriter in the C.S. Lewis suite, for example, and a record player in the one named after the singer Ruby Murray.

This celebration of Belfast alumni and the city's culture is apt for the hotel's location – near to Queen's University, and close to the Lyric Theatre, the Grand Opera House and plenty of smaller music venues. And if you want to know what's on or where to eat, ask Melanie, the cool friend everyone wishes they had, who knows all the best places and latest trends. You can enjoy a cheese or charcuterie board and a drink in the lounge, but for more than that you don't have to go far: the area has plenty of good bars and restaurants, starting with Blank next door.

CONTACT 45 Malone Road, Belfast BT9 6RX • 028 9460 0123
HOW MUCH? Double rooms with breakfast from £110 a night; suites from £170 a night.
ROOMS 16 Guest Rooms.

HARRISON

Titanic Hotel

Nautical-themed luxury accommodation in the heart of the city's old shipyard

Some of the world's most famous passenger liners, including its ill-fated namesake, were designed in this very building, which dates from the late 1880s. The former headquarters of shipbuilders Harland & Wolff has been sympathetically restored to house this luxurious hotel, across from the ship-shaped Titanic Belfast visitor centre. But you don't have to be a Titanorak to appreciate the old shipyard location. Nearby is the Pump House whiskey distillery, the iconic H&W cranes Samson and Goliath, and HMS Caroline, all just a few minutes' walk from the city centre.

Many of the original offices of the directors and senior staff, as well as Drawing Office One, have been repurposed as meeting rooms and event spaces, while retaining all of their charm in the form of antique furnishings, portraits and open-hearth fireplaces. Guest rooms feature plush beds and chic bathrooms, with Paul Costelloe Linen toiletries, and are decorated in a stylish Art Deco nautical-meets-industrial style. You can choose to stay in the original building or a newer addition, and between Standard, Superior and Deluxe rooms. Or 'push the boat out', so to speak, in an Executive or Superior Suite.

On the ground floor, dusty blueprints and charts have been replaced with menus in Drawing Office Two, noted for its spectacular barrel-vaulted ceiling and central island bar. We highly recommend the Punch Romaine (supposedly one of the last cocktails to be served on-board before the rush for the lifeboats), and the hotel's signature Jack & Rose, which is guaranteed to float anyone's boat. Sip while admiring a scale model of the Titanic, original artworks by local artist Colin Davidson and the room's ornate plasterwork, crafted by the same skilled craftsmen who worked on the great liners. The multi-award-winning Wolff Grill offers fine dining choices, along with views of the historic slipways. An excellent buffet breakfast completes the experience, with all the ingredients of the famous Ulster Fry.

CONTACT Queen's Road, Titanic Quarter, Belfast BT3 9DT • 028 9508 2000

HOW MUCH? Double Standard room with breakfast from £129 a night.

ROOMS 119 Guest Rooms.

The Grand Central

Ireland's tallest hotel boasts the best views in town, along with five-star luxury

The transformation of The Grand Central from a soulless, 1970s high-rise office block, into a five-star hotel worthy of presidents and prime ministers was completed in 2018. Borrowing its name from a swish Victorian hotel that shut up shop in Belfast in 1969, the second-tallest building in Ireland dominates the city's skyline. Its 300 rooms over 23 floors are topped off by the Observatory Bar, which offers 360 degree views over Belfast and beyond, along with an extensive cocktail list that has signature concoctions named after local attractions. The hotel's seahorse motif is drawn from the city's coat of arms and adorns many of The Grand Central's surfaces, as do extracts from poet Paul Muldoon's specially-commissioned ode to Belfast. All in all, it's a memorable and convenient base for seeing the city.

The Hastings Suite (named after the late owner) has the distinction of being the most prestigious accommodation in town, having been occupied by Joe Biden on his 2022 Irish tour. Those without an entourage can choose from a wide range of rooms and suites, from Classic to Deluxe, with floor 11 and above offering the best views of the city and mountains beyond. Every guest benefits from a Cloud bed, Espa toiletries, sustainable water bottles and locally-designed and -manufactured furnishings, while Nespresso machines and a pillow menu feature in premium rooms.

The hotel is popular with the movie and TV production crowd, so star-spotting is always a possibility in the light-filled space of the urbane Grand Café or the Seahorse Restaurant: a bright, dramatic contemporary space that makes an excellent place to start the day at breakfast or to enjoy an excellent dinner in the evening.

CONTACT 9–15 Bedford St, Belfast BT2 7FF • 028 9023 1066
HOW MUCH? Double rooms with breakfast from £220 a night.
ROOMS 300 Guest Rooms.

Elephant Rock Hotel

A colourful and very comfortable boutique hotel on County Antrim's Portrush peninsula

People have been holidaying on the Portrush peninsula since Victorian times, drawn by the sea and sand of its beautiful beaches. And, while the natural treasures are perennially popular, modern visitors feel more at home thanks to places like the Elephant Rock Hotel. This independently-owned, boutique hotel – named after a nearby rock formation – is one of a kind. Among a terrace of sea-facing Victorian townhouses in shades of cream, its black-and-pink finish demands attention. Popular with couples, it might just be the coolest place to stay in town thanks to its contemporary design and busy restaurant and cocktail bar.

Each guest room is individually decorated, with upholstered headboards, heavy velvet curtains, and colourful designer cushions adding interest to every room. Bed linen is 400-thread Egyptian cotton, towels are soft and toiletries are locally sourced, vegan and eco-friendly. Every feature, whether functional or fashionable (or in the case of the Lavazza coffee machines, both), has been carefully selected, resulting in rooms that are as comfortable as they are colourful. Whether you opt for a spacious single or a luxurious executive room with a sea view, all of them offer the modern conveniences of wifi, DAB radios and Smart TVs.

After a day on Whiterocks Beach, just 650m away, head back to the hotel and get ready for the evening ahead. You can start it downstairs in the Art Deco-inspired bar, with a signature cocktail (try the 'Ode to Violet', named after the owner's granny). Book a table for dinner in Elephant Rock's 30-seater restaurant, and take your pick from the many other eateries in Portrush on another night.

With the Elephant Rock as your base, this part of the Causeway Coast is yours to explore, with three of Northern Ireland's nine Blue Flag beaches within walking distance of the hotel. Portrush itself is known as a place for traditional seaside fun and there are the amusements and arcades to prove it, but you don't have to look much further for more grown-up pleasures. The Royal Portrush Golf Club is a mile away, Bushmills Whiskey Distillery is less than five miles from here, and a little further takes you to the Giant's Causeway, the famously scenic stone-stacked promontory dubbed by some the 'Eighth Wonder of the World'.

CONTACT 17 Lansdowne Crescent, Portrush, Antrim BT56 8AY • 028 7087 8787

HOW MUCH? Double rooms with breakfast from £100 to £260 a night.

ROOMS 18 Guest Rooms.

Coors
GUINNESS

Ardtara Country House

Country house elegance deep in the Mid-Ulster countryside, with a homely vibe and five-star dining

Getting the balance right between buzzy and peaceful might sound impossible, but Ardtara Country House have struck all the right notes. Its secluded rural location provides every element necessary for relaxation, yet its also boasts a destination restaurant much praised for the locally renowned chef-patron Ian Orr's ever-changing menu, which reflects the kitchen's seasonal homegrown produce.

The building itself is over 120 years old and was the former home of the Clark family, scions of the local linen industry, and guests still experience that family-at-home feeling. Many of the manor's original Victorian features have been carefully restored to sit harmoniously alongside the modern comforts of a top-class hotel. It has just nine guest rooms, almost all of which have a working open fire and are decorated tastefully in period style. Luxurious touches include Italian marble bathrooms and original wooden flooring and all the guest rooms come with king-size beds with high-quality mattresses, robes and slippers, good wifi, flatscreen TVs, and tea and coffee facilities that include Nespresso machines and homemade biscuits. The public spaces are very relaxing, and you can eat very well in the hotel's charming restaurant, where they serve fixed-price lunch and dinner menus and also offer an excellent afternoon tea. The Full Irish breakfast too is worth waking up for.

Ardtara is set among 80 acres of stunning woodland and lakes; fresh air fans will find plenty to do within the grounds. The cities of Belfast and Derry are only an hour away by car, and the Giant's Causeway Coast is only a 45-minute drive. Many of Northern Ireland's other attractions are also within easy reach, including an exhibition centre dedicated to local poet Seamus Heaney just minutes away in Bellaghy.

CONTACT Gorteade Road, Upperlands, Maghera BT46 5SA • 028 7964 44908
HOW MUCH? Double Room with breakfast from £150 a night.
ROOMS 9 Guest Rooms.

The Old Inn

Historic spa hotel with country walks, Belfast Lough and the city on its doorstep

Never was a hotel more aptly named – The Old Inn was established in 1614, which supports its claim to be the oldest hotel on the island of Ireland. The long and low building has understandably seen a few changes since its 17th-century beginnings as a coaching inn. Yet, situated in the small village of Crawfordsburn, a mere 10-minute drive from Belfast, it remains at heart a thoroughly comfortable and also contemporary place to stay.

A section of the building's roof is still thatched and the period charm extends to the sometimes sloping floors of the individually-named bedrooms, ranging from Petite, Highway and Suite, and including a traditionally-styled stand-alone cottage. The luxury Treetop Spa offers a full range of well-being and pampering, with an outdoor pool, sauna, steam room and multiple treatments, and, for those less concerned with their chakras, the 1614 bar serves a range of superb cocktails alongside a roaring fire, while the hearty yet refined French-inspired cuisine at the restaurant is much loved by locals and guests alike. They also serve afternoon tea, host live music on weekends, and even show sports on the telly, making it a thoroughly relaxed place to spend time.

The Old Inn celebrates its links to celebrated author C. S. Lewis, who spent his honeymoon in a cottage here in1958, while musician and near-neighbour Van Morrison has been known to pop in on occasion. And why not? The Old Inn's guest rooms are spacious and have all the amenities you would expect, including big comfy beds, Nespresso machines, satellite TVs, and robes and flip-flops for enjoying the pool and spa facilities. You're also within easy reach of the Belfast Lough and the nearby Crawfordsburn Country Park, so it really is a perfect spot for a country break or as a peaceful base for Belfast.

CONTACT 15–25 Main Street, Crawfordsburn, Bangor BT19 1JH • 028 9185 3255

HOW MUCH? Double Rooms with breakfast and spa access from £165 a night.

ROOMS 32 Guest Rooms.

Lucky Dip

Culloden Estate & Spa

Bangor Road, Holywood, Belfast BT18 0EX

First opened as a hotel in 1962 with only 11 bedrooms, this place was Northern Ireland's first five-star hotel and still promises guests a luxurious stay in an idyllic setting. After recent renovations and extensions, it now boasts 105 luxurious bedrooms and suites and 11 self-catering apartments. Many of the original rooms retain a Victorian charm while newer rooms offer something more contemporary. It also has a lovely spa, a really good restaurant and its own pub!

Europa Hotel

Great Victoria Street, Belfast BT2 7AP

Once the world's most bombed hotel, the Europa was once nicknamed 'The Hardboard Hotel' for its constantly boarded-up windows during the Troubles. But that was a long time ago and nowadays it's one of the largest and most convenient of Belfast's city-centre hotels, nestled beside the Grand Opera House and only a short walk from the main shopping drag and City Hall. There may be trendier places on offer in Belfast these days but The Europa is steeped in history and offers charm in spades. It also sits opposite the legendary Crown Liquor Saloon, which has got to be a bonus!

Galgorm Resort & Spa

136 Fenaghy Road, Galgorm, County Antrim BT42 1EA

Situated in lush woodland, the Galgorm Resort & Spa serves up a tranquil setting for those in search of a luxurious break from the hustle of city life. The hotel is nestled in 380 acres of picturesque park, yet is only a 40-minute drive from Belfast's city centre, making it an ideal base for exploring the region. It has 125 bedrooms and suites, plus a range of self-catering log cabins, cottages and shepherds huts and an outdoor and indoor spa area with hot tubs, saunas and pools. The guest rooms have a contemporary ambience, with a mixture of standard, superior, deluxe and junior suites. Some offer spectacular views over the gently cascading River Maine. Downstairs, the cavernous and charming Gillies Bar & Grill serves high-quality pub food or you can opt for afternoon tea in the Conservatory. For a taste of Italy, book into the resort's family-friendly restaurant, Fratelli, for pizza and pasta in a rustic setting.

The Merchant Hotel

16 Skipper Street, Belfast BT1 2DZ

Belfast's Merchant Hotel is housed in a Victorian Grade A-listed building, originally the headquarters of the Ulster Bank, in the city's historic Cathedral Quarter. A 2010 extension saw the addition of an Art Deco-style wing where both styles seamlessly blend – guests can choose from bedrooms offering Victorian grandeur with luscious velvets or Art Deco opulence with an abundance of features. The hotel oozes elegance and has helped to establish the Cathedral Quarter as Belfast's place to go. Its Great Room restaurant was once the banking hall and provides sumptuous surroundings for guests to enjoy some of Belfast's best dining. Next door, the hotel's award-winning cocktail bar enjoys the dubious distinction of having been featured in the Guinness Book of Records for serving the 'World's Most Expensive Cocktail', while in the rest of the hotel you'll also find the Cloth Ear pub and Bert's Bar with its regular jazz sessions. Guests can also relax in the hotel's spa with its treatment rooms and hydrotherapy area. If you're keen to visit Belfast in style, and budget doesn't apply, this is probably the place to stay.

Ten Square Hotel

10 Donegall Square, Belfast BT1 5JD

Overlooking Belfast City Hall, and a short walk from the Grand Opera House, Ulster Hall and the Waterfront concert hall, Ten Square was Belfast's original boutique hotel. Now renovated and extended to become a 131-bedroom city centre favourite, it offers visitors a chic and contemporary place to lay their head, with a decor that celebrates the location's Linen Quarter – look out for the flax flower motif throughout the interior. Originally a linen warehouse, the building now houses Jospers restaurant, the Linen Bar with its craft beer and local gin menus and a rooftop cocktail lounge with fantastic views of the city centre. The comfortable bedrooms boast good wifi, tea, coffee and water and super-king-size beds.

Galgorm Resort & Spa

Europa Hotel

The Merchant Hotel

Index by Name

Index by Location

Other UK Accommodation Guides from Cool Places

Cool Places: Britain's coolest places to stay, eat, drink... and more!

Dog Friendly Britain: cool places to stay with your dog

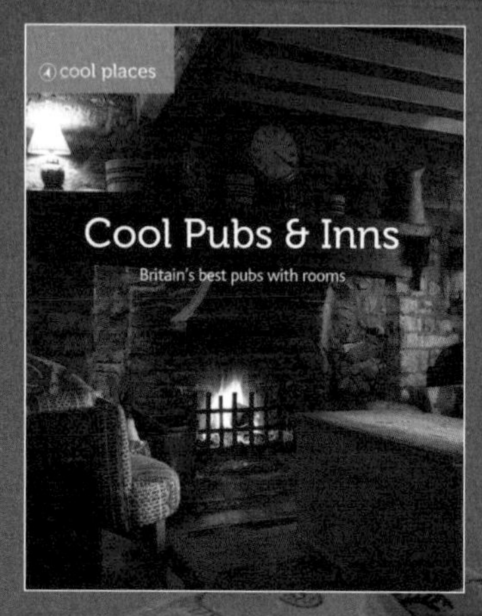

Cool Pubs & Inns: Britain's best pubs with rooms

Glamping Getaways: Britain's Most Stylish Glamping Stays

Acknowledgements and Credits

200 HOTELS: BRITAIN'S COOLEST HOTELS AND B&BS

Published in the UK by Cool Places,
81 Rivington Street, London EC2A 3AY
www.coolplaces.co.uk

A catalogue record of this book is available from the British Library.
ISBN 978-1-906889-74-6

CREDITS

EDITOR Martin Dunford.

CONTRIBUTORS Natasha Blair, Martin Dunford, Laura Evans, Kirsten Henton, Lynn Houghton, David Jones, Portia Jones, Phil Lee, Kathryn Liston, Andrea McVeigh, Beth Pipe, Amy Woodland and the many other UK writers who have contributed to Cool Places over the years.

DESIGN & LAYOUT Diana Jarvis.

PROOFREADING Susanne Hillen, Caroline Osborne

THANKS AND ACKNOWLEDGEMENTS

Thanks to the Cool Places team – especially Laura, David and Jane, Susanne and Caroline for proofreading, Diana for layout and to Caroline, Daisy and Lucy for companionship and inspiration. Thanks above all to the many wonderful hoteliers and property owners who make the UK such a splendid and varied place to stay. Long may you continue!

PICTURES

Images are used with permission from the property owners or the establishments themselves. Cover images: Artist Residence Brighton (front); Belsfield Hotel (back); Berwick Lodge; The Suffolk; Another Place, The Lake (front flap); Fort Road Hotel (back flap).

Page 1 image: The Bell at Saxmundham

Pages 2–3 images (clockwise from top left): The Whittling House; Murrayshall; Old Bell; Losehill House; The 25; Saunton Sands Hotel.

SALES

UK Sales: Compass IPS Limited; sales@compassips.co.uk; www.compassips.london

Printed by Bell & Bain Ltd, Glasgow, Scotland.

This book has been printed on paper made from renewable sources.